CLARENDON PLATO SERIES

General Editor: M. J. WOODS

PLATO

Philebus

Translated with Notes and Commentary

by

J. C. B. GOSLING

FELLOW OF ST. EDMUND HALL
OXFORD

CLARENDON PRESS · OXFORD
1975

Oxford University Press, Ely House, London W. 1

GLASGOW NEW YORK TORONTO MELBOURNE WELLINGTON
CAPE TOWN IBADAN NAIROBI DAR ES SALAAM LUSAKA ADDIS ABABA
DELHI BOMBAY CALCUTTA MADRAS KARACHI LAHORE DACCA
KUALA LUMPUR SINGAPORE HONG KONG TOKYO

CASEBOUND   ISBN 0 19 872044 0
PAPERBACK   ISBN 0 19 872054 8

·

*Printed in Great Britain by
Billing & Sons Limited, Guildford and London*

92781

PREFACE

It may help to make some comments on the purpose of this volume. It is intended primarily for philosophers with no ancient Greek, who wish to study Plato. Such people may like readable English but their need is to get some idea of relationships in the original and ambiguities. So while I have omitted many occurrences of 'O Protarchus', 'O Socrates', for style's sake, much of the English is cumbersome. Thus the translations of *peras* (determinant), *apeiron* (indeterminate), *pathos* (what is undergone) are often barbarous, but, as it is in given passages important for a reader to know that the same word is used, I have preserved the same translation. Sometimes (*psyche* (soul?), *alethes* (true?)) this has proved too much for me, and I have inserted a transliteration of the Greek word in brackets. Where there is dispute about the text or translation, or a note on the meaning of some term, there is an asterisk in the margin of the text, referring the reader to the notes at the end of the text. A word of warning is, however, in order here. So far as possible the line divisions of the English text correspond to those of the Stephanus pagination of the Oxford text. Sometimes, however, there is a lack of correspondence, so since asterisks come against the English that has given rise to comment the reader will sometimes need to be prepared to explore in the notes.

The Introduction is intended to give some idea of the main interpretational problems in the *Philebus*. While a clear line cannot always be preserved, the division of labour between notes and general commentary is that the latter should tackle general problems of interpretation in the relevant sections, the former more particular questions, especially of text and translation. With regard to disputes on the text, I have aimed, except where largish sections are at issue, to give a transliteration and translation of the disputed terms so that a Greekless reader may get some idea of the dispute. Sometimes a passage is too long, or too little hangs on it. In such cases I have been less considerate, more dogmatic. Unless otherwise specified in the notes I have followed the Oxford text. The translation never embodies my own suggested readings, but always one already suggested unless expressly stated. I have given at the end a list of works consulted. While I have doubtless done injustice to most, I should mention Elsa Striker's work in particular. It came to my notice rather late on in the book's preparation, but clearly deserves notice. I have referred to it often, but must say that my reading has been hasty and it is improbable that I have digested all the subtleties or always got her arguments right. It is an important and ingenious work. My intention has been to draw attention to it. I should hate anyone to read it only through my reports.

I should like to thank my colleagues at St. Edmund Hall for giving me leave for a term in 1970, and the authorities at the Research School of Social Sciences, Australian National University, for giving me a visiting fellowship during that period. I had useful discussions with Dr. E. L. Burge, Mr. K. Lycos, Miss E. Reid while there and was enabled to do the greater part of what follows. I am grateful to Dr. Malcolm Brown for starting me thinking on lines that led to the present interpretation of *peras* and *apeiron*. I am also indebted to Mr. M. J. Woods for a number of suggestions and criticisms and especially for prodding not too annoyingly until some minimum standard of clarity was achieved on the main theses.

J. C. B. GOSLING

CONTENTS

INTRODUCTION   ix

TRANSLATION   1

NOTES   73

GENERAL COMMENTARY   139

BIBLIOGRAPHY   229

ADDENDA   231

INDEX   233

INTRODUCTION

The main theme of the dialogue seems clear enough. The question at issue at first is whether a life of pleasure or of intelligence is the good. It is decided that a life combining both is best, and so the argument shifts to the question of whether intelligence or pleasure can take more credit for it. It is argued that intelligence is vital for the production of the right mixture and that various intellectual pursuits will have pride of place within the mixture. Pleasure comes low down in the scale, and so the dialogue ends, with the victory going to intelligence.

This skeleton conceals a good many problems, however. The major ones can be roughly divided into three. First there are problems as to just how we are supposed to think of the contending parties—pleasure and intelligence. Secondly, there is a methodological or metaphysical section where considerable play is made with two technical terms, *peras* and *apeiron*. We seem to be told that understanding the interplay of these two is the key to all our problems. In fact, they seem to create problems, as it is difficult to extract a coherent interpretation of either of the main sections where they occur, and even more difficult to devise an interpretation which either yields the same technical use of the terms in the two passages or makes it clear how Plato could have thought they were the same. Thirdly, there is a problem as to what the connection is supposed to be between the key to our problems and the problems it is to unlock. Obviously the answer to this cannot be independent of the answers to the previous two problems.

It may, of course, be that there is no answer. Perhaps Plato is hopelessly confused, or has put together a rag-bag of arguments and carelessly failed to note their mutual irrelevance. That is a possible conclusion, but it could only be established by showing that no more coherent interpretation is as plausible. I shall therefore proceed on the assumption that the onus of proof is on the rag-bag theory and that the presumption is in favour of saying that Plato thought with some reason that the various parts were relevant to each other. That, however, is for the notes and commentary. For the present I shall take the main problem areas in turn, and try to indicate the main difficulties within them.

1. Pleasure and Intelligence

At first sight the opposition between Socrates and Philebus seems clear enough. They are arguing about what sort of life a man should aspire to. Socrates holds that a life of sheer intellectual activity without any tainting of pleasure is the ideal or at least preferable to Philebus' candidate. Philebus rejects this academic life and insists on a life of pleasure as everyone's aim. Yet how clear is it? It is tempting to interpret Philebus as holding that the actual (or proper?) way of deciding what to do is to ask what is most pleasurable. This is the only criterion usable by men or animals. Consequently, as that is the only goal found desirable, and as the goal is always pleasure, the ideal is obviously a life of nothing but pleasurable activities. Something of this sort seems to have been held by Eudoxus (cf. Aristotle *Nicomachean Ethics* 1172b) who was influential in the Academy. Such a view, however, involves no antipathy to intelligence, only to pleasureless intelligent activity. It could well be held that intelligence is needed to ensure the most pleasant life possible and that some intellectual activities are pleasant or even among the most pleasant. Perhaps, then, the opposition should be seen as between an intellectual life and a life of pleasure according to the common acceptation of that expression. After all, the name 'Philebus' seems to be an invention of Plato's, translatable as 'Loveboy'. One would expect Mr. Loveboy to have sensual interests, and it is notable that at 12b Philebus' goddess is named Aphrodite, and in general he is portrayed as standing up for roughly physical pleasure. In that case the opposition is between an intellectual life and a life given to certain *sorts* of pleasure. If that is so, Socrates should not be opposed to pleasure *simpliciter*, nor Philebus to all forms of intelligence, but the former to a life devoted to certain pleasures, the latter to a life of intellectual activity not geared to the securing of such pleasures. But Socrates could praise the delights of the intellectual life, and Philebus allow of some intelligent activity. By 20e seq., however, the opposition is spoken of as though it were between a life that contained intellectual activity only and no enjoyment, and a life of constant pleasure without the power to remember, recognize, or anticipate one's pleasure, nor to work out means for its attainment. Philebus is by now portrayed as holding that the fact that a life is at all stages enjoyable, is a necessary, sufficient and, with regard to intelligence, exclusive condition of its being good, that 'good' and 'pleasant' are at least coextensive, if not synonymous. It is hard to imagine any hedonist seriously holding this position, and the question arises whether Plato was aware of these different ways of interpreting the dispute. If not, the statement of the issue carries its confusion over to the solution. If so, perhaps he realized the implausibility of Philebus' position in its last form. In that case, it may have been his purpose to draw attention to the fact that if we take strictly the position that the good life is a life that is pleasant and no more, we get this absurd conclusion. The position would be to the effect that pleasure was not simply the criterion for determining what factors constitute a good life, but of itself constituted a good life. The tactic would be similar to that in the early part of the *Theaetetus* where Socrates brings out the absurdity of saying that knowledge is nothing but perception; to be plausible we should take 'perception' to mean 'perceptual judgement'. So here, we must not interpret 'good life' as 'life of pleasure alone'. Here, too, judgement must come in. Otherwise we exclude many pleasures (e.g. of memory) and lack the means to work out better combinations of pleasures. So 'pleasurable' and 'good' are not coextensive with regard to constituents of the good life.

How could we tell where Plato stands on this? One way would be to look for verbal indications of the differences in the various passages cited. Another would be to see whether any use seems to be made of the distinctions in the argument about whether pleasure or intelligence is to be given credit for the good life, and especially in its solution. Unfortunately these areas do not yield any straightforward answer. The only interpretation that seems no longer to feature in the later parts of the dialogue is that which takes Protarchus' position as being that the only fact necessary or relevant to a life's being good is that it be pleasant (but cf. 55a-b and 60a). Both the others seem to be present without Plato's bothering to distinguish them clearly. At least one function of the distinction between the determinant (*peras*) and the indeterminate (*apeiron*) is to distinguish between that which determines that a mixture is good, and that of which the mixture is in some sense constituted. A melody is made up of sounds, but what makes it tuneful, i.e. a good combination of sounds, is the arrangement and proportions that hold between them. This latter is the *peras*, the former the *apeiron*. In general, we can never determine whether or not a combination is good by reference to the *apeiron* but only by reference to the *peras*. Now the good life is a combination and what makes it good is that the constituents are correctly combined. Pleasure is one of the constituents, an *apeiron*, and so one could not determine whether or not the combination was a good one simply by reference to the fact that it had some pleasures in it. At least part of the point of putting pleasure in the category of *apeiron* would seem to be to make it clear that we cannot determine whether or not a life is good by reference to its pleasure properties. It is, of course, according to Socrates, a necessary condition of a human life's being a good one that it contain some pleasures, but that is of no help in deciding which pleasures are to be included. Once the argument of 12-13 is accepted, that 'pleasure' does not denote a point of similarity between pleasures, activities cannot be compared for their power to produce the common ingredient, pleasure. We are left with dissimilar pleasures, and stand in need of a criterion for deciding which are to be included, and how they are to be ordered.

Yet while it is tempting to say that Plato is wanting to make the point that the fact that a life is pleasant does not determine whether or not it is good, when he comes to the final prize-giving at 65 seq., this is not quite the way he talks. Instead we get different types of pleasure spoken of, some of them are given an examination order, others—those espoused by Philebus—are excluded from the list altogether. The procedure is the more puzzling in that it looks as though we have independent contenders, various pleasures, various forms of knowledge, such that when one set is included it is still an open question whether to include the other. Yet the pleasure of doing geometry could not be included while excluding the practice of geometry, and it is a moot point whether Plato did not think that the converse also held. In that case, putting the same items in two different categories might be a clumsy way of making a difference between two facts about the items (viz., that they were branches of knowledge, that they were pleasures), a clumsiness adopted because he is about to make a point against certain forms of pleasure where he wants to be able to have a separate set of items and make a difference between the sets. In short, he seems to be blending the polemic that pleasure does not determine the goodness of a life with the polemic that certain pleasures are bad. The polemics are not incompatible, but then nor are they identical.

I said earlier that it is a moot point whether Plato thought that to include in a life the activity of geometry was ipso facto to include the pleasure of geometry. I do not mean to suggest by this that he thought that everyone who does geometry enjoys it. The point is that there is room for disagreement on how Plato thinks of pleasure. It is natural in English to talk of pleasure as something one gets out of experiences, or that is aroused in one by them, as in some way experientially distinct from its causes. Greek, too (cf. 12d, 66c) has idioms of following, accompanying, and causing which could suggest a similar separation between the activity and the pleasure that results from it. At the same time there is reason to suppose that Plato wished to resist this separation. The arguments at 12c seq., on the multiformity of pleasure, suggest resistance to the view that pleasure is in some sense a single repeated effect of varying activities. This, of course, leaves the possibility that pleasures are mutually dissimilar but are, nevertheless, effects of their activities, though I think the details of the passage suggest exclusion even of that. The argument about false pleasures at 46 seq. on one interpretation also suggests that Plato would reject that, that he would want to say that the pleasure of anticipation consists in the picturing of a future pleasure, and that there is not some further item, the pleasure, resultant on picturing the future pleasure. If he is prepared to consider pleasures as effects of activities, then some of the awkwardness of the final ordering mentioned earlier would be eased. On the other hand that would raise questions about the passage on false pleasures and even about the early section on multiformity.

To sum up: it is not clear whether Plato sees his main objective as rejecting (i) the view that the way to determine whether a given way of life is good is to assess its pleasurableness, (ii) the view that the sybaritic life is the good life, or (iii) the view that a life of which it was only true that it was pleasant—the 'only' serving at any rate to exclude intelligence—would be the only good life. He may, of course, wish to reject all three, but at least at first sight they seem different, and Plato seems to move among them as though they were identical, a fact which makes it difficult to discern the precise aim of various parts of the argument. Underlying this problem is the question of just how Plato thought of pleasure, a question which runs over into other dialogues than the *Philebus*.

2. *Peras and apeiron*

In discussing pleasure I said that at least one function of the distinction between *peras* and *apeiron* was to mark the difference between what determines that a given mixture or combination is a good one, and the ingredients of the mixture. It is, however, only clearly plausible to say this of the later passage (23 seq.) where the distinction is used. Even there the above statement covers a multitude of interpretations. It can hardly be said to be the function of the distinction in the earlier passage (16c seq.). As I said earlier, there are problems about each passage, and about their interrelations, and I propose to take them in turn.

16c.

(The Heavenly Tradition)

This is the first introduction of the terms *peras* and *apeiron*, with the emphasis heavily on the latter. The standard interpretation here is to say that Plato is considering the division of genera into species, and is recommending careful and complete division into subspecies until the point is reached where no further significant differentiations can be made. At that point we abandon ourselves to the unlimited particular instances. It is, however, important to the advancement of knowledge not to be content to think in terms of genera and the particulars that fall under them. Knowledge is advanced by careful and complete classification. Thus we have a picture of the single, undifferentiated covering concept, the multitude of instances, and between them the various subdivisions of the covering concept.

This picture seems to fit the early part quite well, with the possible exception of one sentence to be discussed in the notes; but if we take the talk of species seriously it looks less happy when we come to the illustrations. The high and the low are hardly species of sound. Rather they determine one scale, as distinct from another, the fast and slow. Pitch and tempo are not subspecies of sound, but they are, apparently, in Plato's terminology, subdivisions of the one. But if it is not classification into species that is recommended, what is it? What methodological programme, if any, do we have?

As to this, it may be that it is a mistake to look on the passage in the rather linguistic way suggested. Perhaps Plato is interested not so much in the conceptual apparatus, as, characteristically, in the reality for which it is supposed to cater. It is sound, not the concept of sound, in which the inquirer is interested. It is sound that is in a sense a single entity in which a determinate number of forms is discernible, but is itself a phenomenon that manifests the struggle between the elements of the determinant and indeterminacy. On this interpretation Plato is not, at least primarily, interested in driving a wedge between universals and particulars, or classes and their members, claiming that there is a definite number of the former but an indeterminate number of the latter; rather he is on ground familiar from earlier dialogues claiming that the observable world contains both ordered and disordered elements, or, perhaps better, is the result of the imposition of order on only partially tractable material. There is, once this is recognized, no hope of reducing it to complete order. On the other hand, there is no reason to give up at the beginning. Knowledge is advanced by spelling out the degree of order that can be found, but always the order is to some extent an abstraction. We may talk of b flat, but any two actual notes will, because of the disorderly nature of the material world, differ in ways for which we have no name and which it is not useful to try to specify. The expression '*apeiron*' indicates not the indefinite number of particulars, but the residual intractability of phenomena. The message of hope is that this intractability is limited.

When we try to settle this question there are, of course, particular passages that require special scrutiny within the section itself. There are also three further points to be borne in mind. First, the terms *peras* and *apeiron*, while not common in Plato in a technical sense, were common terms in mathematical discussions in his day. Secondly, the passage occurs in a context, and the claim is that the points about *peras* and *apeiron* will help us with a puzzle about pleasure, so that interpretations should be subjected to the test of relevance to that puzzle. Thirdly, the terms recur at 23 seq. in a way that suggests a recall not simply of the words, but of the doctrine of the earlier passage. Consequently the interpretation of the first ought to be such that Plato could conceivably have thought it identical with the interpretation of the second.

23.

(*The Cosmos*)

In this section the talk of *peras* and *apeiron* is recalled, and we are told that the whole universe can be divided into four elements: *peras, apeiron*, combinations of these two, and intelligence. '*Apeiron*' stands, roughly, for a class of scales—hot and cold, fast and slow, and anything that admits of degrees. The point of the expression '*apeiron*' here seems clearly to indicate the lack of determinateness of the scales. '*Peras*' by contrast stands for precise numbers and proportions which determine a place on the scale and yield a definite temperature, speed, or whatever in place of the indeterminate potentiality. The result of imposing a particular quantity on a given potentiality yields a member of the third class, and intelligence is the cause responsible for the combination.

Each term, with the possible exception of 'intelligence', raises considerable problems. When '*apeiron*' is illustrated the suggestion is very much that any specific temperature such as 32°Fahrenheit is a determination within a range of possibilities. 32 °Fahrenheit is the result of imposing a particular limit on the possibilities of variation within the range. The indeterminateness of the expression 'temperature' is replaced by a specification of a definite temperature, brought about by specifying a precise numerical reading.

As expounded this is most easily put as a point about the analysis of certain concepts. The point will be that certain concepts such as '32 °Fahrenheit', 'b flat', and so on have to be analysed as indicating both a subject-matter of scalar measurement and a determinate point on the scale. 'Temperature', 'angle' give us alternative forms of scale on which 32 ° might be a point, but are themselves indeterminate. '32 °' is a precise mark, but useless until we know the scale on which it is a point. Some concepts just are concepts of a particular determination of a range of possibilities.

There are problems about this interpretation. To begin with there is a close tie (cf. 25d-26a) between the imposition of *peras* and the production of *good* combinations. As elaborated so far the interpretation is a far more general one about concepts that indicate a determination on a scale. But any temperature or note satisfies that point, without qualifying as a good temperature or a melody. This would not necessitate the abandonment of any such view, for it could be reformulated as saying that Plato's claim is that certain concepts, such as those of melody and health, are concepts of proper determinations within certain ranges. This move would, of course, still leave us with the question of whether the early illustrations of '*apeiron*' can be interpreted in other than a purely scalar way, so that the removal of *apeiron* produces harmony. But that is a puzzle anyway.

Even as amended, this seems a very quiet view of *apeiron*. The point being made is just that certain concepts, being concepts of good mixtures, involve reference to a range within which excess and deprivation are possible. Thus in composing a melody the notes have to have the right pitch relative to others. That entails the possibility of a note too high or too low. But this hardly justifies Plato's use of turbulent unruly descriptions of *apeiron*, with the suggestion that only with difficulty is it kept in order (cf. 25e-26a, 30c, 52c-d). Further, the mixtures, on this account, are concepts, and certainly not physical occupants. But the language at 30b-c strongly suggests that if the result of combining *peras* and *apeiron* is not a physical occupant it is at least a good state of a physical occupant. These points have led to attempts to interpret '*apeiron*' as a first move towards something like an Aristotelian concept of matter. The passage now takes on a cosmological air reminiscent of the *Timaeus*. But whereas there Place plays the role of receptacle of forms, in the *Philebus* we have a set of potentialities to determination in given ways, and the determination is brought about by the *peras*, the numerical element. This would give us a place in the dialogues where

Plato starts to elaborate the very mathematicized account of the Forms attributed to his later years by Aristotle.

Briefly, then, and concealing many variations, the tendencies are to interpret Plato either as making points about the analysis of certain concepts, or as speculating on the constitution of the universe, or, of course, as failing to distinguish the two.

3. The two passages compared

If we now turn to the comparison of the earlier Heavenly Tradition and the later passage, one point stands out clearly: in none of the interpretations of the later passage is the expression '*apeiron*' used to indicate the status of particular or member of a species. Its role is either to denote an element in the constitution of particulars, or to denote that of which in a given mixture there could be too much, or too little. Consequently any interpretation of the Heavenly Tradition that makes it the role of '*apeiron*' to indicate the status of instance through the characterisation of instances as not limitable in number, has the consequence that '*apeiron*' has different roles in the two passages. Similarly, on such an interpretation there is no scope in the earlier passage for combining *peras* and *apeiron* to produce either a concept or an individual.

As I have said, the word '*peras*' is hardly used in the earlier passage. On the other hand the word '*poson*' (quantity?) is frequent, and the same word recurs in the later passage constantly in connection with *peras*. One might therefore expect that it is a stand-in for '*peras*' in the earlier passage. On any interpretation, however, its role looks different. To discover the quantity, in the Heavenly Tradition, seems to be to discover the number of subdivisions within a given unit such as sound. In the later passage it does not indicate the number of subdivisions of a more generic concept, but the precise, say, pitches of various notes and the relations between them. In short, the recommendation to seek out the quantity seems different in the two passages, the connection being verbal only and confusing at that. The interpretation of the earlier passage that makes '*apeiron*' indicate the residual intractability of the material world stands some chance of at least seeming to combine with a view of the later passage as cosmological, but neither is free of difficulties within the relevant sections, or free of problems about relevance to the initial puzzle about pleasure. It may seem less costly to accept a lack of cohesion between the passages.

4. Relevance to the solution

Strictly, only the second passage on *peras* and *apeiron* has to be relevant to the conclusion of the dialogue. That is to say, that passage is specifically introduced to help determine whether pleasure or intelligence wins second prize. One would expect, therefore, to witness some examination of an *apeiron* and discussion of the *peras* to be imposed. What we get is distinctions between different general types of pleasure, distinctions between different forms of knowledge, and arguments as to which should be blended together in the good life. The question is: is this what 'finding the *peras* to impose on the *apeiron*' amounts to in the case of the good life? or is the methodological recommendation irrelevant to the procedure followed?

Once again we are left with choices. The irrelevance option ought to be a last resort one unless it can be shown that no relevance is required. On the other hand, the very mathematical description of *peras* at 25a-e gives rise to expectations that receive no fulfilment in the discussion of the good life. Part of the difficulty may be that the discussion is confined to the types of knowledge to be included. We do not reach the question of how frequently and for how long they should be exercised, when some numerical determinations might come in. If we can waive that difficulty, the procedure strongly suggests treating pleasures and forms of knowledge as ingredients of which in the case of pleasure there can be too much or too little, and in the case of knowledge certainly too little. This would suggest treating the various forms of knowledge as *apeiron*, but in fact Plato shies away from any such thing. '*Apeiron*' has overtones of unruliness that make him reserve it, and abusively, for pleasure. Even as regards pleasure, there is no treatment of it as a general scale of more or less pleasurable, as one might expect on analogy with temperature. Instead we get various sorts of pleasure discussed, and the question raised, which should be included? The impression is that to dub pleasure as *apeiron* is not to treat it as a potentiality for determinations, but rather to treat pleasures as items which, relative to the good life mixture, can be over- or underdone. If we take it that the procedure in the last part of the dialogue ought to reflect the immediately preceding recommendations, then the facts of that procedure will reflect back on our interpretation of the preceding section, and will doubtless prove incompatible with some views.

To sum up: each passage on *peras* and *apeiron* has its own problems, even if treated in isolation. Each passage is supposed to bear on other problems raised in the dialogue, and both passages are supposed to purvey the same basic doctrine. Interpretation consequently involves not only attention to the passages themselves, but a complex interplay between all the parts of the dialogue, so that some proposed interpretations call in question in varying degrees the internal cohesion of the work. Nor can one isolate the problems raised at the beginning of this introduction about pleasure, from those on *peras* and *apeiron*. The tendency to speak of *apeiron* as disorderly may be related to a tendency to view the opposition as advocating pursuit of violent pleasures. If *apeiron* is interpreted in terms of potentiality to various forms of determination, one will want to know what bearing if any the characterization of pleasure as *apeiron* has on Plato's view of the nature of pleasure. Only when it is shown that it is impossible to make the various parts of the dialogue cohere can one safely treat it as a set of isolable sections treating separate topics or giving independent treatment to related topics.

None of the above is intended to suggest that there are not other interesting problems of interpretation in the *Philebus*. There are many. What I hope to have done is give some of the major questions to be asked of the dialogue. There are many other consequential questions which any reader who pursues the matter will raise for himself, and other less central ones which are not the less interesting for that. It is probably more helpful, however, for finding one's way about a work to start with the major queries and work to the more detailed points needed for their settlement.

One final comment, on the date of the dialogue. The usual opinion is that it is one of the very latest. It is certainly post-*Republic*, but its relation to the *Politicus* is uncertain, and anyone who wished to date the *Timaeus* early after the *Republic* might be tempted to put the *Philebus* among the early late dialogues also. I have not argued the matter here. The considerations are exceedingly complex. There are stylometric ones, which are not easy to manage even when one waives consideration of the poetic or polemical purpose of a dialogue. Then there are arguments from philosophical development which naturally rely both on detailed interpretation of other dialogues, judgements of relative sophistication, and assumptions about the probability of a philosopher growing more naive; and there are considerations from the history of mathematics. All this is beyond the scope of the present work, and while my own bias is towards putting the *Philebus* among the latest of the dialogues, it does not seem to me obvious nor could I as yet argue it to my own satisfaction.

PHILEBUS

Socrates. I think you would be well advised, Protarchus, to look **11a** carefully at the position you are now taking over from Philebus, and also at the one from our side that you will have to argue against. Make sure you agree to their formulation. Would you like me to **b** summarize them?

Protarchus. That would be a great help.

Soc. Philebus holds that what is good—and this goes for all ***** living things—is enjoyment, pleasure, delight, and all that sort of **5** thing. I hold, by contrast, that intelligence, thought, memory, and other things in that category, correct views and accurate reasoning are, for anything capable of them, preferable and superior to pleasure; indeed to all those capable of a share of them, whether **c** now or in the future, they are of the greatest possible benefit. Is that a fair account of our two positions, Philebus?

Philebus. It couldn't be bettered.

Soc. Are you prepared to accept the position now being offered **5** to you, then, Protarchus?

Prot. I have no choice since our lovely Philebus has cried off.

Soc. And we agree that we should make every effort to get to the truth of the matter?

Prot. Of course. **d**

Soc. I wonder if we could agree on one further point.

Prot. What?

Soc. That at this stage each of us is trying to show that a certain state or condition of a person (*psyche*) is the one capable or providing ***5** all men with the most desirable life. Isn't that right? *****

Prot. Certainly.

Soc. And your position is that this state is one of enjoyment, mine that it is one of intelligence?

Prot. Yes. **10**

Soc. Suppose some other state turns out to be preferable to ***** both of these? Could we agree that if it turns out to be more closely **e** related to pleasure, then while we both lose to the life which

1

12a secures these characteristics, still the pleasant life wins over the life of thought?

Prot. Agreed.

Soc. If, on the other hand, it is plainly more closely related to thought, then thought will win and pleasure will lose? Are you prepared to agree?

5   *Prot.* Yes.

Soc. What about Philebus? Do you agree?

*   *Phil.* My view is, and always will be, that pleasure is the undoubted winner,—but it is for you, Protarchus, to decide.

Prot. As you have handed the argument over to me it is no
10 longer for you to say whether or not to agree to Socrates' proposal.

b   *Phil.* True enough—but I should like to wash my hands of all responsibility in the matter, and I call the goddess to witness that I have no part in it.

Prot. We shall be prepared to bear witness to your saying what
5 you say. Now that is done, Socrates, let's none the less try to thrash the matter out with Philebus' consent, if he gives it, or whatever his wishes may be.

Soc. We must try, then, making the goddess herself our starting point. Philebus calls her Aphrodite, but the most accurate name for her is pleasure.

10   *Prot.* True.

c   *Soc.* The dread that always comes over me, Protarchus, when it comes to naming gods, is not of a human order, but surpasses the greatest fear. So now, if it is Aphrodite who is in question I will call her by whatever name she prefer; but when it comes to pleasure, I
5 am well aware that it is not something simple, and as I said before, we must start by considering pleasure and examining its nature. Mentioned by itself like that, it sounds like a single thing, but it no doubt takes all sorts of forms, which in some way are unlike each
d other. For instance, we describe a rake as getting pleasure, but also a sober man as getting pleasure from his sobriety; then we say that a silly man, full of silly ideas and hopes, gets pleasure, but that it is
5 precisely from being sensible that a sensible man gets pleasure. Yet surely it would be a proof of stupidity to say in these cases that the pleasures in each pair were alike?

Prot. But that's only because they come from opposite things. It is not that they are themselves opposed to each other. How on earth could pleasure be anything but most like pleasure—it's the thing being most like itself.

Soc. That argument will hold just as well for colour being like colour: so far as being a colour goes each one is the same, but we all know that black is not just different from white, but as opposite as can be. The same holds with relationships between figures: in kind they are all one, but when it comes to parts of the kind in relation to other parts, some are as opposite to each other as possible, while others show countless differences—and we shall find many other examples of the same thing. So don't put any trust in this argument, at least, for identifying all the most extreme opposites. In fact, I suspect we shall find that some pleasures are the opposites of others.

Prot. Suppose we did: how would that tell against my position?

Soc. Because I should object that despite their dissimilarity you are applying another term to them in that you are saying that all pleasant things are good. Now no argument will dispute that all pleasant things are pleasant; but although it is my claim that while some are good, most are bad, you are calling them all good, while at the same time, if pressed, admitting that they are not alike. What is the common feature in bad and good pleasures alike that makes you call all pleasures a good thing?

Prot. What do you think you are up to, Socrates? Do you think anyone who puts forward the thesis that pleasure is the good is going to let you say some pleasures are good, others bad?

Soc. Yet you will admit that some are unlike each other at least, and that some are even opposites of others.

Prot. Not at all, at least in so far as they are pleasures.

Soc. That brings us back to where we started, Protarchus. We are not to say in short that pleasures differ, but that they are all alike. Immune to the examples we have just been through, we are to join chorus with the least reputable of philosophical neophytes.

Prot. What on earth do you mean?

Soc. Just that I could counter-attack, taking my cue from you. For I could use your very arguments to prove the rash claim that of all things what is most unlike is most like what is most unlike. That

* would be too glaring a proof of our immaturity and our discussion will get hissed off the stage. Suppose we back up a little. Perhaps if we can get properly to grips with one another we shall be able to reach some agreement.

e *Prot.* What's your suggestion?

 Soc. Pretend that I am having a turn at being questioned by you.

 Prot. Well?

5 *Soc.* Take all the things that I, at the beginning, put forward in answer to the question 'What is the good?', intelligence and knowledge and understanding at the rest—won't they be vulnerable to the same difficulty experienced by your position?

 Prot. How?

 Soc. All the forms of knowledge together will seem to constitute
10 a plurality, and some of them to be unlike others. Even if some turned
14a out to be opposites of others, I should not now deserve to take part in a discussion if I took alarm at the fact and declared that no form of knowledge could be unlike another. The discussion would then collapse like a story that loses its audience, and we should be saved
5 on an absurdity.

 Prot. We must certainly not let that happen, except for the saving part. I am satisfied for my part, so long as both our positions are treated the same. So let us agree that there are many dissimilar pleasures and many different forms of knowledge.

*b *Soc.* In that case let us not conceal the variations shown by the good, whether your candidate or mine. Indeed, we should bring them clearly into the open, and face the possibility that under examination they may make clear whether we should call pleasure the
5 good, or intelligence, or some third thing. For I take it that we are not now just vying to prove my candidate or yours the winner, but shall join forces in favour of whatever is nearest the truth.

 Prot. Of course.

c *Soc.* Then there is a question on which we should get firmer agreement.

 Prot. Meaning?

 Soc. One that has given everyone trouble, which some have at
*5 times been glad to receive, others not.

 Prot. Can't you be clearer?

Soc. I mean the one that has just dropped in our laps which is so
bewildering. For saying many things are in fact one or one many is a
bewildering thing to say, and it is easy to dispute with anyone who
says either.   10

Prot. You mean when someone says of me, Protarchus, that
though I am by nature one thing yet there are many me's, some even   d
opposites of others, claiming that the same person is large and small,
heavy and light, and a thousand other things?

Soc. No. Those are very commonplace puzzles about one and   5
many; but it is pretty well agreed all round not to bother with them.
People realize they are child's play and just a hindrance to discussion.
The same goes for when someone distinguishes the limbs and parts of   e
any given thing and then gets agreement that all these things are the
one thing he started with, then jeers because he has argued one into
the monstrous assertion that the one is indefinitely many things, and
the many things one.

Prot. Then what are these other puzzles on this same subject,   5
which are not yet commonplace nor have agreed solutions?

Soc. When the one a person posits is not a generable or perish-   **15a**
able thing as in these last examples. For it is agreed that about a one
of that sort, as we said just now, there is no need to waste time
arguing. But when someone wishes to posit man, ox, beauty, or the   5
good each as one, a burning interest in making divisions within this
sort of unit is matter for controversy.

Prot. Why?

Soc. First, there's the question whether we should suppose there   b
are any such units in the strict sense; then how they can be such that *
while each is a unit and remains unchanged admitting neither of
generation nor destruction, it is nevertheless unshakeably one but   *
then as found in the indeterminate number of perishable things it is   5
questionable whether it has to be posited as scattered abroad and
become many or, as itself while whole separated from itself, which
seems absolutely impossible, becoming the identical one at once in a
one and a plurality. These are the questions about these sorts of one   c
and many, not those others, that are the cause of all the difficulties
in this area if wrongly, and of all progress if rightly settled.

Prot. Then this must be our first task now?   5

Soc. In my opinion, yes.

Pròt. Then you can take it that all of us here agree with you, though in Philebus' case it would perhaps be best to let sleeping dogs lie, and not ask him.

d   *Soc.* Well then, where shall we begin? There is considerable dispute at a variety of points over this issue. I think I know the place to start, though.

Prot. Where?

*   *Soc.* In my view the identification of one and many by state-
5   ments crops up all over the place in everything that is ever said, and it's not a new phenomenon. Indeed, it seems to me, this is an
*   indestructible and unchanging feature of our statements, which is not only not new but will always be with us. When a young man
e   first savours it, he is delighted, as if he had found some treasure of
*   wisdom. His delight goes to his head and he loves to worry every statement, sometimes rolling it one way and kneading it into a single ball, then unrolling it again and tearing it apart. The result is
5   confusion, first of all for himself, but also for anyone who happens to be by, whatever his age. He has no mercy on his father nor
16a   mother, nor on any of his audience. He hardly spares the other animals, let alone human beings, since he would not even spare foreigners at least if only he had an interpreter.

5   *Prot.* Can't you see, Socrates, that the whole crowd of us are young men? Aren't you afraid that we might gang up with Philebus against you if you are rude to us? Still, we know what you mean. If there is any way of politely keeping the discussion free of such
b   upsets and finding a better way than this to conduct the argument, set your mind to it and we will follow as best we can, for the present dispute is not a trivial one.

5   *Soc.* Indeed not, my children, as Philebus calls you. There could be no finer way than the one of which I have always been a devotee, though often it has slipped through my fingers and left me empty-handed and bewildered.

Prot. What way is that? I wish you would speak out.

c   *Soc.* It is not difficult to expound, but it is very difficult to apply. It has been responsible for bringing to light everything that
*   has been discovered in the domain of any skill. You must examine

the method I mean.

Prot.   Tell us what it is, then.

Soc.   As I see it, it was a gift from the gods to men, thrown down   5
from the gods in a blaze of light by some Prometheus. Our fore-
fathers, superior beings to us as they lived closer to the gods, passed
on this tradition, that those things which are from time to time said   *
to be are made up of one and many, with a determinant and   *10
indeterminacy inherent in them. Since this is how things are con-   d
stituted we should always posit a single form in respect to every one
and search for it—we shall find one there—and if we are successful,   *
then after the one we should look for two, if there are two, or
otherwise for three or whatever the number is; each of these ones
should be treated in the same way, until one can see of the original   5
one not only that it is one, a plurality, and an indefinite number,
but also its precise quantity. But one should not attribute the   *
character of indeterminate to the plurality until one can see the
complete number between the indeterminate and the one. Then one   e
can consign every one of them to the indeterminate with a clear
conscience. As I said, this is the procedure for inquiring, learning,
and teaching each other that the gods have handed on to us. But
present day intellectuals are both too quick and too slow in making   *17a
any one they encounter a plurality. From the one they pass straight
to the indeterminate and the intervening areas slip through their
fingers—and by these is made the difference between our arguments'   5
with each other being philosophical and being sophistical.

Prot.   I think I partly understand what you say, but some things
I need to have put more clearly.

Soc.   The point is clear in the case of letters, so suppose you take
an example where you have had some training.   b

Prot.   How does it go?

Soc.   Vocal sound is, you will agree, just a single thing that comes
out of our mouths, of indeterminate variety, whether you consider   *
an individual or the population at large.

Prot.   Clearly.   5

Soc.   Now we are not as yet experts in virtue of either of these
things, by familiarity either with its indeterminate aspect, or its
unity. What makes a person a lettered person is knowing the

7

quantities of different sounds and their properties.

10　　*Prot.* Obviously.

Soc. What is more, the same holds for what makes a musician.

Prot. How?

*c　　*Soc.* You will grant that vocal sound in the skill of letters also is one.

Prot. Of course.

Soc. And we distinguish two things, high and low pitch, and a

5　　third, even pitch? Or what would you say?

Prot. Yes.

Soc. But you would not yet be a musical expert if you only knew these, although it you did not even know them you would be pretty well worthless in these matters.

10　　*Prot.* Yes indeed.

Soc. Now suppose we take high and low pitch, and you know

d　　the quantities of the intervals and their nature and the notes that limit the intervals, and how many arrangements of them there are— noticing these things our ancestors instructed us their successors to call them scales, and observing other similar characteristics in

5　　physical movements they said that they were to be measured and called rhythms and measures—and at the same time to realize that this was the proper procedure for dealing with every one and

e　　many. For when you have a grasp of them in the way outlined you are already an expert and whenever by this method you get hold of any other one you become an authority on it. But the indeterminate plurality of anything in any case leaves you with an indeterminate

5　　grasp of the subject. It makes you of no repute, of no account—as is

*　　only right for someone who can never give account of anything.

Prot. Socrates seems to me to have made his point very well, Philebus.

18a　　*Phil.* I agree at least on these matters. But what has all this got to do with us? What is he getting at?

Soc. That is a good question of Philebus', Protarchus.

5　　*Prot.* It is indeed. Why don't you answer it?

Soc. I will in a moment. But first I want to pursue this point a little further. If a person grasps any one, then, as I say, he must not turn immediately to its indeterminate character but rather look for

some number. Similarly the other way round, when one is forced to
start with what is indeterminate, one should not immediately look   *b
to the unitary aspect, but again note some number embracing every
plurality, and from all these end up at the one. Let us take up the
present point again in connection with letters.

Prot. How do you mean?   5

Soc. Well, once, I suppose, some god, or some man very like a
god, noticed the indeterminacy of vocal sound. The Egyptians have a
story that it was someone called Theuth who first noticed that in
this indeterminate variety there were several vocables (vowels), not
just one, and then that there were others that could be sounded but   c
were not vowels and that there was a definite number of these, and
finally he distinguished a third class of letters that we now call mutes.
He then distinguished the soundless ones or mutes down to single
letters, and did the same with the vowels and semi-vowels. When he   5
had the full count he gave them, individually and collectively, the
name 'element'. As he realized that none of us would ever learn
about one of them in isolation from the rest, he concluded that this
constituted a single bond that somehow made them a single unit,   d
and pronounced the single skill that covered them 'the art of letters'.

Phil. I have understood these interconnections even more clearly
than the previous ones, Protarchus, but the discussion has the same
shortcoming for me now that it had a little earlier.   5

Soc. You mean you can't see the relevance of it?

Phil. Precisely. Protarchus and I have been trying to see it for
some time.

Soc. Then you have for some time been looking for what's under   e
your feet.

Phil. What do you mean?

Soc. Hasn't the argument always been about whether we should
choose intelligence or pleasure?

Phil. Of course.   5

Soc. And we call each of them one thing?

Phil. Yes.

Soc. Well, that is precisely the problem of our earlier discussion:
how can each of them be one and many? How is it that they are not
without more ado of indeterminate number, instead of each having a   **19a**

precise number before becoming indeterminately many?

Prot. I don't know how he has done it, Philebus, but Socrates
has led us round till we have to face a really difficult question.
Which of us is to answer this one? It may seem ridiculous for me,
after that unconditional promise to take over the argument, to
commission you again, just because I cannot answer it; but it would
be far more ridiculous if neither of us could. What shall we do?
Socrates seems to be asking whether there are forms of pleasure,
and if so, their quantity and of what sort they are, and similarly
with intelligence.

Soc. You have my point exactly. As our recent discussion
warns us, none of us will be worth a straw if we cannot do this for
everything we call one, similar, the same, or the opposite.

Prot. I dare say you are right, Socrates. Still, while it may be
fine for a sage to know everything, it is a good second-best not to
delude oneself. You wonder why I say this at this point? I will tell
you. You are giving us the benefit of yourself in this meeting to
decide what is the best possession a man could have. Philebus says
it is pleasure, enjoyment, delight, and everything of that sort. You
object that it is not these things but those others, which we are
constantly reminding ourselves about, willingly and rightly, so that
bearing both in mind we may test them properly. You, it seems, hold
that a good which will correctly be said to be better than pleasure
at least, is intelligence, knowledge, understanding, skill, and everything in that general category, and that these are what we should
acquire rather than pleasure and the like. When those positions had
been stated, with some argument, we pretended to threaten to
keep you here until the dispute was satisfactorily determined. You
agreed and offered yourself for this purpose, and as children say,
gifts properly given cannot be taken back. So will you please give up
your way of resisting us in the present discussion.

Soc. What are you talking about?

Prot. You keep throwing us into confusion and asking questions
that we won't as yet be able to answer adequately. It is no use
thinking that the confusion of all of us here is our aim in the present
discussion. If we cannot find the answer ourselves, you must, as you
promised. So as to the present point *you* decide whether you must

distinguish various forms of pleasure and understanding, or whether you can let is pass, if in any way you are able and willing to settle our present dispute by some other means.

Soc. As you put it that way, at least I have nothing to be afraid of. That 'if you are willing' removes all foreboding. What is more, by some inspiration I seem to have remembered something that will help us. **b**

Prot. What? **5**

Soc. I am thinking of some discussions I heard, a long time ago now—it may even have been a dream—about pleasure and intelligence. The upshot was that neither of them is the good, but some third thing, distinct from either and better than both. Now if we can come to a clear view of this, pleasure will be deprived of the victory, for the good would not be identical with it. Do you agree? **c**

Prot. Certainly.

Soc. In my view, then, we shan't now need the tools for distinguishing various forms of pleasure. But this will become clearer as we go on. *** 5**

Prot. That's a promising start. Carry on.

Soc. Let us agree on a few small points first.

Prot. What, for instance?

Soc. Is it the fate of the good to be of necessity in the category of the perfect or of the imperfect? ***d**

Prot. In that of the most perfect of all, of course.

Soc. And will the good be something sufficient?

Prot. Of course. More so than anything else. **5**

Soc. One thing about it one cannot readily deny is that everything capable of knowing pursues it, longing to take hold of it and possess it, and they all make no account of anything else unless its accomplishment involves some good. *** 10**

Prot. That's undeniable.

Soc. Let us take the lives of pleasure and intelligence separately and judge each one on its own. **e**

Prot. How do you mean?

Soc. Intelligence must form no part of the life of pleasure, nor pleasure of the intelligent life. For if either of them is the good it must be sufficient by itself. If either turns out to be insufficient, **5**

11

21a then it is not as yet the real good for us.

    Prot. Certainly not.

    Soc. Can we test them on you?

5   *Prot.* All right.

    Soc. You answer my question then.

    Prot. Ask away.

    Soc. Would you, Protarchus, be willing to live your whole life enjoying the greatest pleasures?

10   *Prot.* Of course I would.

    Soc. Granted you have such a life, without any qualifications, would you consider that you lacked anything?

    Prot. Nothing at all.

    Soc. Tell me, then, would you have no need at all of intelligence,

b   thought, calculation of your need, and all that sort of thing?

    Prot. Why? I should have everything if I had pleasure.

*   *Soc.* So you would be glad to live your life like that constantly enjoying the greatest pleasures?

5   *Prot.* Of course.

*   *Soc.* But if you lacked thought, memory, knowledge, and true opinion, surely, to begin with, you couldn't know even whether you were enjoying yourself or not, since you would lack all intelligence.

    Prot. True.

c   *Soc.* What is more, in the same way, as you would lack memory, you would be unable to remember that you did enjoy yourself on any occasion, and no recollection at all of pleasure at one moment would survive to the next. Since you would lack the capacity for true

5   judgement you would not judge that you were enjoying yourself when you were, and lacking the ability to predict you would be unable to predict your future pleasures. It wouldn't be a human life at all, but a jelly-fish existence, or the life of one of those sea things

d   that live (*empsychos*) in shells. Aren't I right? Or can we escape the conclusion?

    Prot. It seems inescapable.

    Soc. Could we consider such a life desirable?

5   *Prot.* Your argument has me thrown for the moment, Socrates. I have nothing to say.

    Soc. We mustn't give up yet. Let's turn now to examine the life of thought.

Prot. How would you describe that?

Soc. The supposed case of someone who agrees to live gifted
with complete intelligence, thought, knowledge, and a memory of 10
everything, but without even the most meagre experience of pleasure, e
or distress either—he is not subject at all to any of these things.

Prot. Neither of these lives seems to me worth choosing,
Socrates, and I think anyone would agree with me.

Soc. What about a joint life, Protarchus, made up of a mixture 22a
of both elements?

Prot. One of pleasure, thought, and intelligence, you mean?

Soc. Yes, and of things of that sort.

Prot. Anyone would choose that in preference to either of the 5
other two, without exception.

Soc. We are clear what follows for our present argument?

Prot. Certainly. There are three possible lives before us, and of b
two of them neither is adequate or desirable for man or beast.

Soc. Then it's surely clear that neither of these at least can be
the good? For it would have to be adequate, complete, and desirable 5
for anything, plant or animal, capable of so living throughout its life.
If any of us chose anything else he would take it in defiance of the
nature of what is truly desirable, in fact really against his will, *
because of ignorance or some unfortunate necessity.

Prot. That seems right.

Soc. That is enough to show that, at least, one should not c
identify the good with Philebus' goddess.

Phil. Nor is your intelligence the good, Socrates. The same
objections hold against it.

Soc. Perhaps that's true of *my* intelligence, Philebus, but I 5
think the case is different with a truly divine intelligence. Still, I
will not champion intelligence for the prize against the combined
life, but we must decide what to do about the second prize. It may d
be that each of us will claim his own candidate as responsible for
this combined life—I intelligence, you pleasure—so that while neither
is the good, one might claim that one of them is responsible for it.
On this point I should be even readier to contest Philebus. I should 5
hold that in the mixed life, whatever it is that makes the life at once

desirable and good, it is intelligence, not pleasure, that is more closely related to it and more nearly resembles it. If I am right, it
e would never be truly claimed that pleasure had a share in either first or second prize. If we can trust my intuition for the moment, it won't even get third prize.

5 *Prot.* I must say pleasure seems to have taken a beating at the hands of these arguments—it's certainly lost the fight for first prize.
23a It shows good sense that intelligence didn't claim first prize, as it would have suffered the same fate. But if pleasure were completely denied the second prize she would be disgraced in the eyes of her
5 lovers; she would no longer seem so beautiful even to them.

Soc. Do you think, then, it might be better to let her be, rather than cause her pain by subjecting her to a thorough and testing examination?

Prot. Don't talk nonsense, Socrates.

b *Soc.* Why is it nonsense? Because it is impossible for pleasure to suffer pain?

Prot. Not just that. You know very well that we shan't let you go until you have settled these questions.

5 *Soc.* Show some mercy, Protarchus. There's a long argument still ahead of us, and by no means an easy one. In fact, it looks as though we shall need different equipment; anyone going for second prize on behalf of intelligence will need other weapons than our earlier arguments, though perhaps some of the old ones will help. We are to carry on then?

10 *Prot.* Of course.

c *Soc.* In that case, we must be very careful to get our starting-point right.

Prot. What do you mean?

Soc. Taking everything at present in the universe, let us make a
5 twofold distinction, or perhaps better, if you don't mind, a threefold one.

Prot. What's the principle of the distinction?

Soc. Suppose we avail ourselves of some of our earlier points.

Prot. Which, for instance?

Soc. We said, if you remember, that God had shown us that part of the things that are is indeterminate, part a determinant.

Prot. Agreed.

Soc. Let's take these as two of the categories. The third is a unit   **d** formed by combining these two. I think I shall be making a fool of myself, distinguishing things into kinds and enumerating them.

Prot. What do you mean?

Soc. It looks as though I need a fourth class.   5

Prot. Why don't you tell us what it is?

Soc. Take what is responsible for the combination of these two, and allow me this as a fourth class along with the other three.

Prot. Won't you need a fifth, capable of dissolving the mixture?   10

Soc. Perhaps—but not yet at any rate. If I do, I hope you will   **e** forgive me going after a fifth?

Prot. Of course.

Soc. First, then, let's take three of the four, and concentrate on two of those three. As they are both split into many parts and are   5 found scattered abroad all over the place, we must round each up in   * turn into a single class so as to see how each constitutes both a one and a many.

Prot. If you could be a little clearer, perhaps I should be able to follow you.

Soc. I am talking of the pair which I put forward as the same   **24a** that we had a little while ago; the indeterminate and the determinant.   * I will try to show that the indeterminate is in a way many. The determinant can wait a while.

Prot. All right.   5

Soc. Be on the look-out, then. What I am asking you to consider is difficult and controversial, but you mustn't let that deter you. First of all, see if you can discern any determinant in relation to hotter and colder; or is it true that so long as the greater and less that inhabit these categories continue there they would not permit   **b** any end to come about? Indeed any such ending would be the end of them?

Prot. True enough.

Soc. Now, we agree that hotter and colder always contain more and less?   5

Prot. Yes.

Soc. The argument suggests that these two are always without end. Being without end they are completely indeterminate.

Prot. I strongly agree.

c   *Soc.* You have taken the point well, Protarchus, and reminded me that this 'strongly' that you just mentioned, and 'mildly', have the same characteristics as more and less. Wherever they are present they exclude any definite quantity. They always imbue activities
5   with greater strength over against greater mildness and conversely, rendering them more or less whatever it may be, and ruling out definite quantity. As we agreed just now, if they do not obliterate
d   definite quantity, but allow degree and measure to appear in the midst of more and less, or strongly and mildly, they in fact abandon the territory they occupied. For in admitting of definite quantity they would no longer strictly be hotter or colder. For the hotter goes on without pause, and the colder in the same way, while a definite quantity comes to a particular point and goes no further.
5   So on the present argument the hotter and at the same time its opposite would come out as indeterminate.

Prot. That seems right, Socrates, though as you said, it's not
e   easy to follow. Perhaps constant repetition would show questioner and questioned to be pretty well in agreement in the end.

Soc. Quite right. We must try to do that. For the moment, though, can we accept one mark of the nature of the indeterminate,
5   to avoid the long business of a complete enumeration?

Prot. What have you in mind?

Soc. Everything we find that can become more and less, and
25a   admits of strength and mildness, too much, and everything of that sort, we are to put in the indeterminate category, as constituting a single class. This is in accordance with our earlier point, if you remember, that we should so far as possible round up things that
*   were found scattered abroad and split up and put the brand of a single characterization on them.
5   *Prot.* I remember.

Soc. Things that don't allow these features, but admit of all the opposite things—equal and equality, and after equal, double
*b   and every proportion of number to number or measure to measure, all these we should be advised to apportion to the determinant. Do you agree?

Prot. Completely.

Soc. Well, then. What shall we say of the third class, the mixture   5
of these two? What is it like?

Prot. No doubt you will tell me.

Soc. Perhaps some spirit will. I shall have to pray for inspiration.

Prot. Try a prayer to one and see   10

Soc. All right. You know, I think we have a friendly one,
Protarchus.

Prot. How do you mean? Let's have your evidence.   c

Soc. I'll tell you. You pay attention to my argument.

Prot. Carry on.

Soc. We talked just now of hotter and colder?   5

Prot. Yes.

Soc. Add drier and moister, more and fewer, faster and slower,
larger and smaller, and everything that earlier we put in one class as   10
characteristically susceptible of degrees.

Prot. You mean the character of indeterminacy?   d

Soc. Yes. But now mix with it the class of determinants.

Prot. I don't understand.

Soc. The one we should have rounded up just now—the class of   5
determining elements, as we rounded up the indeterminate into a
single class—but didn't. Perhaps it will do as well though if with   *
these two rounded up that one emerges clearly.

Prot. What class are you talking about?   10

Soc. That of equal and double, and whatever puts an end to   e
opposites being at odds with each other, and by the introduction of
number makes them commensurate and harmonious.   *

Prot. I see. You appear to be saying that combining these will
result in producing something in each case?

Soc. The appearance is no illusion.   5

Prot. Can you be more specific?

Soc. Well, in the case of disease, isn't it the correct blend of
these that generates the characteristics of health?

Prot. Certainly.   **26a**

Soc. Now take high and low, fast and slow, indeterminate
things—isn't the same true? It at once introduces a determinant and
establishes perfectly the whole art of music.

5 *Prot.* Very true.

Soc. Again, in the case of extremes of cold and heat its advent removes what is far too much and indeterminate and produces what is measured and commensurable.

Prot. Yes indeed.

b *Soc.* So the mixture of indeterminate factors and determinants is responsible for good climate and generally for everything we have

* that is fine.

5 *Prot.* Clearly.

Soc. There are countless other things I could mention: the fineness and strength of health, and many fine points of character

* (*psyche*) and intellect (*psyche*) too. For this goddess, Philebus, saw everyone's arrogance and all their other wickedness, with no deter-

10 minant of pleasures and indulgences, and she established law and

c order as determinants. You, of course, will say she destroyed them, but I think that on the contrary she was their salvation. What's your view, Protarchus?

Prot. I agree with you entirely.

Soc. Well, then, if you've understood, that completes the description of three of the classes.

5 *Prot.* I think I've followed you. You seem to be saying that the indeterminate is one and that the second, the determinant in things, is also one; but I'm not too sure what you are getting at with the third.

Soc. The vast variety of the third class has daunted you. Yet the

d indeterminate manifested a large number of forms, although they constituted a single class marked by the more and less.

Prot. True.

* *Soc.* Again, with the determinant, we did not complain either

5 that it exhibited many forms or that it was not itself one.

Prot. Of course not.

Soc. Well then, my point about the third is this: I am asserting that the whole progeny of these two forms one class—where anything

* comes into being from the measure effected by the determinant.

10 *Prot.* I see.

e *Soc.* Now we said earlier that besides these three there was a fourth class to be examined, and you must help me. So tell me, do

18

you think that in all cases of a thing coming to be something there
must be something responsible for its becoming that thing?   *

Prot. I do. How else could it become anything?   5

Soc. What produces and what is responsible for something, I
take it, differ in name only? We are justified in identifying what
produces something and what is responsible for it?

Prot. We are.

Soc. Again, as in the case just now, we shall find that 'that   27a
which is produced' and 'that which becomes something' are just two
ways of saying the same thing?

Prot. Yes.

Soc. And surely that which produces something has a natural   5
priority, and what is produced follows in its train in coming into
being?

Prot. Surely.

Soc. In fact what is responsible for something and that which is
under its influence in the process of generation are not identical?
They are two different things?

Prot. Of course.   10

Soc. Now the things that come into being and their elements
together make our three earlier classes?

Prot. Yes indeed.

Soc. Can we call the factor which fashions all these a fourth   b
class, that which is responsible for them, now adequately shown to
be different from the others?

Prot. Certainly, it's different.

Soc. It will be a good thing, now we have the four distinguished,
to enumerate them in order to help us remember them.   5

Prot. Fair enough.

Soc. The first class, then, is the indeterminate, the second the
determinant, thirdly there is the sort of thing that is brought about
as a mixture of these, and it would be in harmony with what we have
said to call the fourth what is responsible for this mixture and
generation?   c

Prot. Yes indeed.

Soc. Well, we must now consider the next step in the argument,
and see what is the point of what we have covered so far. The point

5   as I see it is this: we wanted to know whether the second prize should go to pleasure or intelligence. Is that right?

Prot. Yes.

Soc. Now we have made these distinctions we may be in a better position to give a final judgement on the candidates we

10   started arguing about, with regard to both first and second prize.

Prot. Perhaps.

d   *Soc.* Come on, then. We declared the mixed life winner over both pleasure and intelligence, didn't we?

Prot. Yes.

5   *Soc.* Then I suppose we can see which this life is and to which category it belongs?

Prot. Of course.

Soc. We shall have to say it falls into the third category. For this category is not limited to any particular pair, but includes all indeterminates bounded by a determinant. So it would embrace the

10   life which we have declared the winner.

Prot. Certainly.

e   *Soc.* Well, what about the life you advocate, Philebus, of unadulterated pleasure? Which of the categories mentioned would be the right one to put it in? But first answer the following question.

Phil. What?

5   *Soc.* Do pleasure and pain have a determinant or do they admit of degrees?

Phil. They admit of degrees, Socrates. Pleasure would not be completely good if its nature was not to be indeterminate in quan-

*   tity and degree.

28a   *Prot.* Nor, for the same reason, would pain be completely evil. So we must find something other than its indeterminate character

*   to give pleasure a share in goodness. But you can leave that as one of the undetermined things. Now take intelligence, knowledge, and

5   thought. To which of these categories do you two think we could allot these without fear of sacrilege? We must be careful. A good deal hangs on getting the right answer to these questions.

b   *Phil.* You are overplaying the importance of your candidate, Socrates.

Soc. No more than you are yours. But anyway, would you

answer my question?

Prot. Socrates is right, Philebus. We must do as he asks. 5

Phil. Well, haven't you undertaken to answer for me?

Prot. I have indeed, but I am in something of a quandary. Would you be a go-between for us, Socrates, please? We don't want to strike a discordant note by going wrong about your candidate. 10

Soc. All right. You're not asking anything very difficult. Perhaps c when I asked you what category thought and knowledge belong to I put you off your stroke by in fun 'overplaying my candidate' as Philebus put it?

Prot. You certainly did. 5

Soc. Yet the answer's very simple. All men of any claim to intelligence are agreed—really playing up their own importance—that thought has primacy over the whole universe. And perhaps they are right. But unless you object I think we should examine this category more thoroughly.

Prot. You do as you think best—and don't worry about time, d we shan't object.

Soc. Thank you. Let's begin with a question, then.

Prot. Well?

Soc. Should we say that the governing principle of the universe 5 as a whole is irrationality and random chance, or is everything, on the contrary, as earlier generations held, ordered and controlled by some marvellous thought and intelligence?

Prot. Heavens, Socrates, there is no comparison. Indeed, the *e possibility you now mention strikes me as not even reverent. The view that everything is ordered by thought, on the other hand, does justice to the visible order of the sun, moon, and stars and all their 5 revolutions. I should never profess or hold any other view.

Soc. Should we then register our agreement with earlier gener- 29a ations, and instead of just citing other people's opinions without risk to ourselves, stick our necks out too and take our share of the contempt of any hard-boiled thinker who holds there is no order anywhere?

Prot. Certainly. 5

Soc. Come on, then. You must scrutinize the argument that follows.

Prot. Produce it, then.

10   *Soc.* If we examine the constitution of all living bodies we observe fire, water, and air, and also, as sailors say of the sea in a heavy storm, 'the stuff's full of earth'.

b   *Prot.* Too true, and we're all at sea with that bewildering contribution to the argument.

Soc. All right, then, take each element as it occurs in us.

5   *Prot.* And?

Soc. And isn't each, as it occurs in us, a poor thing, all adulterated, lacking its proper natural power? Take one example to illustrate them all. There is fire in each of us, and fire in the universe as a

10   whole, isn't there?

Prot. Surely.

c   *Soc.* In us it is a poor weak thing, but in the universe at large there is a vast amount of it with the full beauty and power of fire.

Prot. That's very true.

5   *Soc.* Tell me, then: is the fire that is at large in the universe kindled and cherished and increased by the fire in us? Or is it the other way round: mine, yours, and that of all living creatures has all these things from it?

Prot. That isn't worth answering.

d   *Soc.* Quite right. And I imagine you'll say the same of the relationship between the earth in animals here and earth in the universe at large, and similarly with the other elements I mentioned just now. Am I right?

5   *Prot.* Would anyone but a lunatic answer otherwise?

Soc. Hardly. But now move on to the next point. Looking at all these elements combined in one thing, we call the result a body—is that right?

Prot. Yes. Certainly.

e   *Soc.* You must conclude the same about what we call the universe: surely this will be a body too in just the same way, since it is made up of the same elements?

Prot. Yes, it will.

5   *Soc.* Then in general is our body nourished, and does it receive and possess all the other things we mentioned about them just now from this body or is it the other way round?

Prot. That's another silly question, Socrates.

Soc. Well, what about my next one? Perhaps it's more sensible? **30a**

Prot. Try me.

Soc. Should we say that the body we have has life (*psyche*)?   *

Prot. Obviously.

Soc. Where does it get it, then—unless, that is, the body of the   5
universe is alive (*empsychos*), since it has the same features as this
body in a wholly superior degree?

Prot. Clearly there could be no other source.

Soc. I agree. Otherwise we should have to say that while there
were these four elements—the determinant, the indeterminate, the   *10
mixture, and fourthly the category of cause—present in everything,   **b**
and this last was in the case of our own elements responsible for life
(*psyche*) and for the development of the body and its recovery when
hurt, and won a name for every form of skill for its varied construc-
tive and beneficial activities, nevertheless while these same elements
were present on a large scale in the universe as a whole and what is   5
more in fine and unadulterated form, in this case intelligence did not
fashion the character of the finest and noblest features of the universe.

Prot. But that would be absurd.   **c**

Soc. In that case we had better say, as this argument suggests,
and as we have said repeatedly, that in the whole universe there is a
good deal of the indeterminate, sufficient determinant, and no mean   5
cause in charge of them, ordering and combining the years, seasons,
and months—a cause that deserves to be described as wisdom or
thought.

Prot. It does indeed.

Soc. But you never find wisdom and thought without life   10
(*psyche*)?

Prot. Certainly not.

Soc. So we must attribute to the divine nature a sovereign form   **d**
of life (*psyche*) and sovereign thought because of the power of
causation involved, and to other spirits other qualities of excellence
according to the descriptions they deem proper.

Prot. We must.   5

Soc. You mustn't think we have been wasting our time with this
argument. To begin with, it bears out the view of our ancestors that

the universe is always under the guidance of thought.

Prot. It certainly does.

10
*e
Soc. But also it supplies the answer to my earlier question, by putting intelligence in the category that was to be cause of everything. So now you have my answer.

Prot. So I have, and an adequate one—though I didn't realize
5
you'd been giving it.

Soc. It's this fooling about. It takes the drudgery out of the work at times.

Prot. I suppose so.

31a
Soc. Anyway, it is now fairly clear what category it belongs to and what its function is.

Prot. Yes.

5
Soc. And similarly the category that pleasure belongs to emerged some time ago.

Prot. Yes.

Soc. Then let's remember these two points about them: that thought is related to cause and that general category, while pleasure is itself indeterminate and in the category of what in itself does
10
not have and will never have any precisely marked beginning, middle, or end.

b
Prot. I am not likely to forget those.

Soc. Next we must see where each is found and what the conditions of their occurrence are. As we examined its category first
5
we might as well start this inquiry with pleasure. But we could never produce an adequate examination of pleasure in isolation from distress.

Prot. If that's the proper way of proceeding let's follow it.

Soc. I wonder if we agree about how they come about?

c
Prot. What's your view?

Soc. I think distress and pleasure occur in nature in the joint category.

5
Prot. Can you remind me which of the ones mentioned you mean by the joint category?

Soc. Heavens! I will try.

Prot. Good.

Soc. Let us understand, then, by the joint category the third of the four we mentioned.

Prot. The one that came after the indeterminate and deter-   10
minant—the one to which you allotted health and, if I am right,
harmony?

Soc. That's right. Now, think carefully about this next point.   d

Prot. Carry on.

Soc. I would suggest that when we get the physical harmony of
an animal being disrupted, there then occur at once disruption of its   5
nature and the coming into being of distress.

Prot. That's very plausible.

Soc. But when the harmony is being restored and it returns to
its natural state, we have to say that pleasure arises, if we have to deal
so briefly with a large question.   10

Prot. I think you're right, Socrates, but can't we try to make   e
the point still clearer?

Soc. I suppose the easiest examples are the obvious everyday
ones.

Prot. Such as?   5

Soc. Well, hunger is a disruption and also distressing?

Prot. Yes.

Soc. While eating, bringing replenishment, is a pleasure?

Prot. Yes.

Soc. Again, thirst is a deterioration and a form of distress, while   10
the power of liquid to replenish a parched throat is a pleasure. To   32a
take another example: heat produces an unnatural separation and
dissolution of elements that is painful, while a cooling restoration
to the natural state is a pleasure.

Prot. True.   5

Soc. And cold produces an unnatural coagulation of the moist
elements of an animal, which is a form of distress, while the natural
return journey of the release and separation of elements is a pleasure.
To sum up, don't you think it's a fair argument that as regards the
form of things whose natural combination of indeterminate and   *
determinant makes them alive (*empsychon*) my point holds, that   b
when this form is disrupted, the disruption is distress, but the move
to their own proper way of being, this return, is always by contrast a
pleasure?

5   *Prot.* I'll grant you that. It seems to me to give a general outline.

    Soc. Then can we agree on this as one form of pleasure and distress occurring respectively in these two conditions?

    Prot. Agreed.

    Soc. Now will you agree about the expectation of undergoing

c   these conditions, that hope of pleasure to come is a pleasurable boost experienced in the mind (*psyche*) alone, while the expectation

*   of suffering is frightening and distressing to the mind.

    Prot. This, then, is another form of pleasure and distress

*5 experienced in expectation by the mind (*psyche*) alone without physical mediation.

    Soc. You have taken my point exactly. And if I am right in

*   these cases, as each appears uncontaminated, as we agree, and not in mixtures of pleasure and distress, it will be clear whether everything

d   in the pleasure category is to be welcomed, or whether that distinction should be given to one of the earlier categories, while pleasure and distress should be treated like hot and cold and the rest—

5   sometimes they are to be welcomed, sometimes not, since they are not themselves goods, but some sometimes acquire the character of good things.

    Prot. I agree with you entirely that that's the direction discussion should now take.

    Soc. Then let's first consider the following point: if what we

e   have said is right (*ontōs*), that a physical deterioration of living things is a pain and restoration a pleasure, what about when they are in a process neither of deterioration nor restoration—what is the state of

5   living things at the time when they are in that condition? Think about it carefully before you say. Doesn't it follow that for any such period any given animal experiences neither distress nor pleasure in any degree?

    Prot. It must follow.

33a *Soc.* Then this is a third possible condition for us besides enjoyment and distress?

    Prot. Certainly.

    Soc. I want you to be sure to bear that in mind. For the assessment of the value of pleasure it is important to keep in mind whether

5   or not this is a possibility. If you don't mind, in fact, I should like to

take the point further.

Prot. In what way?

Soc. You realize that there is nothing to stop one living an intellectual life to this pattern?

Prot. You mean without enjoyment or distress?   b

Soc. Yes. For in the comparison we made of the lives we laid it down that a man who chose the life of thought and intellectual activity should be completely without enjoyment.

Prot. So we did.   5

Soc. So that would be his state, and maybe it would not be surprising if that were the most divine life of all.

Prot. Certainly it's not likely that the gods experience pleasure or its opposite.

Soc. Not at all likely. Either would be quite unfitting. Still we'll   10
consider that later, if it's relevant; and if we cannot put it to intelli-   c
gence's credit for the first prize, we will let it count towards the second.

Prot. Agreed.

Soc. Anyway, the second class of pleasures at least, which we   5
said were purely mental (*psyche*), are wholly dependent on memory.

Prot. How do you make that out?

Soc. It looks as though if we are going to get properly clear on this we must first give an account of memory. Perhaps we should go even further back than memory, to perception.   10

Prot. How do you mean?   d

Soc. Take the way the body is acted on. Let's assume that sometimes the action is extinguished before it reaches the mind (*psyche*), so leaving it untouched by experience, while others penetrate the body and the mind (*psyche*) too and as it were set up a   5
disturbance in each and both together.

Prot. I'll give you that assumption.

Soc. And we shall be right to say that the mind (*psyche*) is oblivious of those that only penetrate as far as the body, but not of those that penetrate both?   10

Prot. Surely.   e

Soc. When I say 'oblivious', you mustn't take me literally to be talking of oblivion coming on one. For that is loss of memory which

5 so far as the present illustration goes does not exist yet. It would be absurd to speak of the loss of something that does not exist, nor has existed.

Prot. Certainly.

Soc. Suppose we change our terminology, then.

Prot. In what way?

10 *Soc.* Instead of calling the mind (*psyche*) oblivious when it undergoes nothing from the disturbances in the body, I want you to

34a substitute 'insensibility' for 'oblivion'.

Prot. I see.

* *Soc.* When mind (*psyche*) and body jointly undergoing one effect
5 are jointly aroused, it would surely be right to call this arousal perception?

Prot. Surely.

Soc. We are clear now, then, what we mean by perception?

Prot. Quite.

10 *Soc.* Then in my view 'retention of perception' would be a good definition of memory.

b *Prot.* Certainly.

Soc. And surely we can distinguish between memory and recollection?

Prot. Possibly.

Soc. Wouldn't it go like this . . .

5 *Prot.* Well?

Soc. When the mind (*psyche*) of itself, without sensory stimulation, recovers as far as possible what it once underwent in conjunction with the body, we say it recollects.

Prot. That's true.

10 *Soc.* Further, when, on its own, the mind (*psyche*) regains memory of some sense-experience or piece of knowledge which it

c had lost, all such cases we call recollection.

Prot. That's true.

Soc. There is a point to all this.

5 *Prot.* What?

Soc. To get as clear as possible about pleasure experienced by the mind (*psyche*) independently of the body, and at the same time about desire. These points are likely to clarify both.

Prot. Come on, Socrates. Get on to the next stage.

Soc. It looks as though we have to do a good deal of work in our discussion on how pleasure comes about and on all the forms in which it does so. Indeed, even before that, I think we must now consider the nature and location of desire. *d

Prot. All right, then. After all, we've nothing to lose.

Soc. Well, something. If we find the answer we shall lose our 5 problem.

Prot. Fair enough. But let's get on to the next step.

Soc. Just now we spoke of hunger, thirst, and a number of 10 things of that sort as desires, didn't we? e

Prot. Yes indeed.

Soc. What was the common feature we had in mind to persuade us to call these very different things by the same name?

Prot. Heavens! Perhaps that is not easy to answer, though I 5 suppose we must.

Soc. Let's go back and start from those cases, then.

Prot. What do you mean?

Soc. I take it that we say of a man on occasion 'he is thirsty'?

Prot. Of course. 10

Soc. In fact this means 'he is deprived'.

Prot. Yes.

Soc. Now thirst is a desire?

Prot. Yes. For drink.

Soc. For drink, or to be replenished by drink? 35a

Prot. To be replenished, I suppose.

Soc. So it seems that when one of us is deprived he has a desire for the opposite of what he is undergoing: for when deprived he longs for replenishment.

Prot. Clearly. 5

Soc. Well, then. Consider someone being deprived for the first time. Could he have any contact with replenishment from either perception or memory of something he is neither undergoing at the moment nor has ever undergone before?

Prot. How could he? 10

Soc. Yet we agree that anyone who has a desire has a desire for b something?

Prot. Of course.

Soc. Now he doesn't desire what he is actually undergoing. For he is thirsty and that is a deprivation, whereas his desire is for replenishment.

5 *Prot.* Yes.

Soc. So something about the man who is thirsty has some contact with replenishment.

Prot. That follows.

Soc. It cannot be his body, for that is in a state of deprivation.

10 *Prot.* True.

Soc. That leaves the mind (*psyche*) to have contact with the
c replenishment, and clearly through memory—after all, what else could it do it with?

Prot. There isn't anything else.

Soc. Do you see the result of this argument?

5 *Prot.* What?

Soc. It tells us that desire does not belong to the body.

Prot. I don't see that.

Soc. Because with every animal desire indicates an effort in a
10 direction opposed to what the body is undergoing.

Prot. True.

Soc. The drive towards the opposite of the things it is undergoing shows, surely, that there is some memory of the opposites of what it is undergoing.

Prot. Agreed.

d *Soc.* In fact, in showing that it is memory that supplies the drive to the object of desire the argument proves that all impulse, desire, and initiation of activity in every living thing is a function of the mind (*psyche*).

Prot. True.

5 *Soc.* In fact, the argument rules out the body as what undergoes thirst, hunger, or anything of that sort.

Prot. Very true.

Soc. There is another point for us to note about these things. The tendency of the argument seems to me to be in the direction of
10 indicating to us a form of life consisting in these activities.

e *Prot.* What activities? I don't see what life you are talking about.

30

Soc. The activities of deprivation, replenishment, and everything to do with the well-being or harm of living things, and any
pain or pleasure accompanying either according to the physical   5
changes any of us may be undergoing.

Prot. Those occur, certainly.

Soc. What happens if one falls in between those two?

Prot. In what way between?

Soc. Suppose someone, because of what he is undergoing, is in
pain, but can remember the pleasant things at whose occurrence he   10
would be relieved of pain, though he still lacks that replenishment.
What then? Would we say, or not, that he is at a mid-point with   **36a**
regard to what he undergoes.

Prot. Yes, we would.

Soc. Would he, without qualification, be suffering or enjoying
himself?

Prot. Certainly not enjoying himself. He would be suffering
twice over, physically in what he is undergoing and mentally from   5
his expectant craving.

Soc. Why do you say he suffers twice over? Isn't it possible for
someone in a state of deprivation sometimes to have a firm hope of
replenishment, sometimes to be without hope?   **b**

Prot. Certainly.

Soc. But surely in so far as he has hope of replenishment you
agree he must get some pleasure from remembering, although at the   5
same time he suffers from the deprivation?

Prot. Yes, he must.

Soc. In these circumstances, then, a man or animal simultaneously experiences distress and pleasure.

Prot. It looks like it.   10

Soc. But suppose he has no hope of any replenishment when
deprived. In that case surely he undergoes the doubling in his
sufferings, which when you noted it just now you thought to be in a
simple way double.   **c**

Prot. That's a good point, Socrates.

Soc. I now want to put this analysis of these things we undergo
to work in the following way.

Prot. In what way?   5

Soc. Are we to say that these forms of distress and pleasure are true (*alethēs*) or false? Or are some one, some the other?

Prot. How on earth could pleasure or distress be false?

10 *Soc.* How, in that case, can fears be true (*alethēs*) or false, or expectations, or judgements?

d *Prot.* I don't think they can, except for judgements.

Soc. What? It looks as though we are in for a long argument.

5 *Prot.* It certainly does.

Soc. Still, if, as your master's pupil, you accept that it is relevant to what we have been arguing, we must persevere.

Prot. I suppose so.

10 *Soc.* But we must avoid any digressions, and anything that is not to the point.

Prot. Agreed.

e *Soc.* Tell me, then. I have been puzzled for a long time about the same problems that we have just raised. What is your position? Not that some pleasures are false, others true (*alethes*)?

Prot. How can they be?

*5 *Soc.* So on your view no one ever, in waking life or asleep, even if mad or deranged, thinks he is enjoying something when he is not, or thinks himself distressed about something when he is not?

10 *Prot.* We all take it that these things happen, Socrates.

Soc. But are we right, or do you think we should examine the view?

Prot. I think we should examine it.

37a *Soc.* Let's be more precise, then, in what we said just now about pleasure and judgement. We are agreed that there is such a thing as judging?

Prot. Yes.

*5 *Soc.* And as being pleased?

Prot. Yes.

Soc. Further, there is something that is judged?

Prot. Of course.

Soc. And also something that a pleased person is pleased about?

10 *Prot.* Certainly.

Soc. With a subject judging, whether or not he is judging correctly, at least that he is really (*ontōs*) judging he never loses.

32

Prot. Obviously.   b

Soc. Similarly with someone who is pleased, whether he is rightly pleased or not, at least that he is really (*ontōs*) pleased he never loses.

Prot. Yes, that's true too.

Soc. Then we must examine how it is that judgement is   5
commonly false, as well as being true (*alethes*), while pleasure is only true (*alethes*), although in these cases both remain genuine (*ontōs*) examples of judgement and pleasure.

Prot. We must indeed.

Soc. Your point is that judgement is capable of truth (*alethes*)   10
and falsity, and consequently is not simply judgement but judgement   c
with a certain quality, and this you say we should examine?

Prot. Yes.

Soc. In addition we shall have to reach agreement on whether we really can accept that some things admit of qualities, but   *5
pleasure and distress just are what they are, and do not allow of qualities.

Prot. Clearly.

Soc. Yet it's easy to see that they do in fact admit of some qualities. For some time ago we said that pleasure and distress become considerable, minor, and violent.   10

Prot. Very much so.   d

Soc. Further, if badness accrues to one of these, we shall say that the result is a bad judgement or a bad pleasure, as the case may be.

Prot. Of course.   5

Soc. And what if correctness or its opposite accrues to one of them? Shall we not speak of correct judgement in the case of judgement, and similarly with pleasure?

Prot. We should have to.

Soc. But suppose the object of the judgement is misrepresented,   *e
we must agree that the judgement that is then mistaken is incorrect and does not judge correctly?

Prot. Naturally.

Soc. Now suppose we notice that some distress or pleasure   5
misrepresents the object of distress or the opposite, could we call it correct or good or use any complimentary term of it?

Prot. Certainly not, if, that is, pleasure turns out to be capable of mistakes.

10   *Soc.* Well, pleasure often seems to go along not with correct but with false judgement.

38a   *Prot.* Of course. And in such cases and on those occasions, Socrates, we call the judgement false, but no one would ever call the pleasure itself false.

Soc. You've become a very keen protagonist of pleasure, Protarchus.

5   *Prot.* Not really. I'm repeating what I've heard other people say.

Soc. Would you say, then, that it makes no difference whether our pleasure is based on true judgement and knowledge or founded on error and ignorance, as commonly happens with us?

b   *Prot.* It makes a considerable difference.

Soc. Then let's examine the difference.

Prot. Proceed as you think best.

Soc. I think, perhaps . . .

5   *Prot.* Well?

Soc. We agree, don't we, that some judgements are true (*alethes*), some false?

Prot. Certainly.

Soc. And as we just said, pleasure or distress often accom-
10   panies these—accompanies a true (*alethes*) or false judgement, that is.

Prot. Yes.

Soc. And in every case our judgements, our efforts to come to a firm conclusion, depend on memory and perception.

c   *Prot.* That's true.

Soc. Are we agreed that the following must hold in these cases?

Prot. What?

5   *Soc.* Would you say that often a person seeing something from a distance doesn't see it very clearly and wants to decide what it is he is seeing?

Prot. I would agree about that.

Soc. Our man might then ask himself a few questions, like this.

Prot. How do you mean?

Soc. He might say 'What's this that seems to be standing by the
d   rock under a tree?' Does that seem to you a plausible account of what

a person might say to himself if ever he observed some such appearance?

Prot. Yes, it seems quite plausible.

Soc. A man in such a case might next make a guess at it. 'It's a   5
man' he might say, in answer to himself.

Prot. Certainly.

Soc. Or he may mistakenly suppose what he sees to be the work   10
of some shepherds and say 'It's a carving'?

Prot. That's possible.

Soc. Now suppose there is someone else with him, and he says   e
out loud to this man what he had been saying to himself. In that
case what we previously called a judgement comes out as a statement?

Prot. Of course.   5

Soc. But if he is by himself when he has these thoughts, it might
well be that he would continue for some time with them in his mind.

Prot. It might, yes.

Soc. Well, would you agree with me, then?   10

Prot. What about?

Soc. I think our mind (*psyche*) is like a book on that occasion.

Prot. What do you mean?

Soc. I think memory interacting with perception together with   *39a
the things undergone in connection with them write as it were
statements in our minds (*psyche*). When what is undergone writes
the truth (*alethes*) we acquire true (*alethes*) judgements or state-   5
ments; when this as it were internal scribe of ours writes falsehoods,
the result is the opposite of the truth (*alethes*).

Prot. I'd accept that. It seems quite right to me.   b

Soc. Then I want you to accept the presence of another worker
in our minds (*psyche*) on that occasion alongside the first.

Prot. What is that?   5

Soc. A painter, who follows the scribe and paints pictures in the
mind (*psyche*) of what the scribe writes.

Prot. I am not sure what you are referring to now, or when this
painter operates.

Soc. I am thinking of when a person isolates what he previously
judged or said from sight or any other form of perception and as it   10

were sees in his mind's eye the images of what was judged and
c   stated. Or don't you think this sort of thing can happen?

    Prot. Of course it can happen.

    Soc. And the pictures corresponding to true (*alethes*) judge-
5   ments or statements are true (*alethes*), those corresponding to false
ones false?

    Prot. Certainly.

    Soc. If we are right so far, there's a further point to consider.

    Prot. What's that?

10   *Soc.* Whether this phenomenon is confined to present and past
events, or whether it occurs with future ones as well.

    Prot. It holds with them all alike.

d   *Soc.* Well, then, earlier we said of the forms of pleasure or
distress that were purely mental (*psyche*) that they preceded
physical pleasure or distress. In other words we feel pleased or
5   distressed in advance about the future?

    Prot. Certainly.

    Soc. Now take the writings and pictures which just now we
e   posited as occurring in our minds. Are these connected with the
past and present only, not with the future?

    Prot. But they are very much connected with it.

    Soc. I take it you say 'very much' because these are all examples
5   of hopes for the future, and all our life through we are always filled
with hopes?

    Prot. Quite.

    Soc. Well now, I want you to answer a further question.

    Prot. What?

10   *Soc.* Would you agree that a man who is just, pious, and in
every way good, is sure of the gods' blessing?

    Prot. Of course.

    Soc. Whereas quite the opposite holds of someone who is unjust
40a and utterly wicked?

    Prot. Certainly.

    Soc. As we said just now, all men are in turmoil with countless
hopes?

5   *Prot.* Yes indeed.

    Soc. What we call hopes are in fact statements made internally, aren't they?

Prot. Yes.

Soc. And especially the painted images; so that often a man has   *
a vision of himself getting a vast sum of gold, and numberless   10
pleasures in consequence; and central to the picture is himself hugging
himself with delight.

Prot. Naturally.   b

Soc. Should we say that, as they are assured of every blessing,
good men for the most part have the truth (*alethes*) written in their
minds, and wicked men quite the opposite? or should we not say
that?

Prot. Of course we should.   5

Soc. So wicked men have these painted pleasures as much as   *
anyone but they will be false ones.

Prot. Certainly.

Soc. In fact for the most part the pleasures that the wicked   c
delight in are false, while good men enjoy true (*alethes*) ones.

Prot. You're very compelling, Socrates.

Soc. So according to the present argument men's minds (*psyche*)
harbour false pleasures, caricatures of the true (*alethes*) ones, and   5
similarly with distress.

Prot. Yes.

Soc. Now it emerged that it is possible for a person making a
judgement at all always to be genuinely (*ontōs*) making a judgement,
even though on occasion about something that is not present or has
not happened, or is never going to happen.   10

Prot. That must be so.

Soc. And it was this that made the judgement false and resulted   d
in error of judgement. Isn't that right?

Prot. Yes.

Soc. Well then, don't we have to allow to distress and pleasure   5
an analogous condition in similar circumstances?

Prot. What do you mean?

Soc. Just that it emerged that it was possible for someone who
was at all delighted about anything in any way however fortuitous
always to be genuinely delighted, although on occasion not about
anything that had happened or was present, and often, even perhaps

10   usually, about what is never going to happen?

e   *Prot.* That must be possible.

        Soc. The same would hold of fear, anger, and the rest, too, would it—that they are all on occasion false?

5   *Prot.* Certainly.

        Soc. Have we any other criterion of the value or worthlessness of judgements than their susceptibility to error?

        Prot. None.

        Soc. Nor, I take it, can we give any other test of the worthlessness

10   of pleasures than their falsity?

41a   *Prot.* On the contrary, Socrates. Hardly anyone would say that falsity itself affects the worth of pleasure or distress, but only their involvement with other serious forms of worthlessness.

5   *Soc.* We will come to worthless pleasures, and ones that are so through actual worthlessness a little later, if we see fit. For the moment we must consider another way in which many false ones are

b   to be said to be often present and come about in us. We might find it useful in our final judgement.

        Prot. Of course we must consider them; that is, if there are any.

5   *Soc.* If I am right, there are. But it's a view that cannot be freed from questioning until we come to some agreement on it.

        Prot. All right.

        Soc. Let's tackle the question in the best Olympic style.

10   *Prot.* Right you are.

c   *Soc.* Now if you remember, we agreed just now that when we have what are called desires, the body's reaction is quite separate and distinct from the mind's (*psyche*)

        Prot. I remember. That's what we agreed all right.

5   *Soc.* But what desires, we said, is the mind (*psyche*), and it desires a state opposite to whatever one the body is in, while it is the body that is responsible for the pain or it may be some pleasure from the way it is affected.

        Prot. True.

        Soc. Do you see what follows in such cases?

10   *Prot.* You tell me.

d   *Soc.* When this happens we get a situation of simultaneous pleasure and distress, and the experience of both at once, opposites though they are, as we agreed not long ago.

Prot. We did, certainly.

Soc. Are we to stick by a further point we agreed to?   5

Prot. Which is that?

Soc. That pleasure and distress both admit of degrees, and belong to the indeterminate category.

Prot. We have settled that. There's surely no doubt about it.   10

Soc. Have we a means, then, of assessing them correctly?

Prot. What's the difficulty now?   e

Soc. Just whether in such cases the aim of our judgement is on every occasion to decide which, when they are compared with each other, is greater, which less, which more, which of greater intensity,   5 pleasure compared with distress, that is, or distress with distress or pleasure with pleasure.

Prot. They fall into that category, certainly, and that is what we aim to judge.

Soc. Well, is it the case that so far as vision goes, seeing things from different distances destroys true judgement of size and leads us **42a** to make false estimates, but the same thing doesn't happen with pleasure and distress?

Prot. On the contrary, it is even more in evidence there.

Soc. So now we have the opposite situation to the one we had a   5 minute ago?

Prot. What do you mean?

Soc. We then found that judgements at the same time infected the pleasure or distress with their own truth or falsity.

Prot. True.   b

Soc. But now, from being viewed respectively close to and at a distance, and being compared, various pleasures seem greater and more intense when set against the distress, and the opposite with   5 the distress set against the pleasures.

Prot. That sort of thing is bound to happen on this account.

Soc. So to the extent that either seems greater or less than it really is, if you wish to isolate that portion which is apparent and not real, you will not be justified in claiming that it appears correctly,   c nor I imagine will you go so far as to suggest that that part of your pleasure or distress that was directed to that misgauged pleasure was itself justified or true.

Prot. Of course not.

5 *Soc.* Next I want to see whether there are not some examples of pleasure and distress that creatures experience that seem and indeed are even more false than these.

Prot. What sort of examples are you thinking of?

10 *Soc.* We have often said that when a thing's constitution is being
d disrupted by compression or dissolution of elements, or by satiety or deprivation, or by excessive growth or wasting, then distress, pain, suffering, everything of that sort, follow these in their train.

Prot. Yes, that's familiar doctrine.

5 *Soc.* But when a thing's proper constitution is being restored we agreed among ourselves that this restoration was pleasure?

Prot. We did.

10 *Soc.* What of when neither of these things occurs in relation to our body?

Prot. When would that happen?

e *Soc.* That question's not relevant, Protarchus.

Prot. Why not?

5 *Soc.* Because it wouldn't stop me putting my question to you again.

Prot. What do you mean?

Soc. I should simply ask: suppose no such thing did happen, what would follow of necessity?

Prot. You mean if the body were free of both processes?

10 *Soc.* Right.

Prot. This at least is clear, that no pleasure would occur in one in such a state ever, nor any distress.

43a *Soc.* Very carefully put. I suppose you mean that in fact everything must always be undergoing one or other of these processes? That's what the experts say: everything is in a process of constant change.

5 *Prot.* Certainly, and it's not a frivolous view, either.

Soc. That's not surprising. They are not exactly frivolous men. But I want to sidestep the thrust of this objection if possible. I think I've a way of avoiding it if you are prepared to go along with me.

Prot. Tell me how.

Soc. To these men, let our comment be 'Let it be as you say';   10
but now you tell me whether every living (*empsychos*) thing is   b
always aware of everything that happens to it, so that we don't
even grow or undergo anything of that sort without noticing it, or
whether quite the opposite isn't true.

Prot. But of course it is. We hardly notice any of those things   5
happening.

Soc. In that case, we were wrong just now when we said the
changes this way and that in us result in pleasure and distress.

Prot. Of course.   10

Soc. It would be better and safer to rephrase it as follows.   c

Prot. How?

Soc. By saying that big changes produce distress or pleasure in us   5
but moderate and quite small ones produce neither.

Prot. That would certainly be a more accurate formulation than
the other.

Soc. In that case, the form of life I mentioned just now would
become a possibility again.

Prot. What one is that?   10

Soc. The one we said to be without distress or enjoyment.

Prot. Certainly it would.

Soc. To sum up then, let us posit three forms of life, one
of pleasure, one of distress, and one of neither. What would you say   d
on the subject?

Prot. Just what you have said, that there are these three lives.

Soc. Now not being in distress would hardly be the same as
enjoying oneself, would it?   5

Prot. Of course not.

Soc. So when you hear people say that the pleasantest thing is
to live all one's life free of distress, what do you think they are
saying?

Prot. They seem to be saying that not being in distress is   10
pleasant.

Soc. Take any three things now, say one gold, one silver, one   e
neither, just to have fine names.

Prot. All right.

Soc. Could the one that is neither possibly become either gold   5

or silver?

Prot. How on earth could it?

Soc. Similarly, it would be a mistake for anyone to believe and therefore to say that the mid-way life was either pleasant or dis-

10 tressing; at least if we are to be strict.

Prot. How could it be?

44a *Soc.* Yet we find people who say and believe these things.

Prot. Certainly.

Soc. Do they then think they are enjoying themselves on the

5 occasions when they are not in a distressed condition?

Prot. That's what they say, at any rate.

Soc. So they believe they are then enjoying themselves, or they wouldn't say it.

Prot. Probably.

Soc. Yet they are making a false judgement about enjoyment if,

10 that is, enjoyment and lack of distress are two quite different things.

Prot. But they turned out to be quite different things.

Soc. We have a choice then. We could hold as we did just now,

b that there are three alternatives, or that there are only two, first distress, which we would say was a human evil, and secondly release from distress, which being itself good, we should call pleasurable.

5 *Prot.* Why are we raising this question at this stage, Socrates? I don't see what you are getting at.

Soc. Don't you know the real enemies of Philebus here?

Prot. Who are you referring to?

Soc. People with a considerable reputation as scientists, who

*10 completely deny that they are pleasures.

Prot. How do they do that?

c *Soc.* According to them, what Philebus and his friends at present call pleasures are nothing but cases of release from distress.

Prot. So do you think we should accept their view, Socrates, or what?

5 *Soc.* No, but we should take them as providing an insight, one
* which is derived not from their science but from a certain difficulty due to nobility of character. They have an inordinate hatred of the power exercised by pleasure and consider it quite unhealthy, indeed they think of its very attractive power as a form of witchcraft rather

than pleasure. To this extent you may find them useful, when you **d** have considered the rest of their difficulties. After that I will tell you which pleasures I think are true ones. Then we shall be able to judge the power of pleasure from a consideration of both sets of arguments.

Prot. Agreed. 5

Soc. Let's then follow in the track of these people's difficulty with pleasure, treating them as allies. Their argument goes something like this: they start with a more basic point, asking whether, if we want to get clear about the nature of a given kind of thing, say hardness, **e** we should understand it better if we examined the hardest things rather than examples low down on the scale of hardness? Come on, Protarchus, you must answer these difficult people as though they were me.

Prot. Oh yes. I should say we should examine the top of the **5** scale.

Soc. So if we wanted to get clear about the nature of the class of pleasures we should have to examine not those examples that are only just pleasures, but ones at the top of the scale that are said to be the **45a** most intense.

Prot. Everyone would agree with you on this present point.

Soc. And surely the familiar pleasures, that are also greatest, are, **5** as we repeatedly say, the physical ones?

Prot. Of course.

Soc. Do these occur in and reach their most extreme forms among sick or healthy people? We want to be careful. We might slip up if we rush in with an answer. We should probably answer 'among **b** healthy people'.

Prot. Very likely.

Soc. And yet, surely, the pleasures that exceed all bounds are those that are also preceded by the most intense desires?

Prot. That's true. **5**

Soc. But surely people suffering from fever and similar illnesses experience more severe thirst and cold and all the other physical experiences? and being more closely acquainted with want they ***** surely get greater pleasure from replenishment? Or shall we declare **10** that untrue?

Prot. Now you have said it that seems very much the case.

Soc. Well then, should we seem justified in saying that if anyone **c**

43

wants to examine the greatest pleasures he should look not at the healthy, but at the sick? You must be clear that I am not asking whether the very sick have more pleasures than healthy people. I am interested in the degree of pleasure, in locating in this sort of case the high point of intensity on any occasion. For we have to see what sort of thing it is and what people who deny that it really is pleasure are saying about it.

Prot. I think I follow you pretty well.

Soc. Soon you will lead as well. Tell me: if you compare an unrestrained life with a temperate one, do you notice greater pleasures in the former than the latter—I don't mean a greater number—I am thinking of degree or intensity. Think carefully and tell me.

Prot. I see what you mean. There's no comparison. Temperate people are of course constantly restrained by the proverbial maxim they all follow, bidding them do 'Nothing in excess'. But with intemperate, unrestrained people the intense pleasure that possesses them sends them roaring about like lunatics.

Soc. I agree. And if so, then it is clear that for the occurrence of the greatest forms of pleasure or distress we have to look to degenerate states of mind (*psyche*) and body, not to where they are in good condition.

Prot. Quite.

Soc. Let's take some of them, then, and see what it is about them that made us call them the most intense.

Prot. We must.

Soc. Then let's take the pleasures of some forms of illness and examine their characteristics.

Prot. What ones have you in mind?

Soc. Those of the more disreputable diseases, which are utterly hateful to those difficult people we mentioned a little while back.

Prot. Can you specify?

Soc. The relief of itching, for example, by scratching, and any others like that that need no other treatment. How in heaven's name are we to describe this experience we have? Should we call it a form of pleasure or distress?

Prot. This seems clearly to be a mixed experience, Socrates, a bad affliction.

Soc. Well, I didn't make the point to please Philebus exactly. *b
But we could hardly hope to settle the present question without a
look at these pleasures and the ones to follow.

Prot. Then we must move on to others of the same clan. 5

Soc. You mean those that are combined experiences like that?

Prot. Yes.

Soc. Well, some of these combinations are at the purely physical
level, and others are purely mental (*psyche*). Further, we shall find c
with the mind and the body combinations of distress and pleasure
sometimes lumped together under a single heading as pleasure,
sometimes as distress.

Prot. Can you illustrate that? 5

Soc. Take a case where in a process of restoration or disruption
someone simultaneously undergoes the opposite experience. For
instance, sometimes a person who is cold is warmed, or someone who
is warm is cooled, and he wants to achieve the one condition and
escape the other, the proverbial bitter-sweet situation, and if the d
condition is persistent it induces first irritation and in the end severe
frustration.

Prot. That's very true.

Soc. These sorts of mixtures are sometimes equally balanced
between distress and pleasure, sometimes one is preponderant. Isn't 5
that so?

Prot. Certainly.

Soc. Do you agree, then, that with some, when distress pre- *
ponderates over pleasure—as, in the cases of itching referred to just
now, or tickling—when this sensation of seething ferment is internal 10
and one fails to reach it by rubbing and scratching, only managing to e
disperse the surface parts, people then by bringing these near a fire
and because of their distress changing about to the opposite extreme
sometimes produce the most intense pleasures, and then by violently
dispersing what is bound together or binding what is dispersed,
produce distress mixed with pleasure, the opposite in the inner
parts relative to the outer, according to the direction in which these 5
are veering, and so these cases serve up distress alongside pleasure? 47a

Prot. True.

Soc. When pleasure predominates in such cases, the slight
admixture of distress sets up a tingling sensation of mild irritation,
but the prevailing pleasurable element takes possession of a man
sometimes making him leap about in his ecstasy, so that he changes
complexion, takes up all kinds of strange positions, pants in strange
ways, and is driven completely out of his senses with mad cries and
shouts.

Prot. How right you are.

Soc. He feels bound to say of himself, as do others, that he is
almost dying with enjoyment when he indulges in these delights. The
more unrestrained and intemperate he is the more fervently he goes
after them in wholehearted pursuit. He dubs them the greatest of
pleasures and counts as most blessed with good fortune the man who
lives as great a part of his life as possible indulging them.

Prot. That fully covers what follows from most people's views
on the subject.

Soc. Well, at least as far as mixed pleasures of the body itself
are concerned, from the interaction of its surface and inner parts.
As for those where the mind's contribution is the opposite of the
body's, distress in contrast with physical pleasure, or pleasure in
contrast with physical distress, so that both form one combined
experience, we went through them earlier. If you remember, when a
person is deprived of something he wants replenishment. In that he
is hoping he gets pleasure, in that he is deprived, distress. But there
was one point we did not testify to before, but should state now,
that although in all these cases, and there are thousands of them, the
mind (*psyche*) is at odds with the body, still the result is a single
combination of pleasure and distress.

Prot. You are probably right.

Soc. That still leaves us with one form of distress-cum-pleasure.

Prot. What's that? Tell me.

Soc. A combined experience that we said the mind (*psyche*) often
achieves by itself.

Prot. What sort of account can we give of that?

Soc. Take anger, fear, yearning, sorrow, love, envy, malice, and
the rest,—aren't these forms of purely mental (*psyche*) distress?

Prot. Certainly.

46

Soc.   Yet don't we find that they are imbued with an unexpected   5
degree of enjoyment? Or do you need reminding of the point about
anger and indignation

> that stirs the wisest man to fury's foam
> yet is sweeter than honey dropping from the comb

or of the fact that sorrow and yearning both contain an element of **48a**
pleasure along with the distress?

Prot.   Certainly not. I agree these feelings are just as you describe
them.

Soc.   Remember too, how the audience at a tragedy actually   5
enjoy their tears.

Prot.   Of course.

Soc.   And did you realize that with comedies too the state of
mind (*psyche*) is one of combined distress and pleasure?

Prot.   I don't see how that's true.   10

Soc.   No. It's not at all easy to realize that this situation always   **b**
holds there too.

Prot.   It certainly isn't so far as I can see.

Soc.   Then let's take it, the more as it is a more obscure case.   5
That will make it easier for people to grasp the phenomenon of
combined pleasure and distress elsewhere.

Prot.   Perhaps you could say how?

Soc.   Take what we mentioned just now—malice. Would you say
that was a form of mental (*psyche*) distress, or what?

Prot.   A form of distress.   10

Soc.   Now, a person's malice shows itself, doesn't it, in pleasure
at the misfortunes of those around him?   *

Prot.   Certainly.   c

Soc.   And surely that ignorance which we call a state of silliness   *
is a misfortune?

Prot.   Of course.

Soc.   Next, consider the facts about the nature of what we
ridicule.

Prot.   You say.   5

Soc.   Briefly, that it is always a failing, one that takes its name   *
from a state of character, and is that specific form of failing with the
characteristic quite opposed to what the oracle at Delphi recommends.

10   *Prot.*   The 'Know yourself' oracle, you mean?

d   *Soc.*   Yes. And clearly for the opposite of that the oracle would have to say in no way knowing oneself.

    Prot.   Of course.

    Soc.   I want you to try to make a threefold distinction.

5   *Prot.*   How? I'm sure I can't think of one.

    Soc.   You are saying that I have now got to make it in fact?

    Prot.   Yes. But I'm not just saying you must, I'm asking you.

    Soc.   Aren't there, then, just three respects in which anyone with this failing might be under a misapprehension about himself?

10   *Prot.*   What three?

e   *Soc.*   To begin with there is money: people think they are richer than their possessions in fact justify.

    Prot.   A good many people are in that condition, certainly.

    Soc.   But there are even more who think they are stronger or

5   more handsome than they really are, and that in every physical respect they surpass their actual state.

    Prot.   True.

    Soc.   But the largest category is of those who are under some

*   delusion on the third count—their moral and intellectual equipment

10   (*psyche*)—and consider themselves notable for some excellence they don't have.

    Prot.   I could not agree more.

49a   *Soc.*   And of all excellences surely the one that most people lay unqualified claim to is intelligence. They are full of rivalry on this score and a false pretence of intelligence.

    Prot.   How right you are.

5   *Soc.*   And surely we should be right to call every such state a misfortune?

    Prot.   Heavens yes.

    Soc.   Now we need to make one further distinction if we are to get clear the unexpected combination of pleasure and distress when we look at malice in entertainments. I can hear you asking: how do

b   we draw the distinction? Well, it is necessary that all those who make this particular silly mistake about themselves be divided, as must all men, but these especially, into those with power and influence and those with none.

Prot. Of course. 5

Soc. Divide them in this way, then: all those in this state who are weak and unable to stand up for themselves when mocked you may rightly call ridiculous. As for those strong enough to stand up * for themselves, on the other hand, you will have the most accurate c account of them if you describe them as frightening, not to say as enemies. For the ignorance of powerful people is dangerous as well as shameful—it is a menace to anyone near whether in real life or in fiction. In weak people, on the other hand, it acquires for us the rank 5 and character of the ridiculous.

Prot. I agree completely, but I don't yet see clearly how pleasure and distress are combined in these cases.

Soc. Then first of all consider how malice works.

Prot. Carry on.

Soc. It is, surely, an unjustifiable form of distress, and also of *d pleasure?

Prot. Certainly.

Soc. But it is neither unjustifiable nor malicious to rejoice at the misfortunes of one's enemies, I take it?

Prot. Of course not. 5

Soc. Yet surely it is unjustifiable, as sometimes happens, to be pleased instead of distressed at the misfortunes of one's friends?

Prot. Of course it is.

Soc. We said, didn't we, that ignorance is for all people a misfortune?

Prot. And rightly. 10

Soc. In that case if we take delusions of intelligence, good physique, and the rest that we went through just now and said to e occur in three forms, dubbing them ridiculous in weak subjects and detestable in powerful ones—should we still say, or not, that when one of our friends has this condition in a form harmless to others, it is a subject for ridicule?

Prot. Certainly. 5

Soc. But we agree, too, that it is a misfortune, in so far as it is a state of ignorance?

Prot. Very much so.

Soc. Do we enjoy laughing at it, or does it distress us?

50a *Prot.* We enjoy it, of course.

Soc. But didn't we say that it was malice that produced pleasure at the shortcomings of our friends?

Prot. It must be.

5 *Soc.* It follows from this argument, then, that when we laugh at the ridiculous aspects of our friends, the admixture of pleasure in our malice produces a mixture of pleasure and distress. For we agreed some time ago that malice was a form of distress; but laughter is enjoyable, and on these occasions both occur simultaneously.

10 *Prot.* True.

b *Soc.* In fact, this argument suggests that in dirges, tragedies, and comedies, not only on the stage, but in the whole tragi-comedy of life, distress and pleasure are blended with each other, and the same goes for countless other cases.

5 *Prot.* It is impossible not to agree with that, however much the needs of controversy pull one in the opposite direction.

c *Soc.* Earlier we put forward anger, yearning, sorrow, fear, love, envy, and malice, and everything of that sort as cases where we should find the combined experiences we have gone over *ad nauseam*. Do you agree?

Prot. Yes.

5 *Soc.* You realize that all our recent discussion has dealt with sorrow, malice, and anger?

Prot. Of course I do.

Soc. Does that leave a lot to be discussed?

Prot. Yes indeed.

10 *Soc.* Then why do you think I illustrated the combination of the two in comedy for you? Surely it was in the hope of convincing

d you that it would be even easier to show how they combined in fear, love, and the rest. I was hoping that you would take this example as enough to let me off extending the discussion further to cover the others, and would simply accept that the body without

5 the mind (*psyche*), the mind (*psyche*) without the body, and both in combination with each other in these experiences are full of pleasure mixed with distress. Now, are you going to let me off, or are you going to keep me here till midnight? One small point, and perhaps

you'll let me off: I shall be prepared to go through all these cases
tomorrow for you, but for the moment I want to get on with what   e
is left of the points needed for the judgement enjoined by Philebus.

Prot. Fair enough. You go through what is left for us to do, as
you think best.

Soc. The natural procedure, indeed the required one, would be   5
for us to follow consideration of mixed pleasures with discussion in
turn of unmixed ones.

Prot. That's a good idea.   51a

Soc. Then I'll move on and try to indicate for both our sakes
which they are. I am not altogether convinced by those who say that
all pleasures are relief from distress. As I said, I use them as witnesses
to show certain pleasures to be apparent but not real (*ousas*), and   5
certain others that seem both intense and numerous, though in fact
they are discomforting states kneaded together with distress and
relief from the most extreme physical and mental (*psyche*) pain.

Prot. But now, which ones would one rightly understand to be   b
true (*alethes*) ones, Socrates?

Soc. Those related to colours we call beautiful, for instance, or
to shapes, most pleasures of smell, and those of hearing, and
generally any where the deprivation is imperceptible and which   5
supply perceptible replenishments which are both without pain and
pleasant.

Prot. I don't see how that description fits these cases.

Soc. That's because I haven't put my point very clearly. I must
try to make it clearer. By 'beauty of shape' I don't in this instance   c
mean what most people would understand by it—I am not thinking
of animals or certain pictures, but, so the thesis goes—a straight line
or a circle and resultant planes and solids produced on a lathe or   5
with ruler and square. Do you see the sort of thing I mean? On my
view these things are not, as other things are, beautiful in a relative   *
way, but are always beautiful in themselves, and yield their own   d
special pleasures quite unlike those of scratching. I include colours,
too, that have the same characteristic. Have you got my point, or not?

Prot. I am trying to understand it, Socrates. Could you try to
put it a little more clearly still?   5

Soc. Well, with sounds, it is the smooth clear ones I am thinking of, ones that produce a single pure tune, and are beautiful not just in a certain context but in themselves—these and their attendant pleasures.

10 *Prot.* There are certainly sounds that meet that description.

*e *Soc.* Pleasures of smell are a more earthy set. I consider all cases correspond to those others in so far as they do not have distress as a necessary part of them, however this comes about and from

5 whatever source they reach us. So that makes two classes of pleasure of the sort I mean. Do you follow that?

Prot. I do, yes.

Soc. Then we have still to add the pleasures of discovery,

52a granted we agree that they do not involve any actual hunger for learning, and that there is no distress from the start through hunger for knowledge.

Prot. I'll agree to that.

5 *Soc.* Suppose, then, someone is replete with learning and then loses it, forgets it. Is there, so far as you can see, any distress involved in the loss?

Prot. Not intrinsic to the nature of the occurrence, but in

b reflection on what has happened, when a man is distressed at the loss of it because of its value.

Soc. All right. But at present at any rate we are after a thorough description only of the nature of what happens without regard to any reflection on it.

Prot. In that case you are right. Loss of memory in matters of

5 learning is something that always come on us without pain.

Soc. These pleasures of learning, then, must be said to be unmixed with distress, and to be the preserve of very few, certainly not of the majority of people.

Prot. They must indeed.

*c *Soc.* So now we have an orderly sorting out of the purified pleasures from what should be called unpurified cases. As a further point we ought to add that violent pleasures are disordered, while

5 the others exhibit order. Those that admit of great degrees and

* intensity, whether becoming such commonly or only rarely, we should put in the category mentioned earlier of that which is indeterminate and more and less and in varying degrees permeates

both body and mind (*psyche*). The others we should put in the   **d**
category of ordered things.

Prot. That seems absolutely right.

Soc. There is a further point to consider about them next.

Prot. What's that?   5

Soc. How should we say they stand with regard to truth   *
(*aletheia*)? Are the purified, unadulterated, and adequate cases better
off, or the intense, large, and extreme?

Prot. I'm afraid I don't see what you are getting at with that
question, Socrates.

Soc. I don't want any stone left unturned in our examination   10
of pleasure and understanding, in case each has purified instances   **e**
and others that are only unpurified instances, so that you and I and
others here may find it easier to judge between them as each comes
for judgement in its purified form.

Prot. Quite right.   5

Soc. Then let's consider the purified classes in general as
follows: first, let's select one for examination.

Prot. Which should we select?   **53a**

Soc. Perhaps we could start by examining the class of whites.

Prot. All right.

Soc. How would we select a purified example of white, what   5
would it be? What constitutes it as such? Is it quantity and bulk, or
lack of adulteration, where there is not the slightest bit of any
other colour in it?

Prot. Obviously, it is the least adulterated example of white
we want.

Soc. Quite right. Shouldn't we then reckon this as the truest
(*alethes*) and at the same time the finest of all whites, rather than   **b**
one that won on quantity or bulk?

Prot. Surely.

Soc. The completely right answer, then, is that a spot of
purified white is whiter—finer, truer (*alethes*)—than any amount of   5
broken white.

Prot. Certainly.

Soc. Well, then, I don't think we shall need many illustrations
like that for our argument about pleasure. It is enough for us to   10

c note straight away that any pleasure however slight and inconsiderable it may be, so long as it is purified of all distress, is pleasanter, truer (*alethes*) and finer than any other whatever its size or quantity.

Prot. Very true. That example is quite adequate.

Soc. What about the following? On pleasure, haven't we heard

5 people say that it is always a process of becoming—that with

* pleasure there is no such thing at all as being? The people who try to draw our attention to this argument are clever men, and we should be grateful to them.

Prot. Why?

d *Soc.* I will expound that for you by pursuing some questions with you.

Prot. Tell me. Just put your questions.

Soc. Let's postulate two classes: things that are in themselves and things that yearn after something else.

5 *Prot.* How? What are these two?

Soc. The first has always a natural claim on devotion, the second is incomplete without the first.

Prot. You will have to be clearer than that.

Soc. I take it we have all seen fine well-born boys about along

*10 with their virile lovers?

Prot. Who hasn't?

e *Soc.* Then look for other pairings analogous to this one over the whole range of what we say there is.

Prot. Have I got to ask you a third time, Socrates? Say what you have to say more clearly.

Soc. It's nothing complicated, Protarchus. It's just that the

5 exposition is making fools of us. The point being made is that everything there is is always either directed to something else, or else is that towards which in any case that which is directed to something is in process of being directed.

Prot. With all this repetition I am almost there.

54a *Soc.* Perhaps we shall understand better as the argument develops.

Prot. Doubtless.

Soc. Take this other pair.

Prot. Which?

Soc. In all cases coming to be is one thing and being is another. 5
Prot. I'll give you that pair: being and becoming.
Soc. Right. Which of these would you say is directed to the other? Is becoming directed towards being or being directed towards becoming?
Prot. You are talking of being and asking me whether it is 10
through being directed at becoming that it is what it is?
Soc. That sounds right.
Prot. Heavens above. Why don't you try me with this one: b
'Tell me, is the process of ship-building directed to ships, or are ships, rather, directed to ship-building?'—and so on with the rest?
Soc. That's precisely what I am doing? 5
Prot. Then why didn't you answer for yourself?
Soc. No reason at all; but you must take your share of the discussion.
Prot. All right.
Soc. I should say, then, that the supply to anyone of drugs c
and all tools and materials is directed to some process of becoming, but that each process of becoming is being directed to some particular being, one to one, another to another, and becoming as a whole is in process of being directed to being as a whole.
Prot. Obviously that's so. 5
Soc. Then if pleasure is indeed a process of becoming, it would necessarily be *being* directed to some being.
Prot. What of it?
Soc. Well, that to which anything that is at any time being directed to something might be directed is classified as a good; 10
whereas that which is being directed to something should be put in a different category.
Prot. There's no avoiding that.
Soc. So if pleasure is a process of becoming, surely we shall be d
right to put it in some other category than that of good?
Prot. Absolutely right.
Soc. As I said, then, at the beginning of this discussion, we 5
should be grateful to the person whose charge against pleasure is that with it there is becoming, but no being at all. For clearly such a man will ridicule those who call pleasure (the) good.

Prot.   Obviously.

e   *Soc.*   Further, this same man will also ridicule those whose life's fulfilment is in processes of becoming.

Prot.   How? What sort of people do you mean?

5   *Soc.*   All those who cure their hunger or thirst or anything like that that is cured by some process, and are delighted because of the relevant process, because it is a pleasure; and they say they couldn't bear to live without hunger and thirst and without experiencing all the experiences anyone might mention that follow such conditions.

55a   *Prot.*   They certainly talk that way.

Soc.   Now, I take it we should all agree that the opposite of becoming is ceasing to be?

Prot.   There is no option.

5   *Soc.*   In that case, in making such a choice a man is opting for the processes of becoming and ceasing to be as distinct from the third life which contained neither pleasure nor distress but thought in as unadulterated a form as possible.

Prot.   So far as I can see, Socrates, anyone who proposes

10   pleasure as our good is involved in considerable absurdity.

Soc.   Very considerable, if we add a further point.

Prot.   What is that?

b   *Soc.*   Surely, it must be absurd to hold that there is nothing good or fine in bodies or many other things, but only in the mind (*psyche*), and even here to allow pleasure only, while courage, temperance, intelligence, and other goods a mind (*psyche*) possesses are no such

5   thing? On top of all this, one is forced to say that someone who instead of enjoying himself is in distress is evil for the period of his distress, even if he is the most virtuous man in the world, while

c   anyone who enjoys himself, for the period of his enjoyment excels in virtue in proportion to his enjoyment.

Prot.   These conclusions are all as absurd as you can get.

Soc.   We must not, though, try to make a complete examination

5   of pleasure and then turn out to be very sparing of intelligence and knowledge. Like honest men we must subject them to a thorough test for possible faults, so that we can examine them in their naturally most purified form. Then we shall be able to use the really genuine forms both of these and of pleasure for the judgement

between them.

Prot. That's fair.   10

Soc. Well, knowledge that is an object of study has two parts,   d
one concerned with crafts and one with education and nurture. Do
you agree?

Prot. Yes.

Soc. We must consider first whether one class of skills is nearer   5
to knowledge, while another is less so, and whether the first should
be considered as absolutely purified cases, the others less fully
purified ones.

Prot. Then we must tackle that.

Soc. The dominant examples of each must be taken separately.   10

Prot. Which, for example, and how do you propose treating
them?

Soc. Suppose for instance that one abstracted arithmetic,   e
measurement, and weighing from all branches of knowledge. The
remnant in each case would be pretty meagre.

Prot. It would indeed be meagre.

Soc. After that one would be left with guessing, by constant use   5
and experiences training one's senses and then using one's capacities
for estimating, which many people call skills—capacities that develop   **56a**
their power with laborious practice.

Prot. That would be inevitable.

Soc. For a start, then, music is full of this, in so far as it
determines which notes are concordant on estimates born of practice
rather than by measurement. Of music all flute-playing falls into   *5
this category and lyre-playing, for it involves searching by guess for
the proper point on each string as it sounds. Consequently there is a
considerable admixture of imprecision, and little to rely on.

Prot. True enough.

Soc. We shall find further that the same holds of medicine,   b
farming, piloting, generalship.

Prot. Certainly.

Soc. Building on the other hand uses a great many measures
and tools, and these things, which give it considerable precision,   5
make it more scientific than most branches of knowledge.

Prot. How do you mean?

Soc. Take shipbuilding, house-building, and many other building
c   crafts. They use straight-edges, compasses, stonemason's rules,
weights, and precision-made squares.

Prot. That's very true.

Soc. Then let's put the so-called skills into two categories, one
5   consisting of those which like music involve less precision in their
operations, the other consisting of the more precise ones such as
building.

Prot. Agreed.

Soc. The most precise of these skills are the ones which a little
way back we mentioned as of first importance.

10   *Prot.* I take it you mean arithmetic and the skills you mentioned
just now along with it.

d   *Soc.* Exactly. But shouldn't we say that these also fall into two
classes—what do you think?

Prot. What sort of distinction do you mean?

5   *Soc.* First of all, isn't there an arithmetic of the vulgar and
*   another of the academics?

Prot. How would one ever distinguish the one kind of arithmetic from the other?

Soc. It is an important distinction, Protarchus. The first kind of
10   arithmetician calculates with unequal units, for instance pairing
camps or oxen, or the most minute and the vastest objects in the
e   world. The others would have nothing to do with them except on the
postulate that none of the myriad units under discussion is in any
way different from any of the others.

Prot. You are quite right. There is an important difference
5   among people who busy themselves with arithmetic, and it is only
sense to put them in different categories.

*   *Soc.* Well, then. Comparing the calculation and measurement
that is found in building and in the market-place with academic
57a   geometry and calculation, are we to put them into a single category,
or should we posit two?

Prot. In line with what we said before I'd vote for each of these
taking two forms.

5   *Soc.* You'd be right. Do you realize why I brought these considerations before the meeting?

Prot. Possibly, but I should be glad if you would make clear the answer to what you are now asking.

Soc. We began this argument in search of an analogue to the case of pleasures, and now it seems to have thrown up these considerations as part of an inquiry as to whether one form of knowledge is a more purified form than another, as some pleasures were than others.

Prot. At least that that's why it embarked on these questions is clear.

Soc. Come now. Surely in the earlier part of the discussion it was uncovering the fact that different skills on different topics were some more, some less precise than others?

Prot. Certainly.

Soc. And in these cases surely the argument first gave a skill a single name, giving the impression that it was the name of a single skill, and then, suggesting it is the name of two, raises the question of the state of precision and purification of these two on the matters in hand, whether the academic or non-academic version is the more accurate.

Prot. Certainly the discussion seems to me to raise that question.

Soc. How are we to answer it then?

Prot. But we've already found an amazingly vast difference in accuracy between forms of knowledge.

Soc. Then it will be easy to answer?

Prot. Certainly. Let's make no bones about it. The ones we have just been considering are far ahead of the others and among these in turn those practised in a genuinely academic way are streets ahead of the rest so far as precision and accuracy of measurement and calculation are concerned.

Soc. Let's accept your decision, then, and putting our trust in you we can give a confident answer to the experts in ambiguity.

Prot. What answer have you in mind?

Soc. That there are two forms of study of number and measurement, and the countless other branches of study that follow in their train share the same duality despite having but one name.

Prot. Then let's give that answer with all best wishes to the experts you mention.

Soc. Our position is, then, that these branches of knowledge are pre-eminent in precision?

5   *Prot.* Certainly.

Soc. But surely we shall be disowned by dialectical ability, Protarchus, if we give judgement in favour of any other.

Prot. Which one, now, must one call dialectic?

*58a   *Soc.* Clearly the one that would understand at least every ability now being mentioned. In my view, at least, anyone who possesses the slightest intelligence will agree that the discipline concerned
*   with the final truth, the real nature of things and unchanging reality
*5   is the most genuine (*alethes*) knowledge. But what of you? What would your judgement be, Protarchus?

Prot. Well, Socrates, I have always heard Gorgias insist again and again that the art of persuasion is preeminent over all others—
b   after all, it would bring everything into voluntary subjection, without coercion, and be far superior to any other skill—but now, I would not want to be in conflict with you, or him either.

Soc. It sounds as though you would like to cry 'To arms', but
5   respect makes you drop your arms instead.

Prot. Well, have it your way.

Soc. Perhaps it is my fault that you did not see the point.

Prot. What point?

c   *Soc.* I was not as yet asking, you see, what skill or branch of knowledge outstripped the rest in being greatest or best or most beneficial to us; our present inquiry is: which has as its province the clearest, most precise, and true (*alethes*) subject-matter, however
5   little its power to benefit us? But look, Gorgias, after all, will not object, so long as you grant that his favoured skill wins so far as usefulness to men is concerned; but as to the discipline I mentioned just now—remember what I said earlier about white, that even a small amount, so long as it is pure white, is better than a large
d   amount that is not, at least in being most truly (*alethes*) white; similarly now with branches of knowledge we should give them concentrated thought and a thorough auditing, considering not their profit or prestige, but whether there is not innate in the human mind
5   (*psyche*) a capacity to love the truth (*alethes*) and do everything needed to acquire it, and having examined this capacity thoroughly,

let's say whether the probabilities are in favour of the purified form of comprehension and understanding being acquired through its methods or whether we should look for another more powerful discipline.

Prot. On consideration I think it is hard to accept that any   e other branch of knowledge or any other skill has a firmer hold on the truth (*aletheia*).

Soc. I wonder if you say that because you have noticed the following fact: that most skills, and those who have laboured on   5 these matters, first of all use common opinions and eagerly inquire ***59a** on matters relevant to them? Even when someone thinks his inquiry is about nature, you can be sure that he never gets beyond questions about the universe around us, its origin and its passive and active modes of change, and spends his life on these inquiries. Should we say that, or what?   5

Prot. Certainly.

Soc. Our man, in fact, has undertaken a labour on present, future, and past events, not on unchanging truths (*onta*).

Prot. Exactly.   10

Soc. By the most accurate standards of truth (*aletheia*) can any clear results emerge on these matters which never have shown and   b never will show and do not in the present show any unalterable stability.

Prot. How could they?

Soc. How in fact can we obtain any stable results whatever in areas which have achieved no stability of any kind?   5

Prot. I don't think it's at all possible.

Soc. So there is no understanding or branch of knowledge relating to them that has the complete truth (*alethes*).

Prot. Apparently not.

Soc. In that case, we must put right on one side the matter of   10 you and me and Gorgias and Philebus. Look instead to the argument and stand up in court for one point.

Prot. Which?   c

Soc. That stable, purified, true (*alethes*), and what we call unadulterated results are confined either to matters that are unchangeably and uniformly the same in the least tainted form possible or to

5   those most closely related to them; all the rest must be said to be secondary and derivative.

Prot. Very true.

Soc. And isn't the fairest thing to allot the most laudatory names in this area to the most laudable candidates?

10   *Prot.* That's only proper.

d   *Soc.* And surely 'thought' and 'intelligence' are the highest terms of praise here?

Prot. Yes.

Soc. In all accuracy, then, these are the names for thinking

5   engaged on the real truth (*to on ontōs*).

Prot. Certainly.

Soc. Yet these are the very names which earlier I put forward as contestants.

Prot. No one's questioning that.

10   *Soc.* Well, then, it would be a fair enough image to compare us

e   to builders in this matter of the mixture of intelligence and pleasure, and say we had before us the material from which or with which to build.

Prot. That's a good comparison.

5   *Soc.* Then our next business must be to try to mix them?

Prot. Naturally.

Soc. Wouldn't it be more correct procedure to give ourselves these preliminary reminders?

Prot. Such as?

10   *Soc.* We have already given them. Still, it's a good maxim:

60a   that a fine phrase should be repeated two or three times in a speech.

Prot. Certainly.

Soc. Let's get on with it, then. What we said went, I think,

5   something like this.

Prot. Go on.

Soc. Philebus says that pleasure is the proper goal for all living things and they should all aim for it, and especially that this constitutes the good for all of them, and that these two names 'good'

10   and 'pleasurable' are correctly assigned to a single thing, a single

b   characteristic. By contrast Socrates holds that there is not one thing here but two, as the two names suggest, that goodness and

pleasure have distinct natures, and that intelligence has more part
with goodness than pleasure has. Aren't those the positions, and   5
isn't that how we expressed them earlier?

Prot. Exactly.

Soc. Can we agree to a further point as accepted both then and
now?

Prot. What point is that?

Soc. That in one respect the good of its nature differs from the   10
other two.

Prot. In what respect?   c

Soc. In that any living thing that had complete, unqualified,
and permanent possession of it would never need anything further—
it would have what was perfectly sufficient. Do you agree?

Prot. I do.   5

Soc. And so we tried to describe each one as separately
constituting everyone's lives—pleasure without any intelligence and
intelligence without a scrap of pleasure.

Prot. We did indeed.   10

Soc. And did we consider then that either would satisfy anyone?   d

Prot. How could they?

Soc. If, then, anyone thinks we overlooked anything at that
stage, I hope he will now go back and state the matter more
accurately. He will have to put memory, intelligence, knowledge, and 5
true opinion in the same class and see whether anyone would agree
to accept the possession or acquisition of anything if he lacked them,
even the greatest quantity or most intense degree of pleasure, if he
were deprived both of the ability correctly to judge that he was
enjoying himself, and of any knowledge of what he was ever undergoing, and of any memory of his experience however short. The   e
same argument will have to be gone through with intelligence as to
whether anyone would prefer to have intelligence, without even the
briefest pleasure, in preference to having some pleasures as well, or
all possible pleasures without intelligence in preference to the same
with a modicum of intelligence.   5

Prot. No-one could, Socrates. There is no need to go over these
questions again and again.

Soc. In that case, neither of these is beyond criticism as   **61a**

complete, desirable to all, and absolutely good?

Prot. Certainly not.

Soc. We need, then, either a clear account or at least a sketch
of the good, in order, as we said, to know to which to give second
prize.

Prot. That's true.

Soc. I wonder if we already in fact have a lead to the good.

Prot. What do you mean?

Soc. Well, if you were looking for someone and first discovered
the exact whereabouts of the house he lived in, you would be a fair
way to finding the man you were looking for.

Prot. Obviously.

Soc. Now the argument still indicates, as earlier, that we should
look for the good not in a single component life, but in a mixed one.

Prot. Agreed.

Soc. Indeed, there will be more hope of what we are looking for
being clearly discernible in a life where the ingredients are appropriately mixed than in one where they are not?

Prot. Far more.

Soc. Then let's set about the blending, Protarchus, with proper
prayers to Dionysus or Hephaestus or whichever god has the office
of overseeing it.

Prot. Yes indeed.

Soc. It is like being cup-bearers at table faced with streams
of—well I suppose we might call the stream of pleasure the honey,
and pretend intelligence's is something sobering and non-alcholic, a
bracing and healthy element like water—and we must do our best
to produce the finest blend of them that we can.

Prot. Of course.

Soc. First, though, would our best chance of hitting the right
blend be to mix in every pleasure with every form of intelligence?

Prot. Possibly.

Soc. There is a risk, though. I think I have a suggestion for a
safer way of going about the mixing.

Prot. Tell us what it is.

Soc. Some pleasures turned out so far as we can see to be more
truly (*alethes*) pleasures than others, and some skills to be more

accurate than others, didn't they?

Prot. Obviously they are.

Soc. And branches of knowledge also differed. Some set their   10
sights on things in the process of generation and decay, others on   e
what was not subject to these processes but is always unchangingly
the same. Taking the truth (*aletheia*) as our standard, we thought
the latter truer (*alethes*) than the former.

Prot. Quite right, too.   5

Soc. Suppose then we look out the truest (*alethes*) segments
from each set and first mix them together. We could then ask
whether these together were enough to provide us with the most
desirable life possible or whether we should still need something of a
different sort.

Prot. That sounds a good plan.   62a

Soc. Let us then posit a man with an intellectual grasp of what
justice is, powers of reasoning to match his understanding, and,   *
further, in the same condition as regards his thoughts on all such   5
truths.

Prot. All right.

Soc. Is such a man adequately equipped with knowledge? He
can give an account of the divine circle and sphere in themselves, but
when it comes to the sphere and circles in our human world he is
just ignorant even when it comes to using circles and other measures   b
alike in building.

Prot. We've posited an absurd condition for him Socrates,
confining him to divine branches of knowledge like that.

Soc. What do you mean? Should we throw in skills involving   5
inaccurate measures and circles, which are not reliable nor purified
skills, and add them to the mixture?

Prot. We shall have to if anyone is even going regularly to find   *
his way home.

Soc. And what about music which just now we said failed to   c
get purified status because it was full of guess-work and imitation?   *

Prot. I think we shall have to add that too, if our life is ever to
be any life at all.

Soc. In fact you want me, like a doorman pushed and pressured   5
by the crowd, to throw open the doors in surrender and let all forms

of knowledge rush in, mixing in the inferior with the purified cases.

d   *Prot.*   For my part I cannot see what harm it would do anyone to have all the other forms of knowledge, so long as he had the first we let in.

5   *Soc.*   Shall I let them all flow then into what Homer poetically calls 'the waiting arms of the watersmeet'?

Prot. Yes, certainly.

Soc.   In they go, then. Now we must turn back to the other stream, pleasure. Of course the blending hasn't happened as we first intended, with the true items of each first. Our enthusiasm for

10   all forms of knowledge has led us to let them in *en masse* even before

e   any of the pleasures.

Prot. , That's very true.

Soc.   So it's time to take thought about the pleasures too. Should

5   we let all these in in a bunch as well, or should we in this case first let in only the true (*alethes*) ones?

Prot.   It would be far safer just to let in the true (*alethes*) ones first.

Soc.   Then in they go. Now what? Surely if there are any that are necessary we should add them too as we did in the other case?

10   *Prot.*   Of course; that is, any necessary ones at any rate.

63a   *Soc.*   With skills we decided that it was harmless and indeed beneficial to know them all throughout life. I suppose that if we now say the same of pleasures, that it is beneficial and quite harmless for everyone to enjoy them all throughout life, we must add them all to

5   the mixture.

Prot.   What should we say about them, then? What should we do with them?

Soc.   That is not a question we should put to ourselves, Protarchus. Instead, let's put it to the various forms of intelligence and pleasure

10   themselves by asking them about each other.

b   *Prot.*   Asking what, for instance?

Soc.   'Come, pleasures, my friends (or some other name, if "pleasures" is not right), would you prefer to cohabit with every form of intelligence, or to live apart from intellectual activity?'

5   There is only one answer, I think, that they can possibly make to that.

Prot. What is that?

Soc. What was said earlier 'It is neither possible nor beneficial for any category to be isolated by itself in its pure form; but if we   c have to choose one to live with, then out of them all we consider the best would be the one that brought knowledge of everything else but especially as perfect knowledge as possible of each one of us.'

Prot. 'Your present answer is excellent' we shall tell them.

Soc. It is indeed. So now we should question intelligence and   5 thought. 'Do you need any pleasures as well in the mixture?' we should say in our interrogation of thought and intelligence. 'What sorts of pleasure have you in mind?' they might say.

Prot. Very probably.

Soc. Our next contribution will be as follows: 'In addition to the   d true (*alethes*) pleasures already mentioned, do you also want the most intense and violent ones living with you?' And they might say 'How could we possibly, seeing that they put countless obstacles in   5 our way, their madness wreaks havoc in the minds (*psyche*) in which we live; they prevent our growth in the first place; and since their   e lack of interest brings forgetfulness, they for the most part completely destroy our offspring? It is different with the true (*alethes*) purified pleasures you mentioned; you can take it that those are generally congenial to us, as also those that go with health and self-control, and especially all those that, like attendants on a   5 goddess, always accompany all virtue. All these you can mix in. But as to those that from time to time are found to accompany stupidity and all other deplorable characteristics, it would surely be quite irrational for anyone to mix them with thought if he wanted to examine the finest and most harmonious blend and   *64a mixture so as to try to learn from it what is by nature good both in man and the universe at large, and to divine its form.' Surely we must admit that thought has answered sensibly, showing possession of itself on behalf not only of itself but of memory and true opinion   5 too?

Prot. Very sensibly.

Soc. Yet this, at least, is a necessity, and without it nothing at all would ever become anything.

Prot. What's that?   b

*   *Soc.* If we will not mix truth (*aletheia*) in with whatever we have in hand it would not truly (*alethes*) come to be or, having come to be, persist.

       Prot. Obviously.

5   *Soc.* As you say. Now if there is anything else we ought to add to this blending, you and Philebus must say. So far as I can see the description is complete, a sort of incorporeal design for the proper direction of a living (*empsychos*) body.

       Prot. You can put me down as agreeing with that, Socrates.

c   *Soc.* Should we perhaps somehow be right in saying, then, that we are now on the very threshold of where the good is to be found?

       Prot. I think so.

5   *Soc.* In that case, which element would you say at once took pride of place and was more particularly responsible for this condition's being attractive to all and sundry? When we have decided that, we will go on to see whether its role in the total structure shows greater natural kinship with pleasure or with thought.

d   *Prot.* Certainly nothing could be more relevant for deciding the issue before us.

       Soc. Yet it doesn't seem difficult to see what is responsible in

5 every mixture for its being either priceless or valueless.

       Prot. How do you mean?

       Soc. Surely no man is ignorant of it.

       Prot. Of *what?*

       Soc. Simply that any blend whatever that fails of measure and

10 commensurability necessarily by that very fact says good-bye not only to its ingredients but most importantly to itself. It ceases in

e these circumstances to be a blend of anything, and becomes a genuinely unblended hotch-potch, the real ruination always of what is afflicted by it.

       Prot. True enough.

5   *Soc.* So now it looks as though the power of making something good has gone into hiding in the cover of what makes a fine something. For measure and commensurability emerge always as what constitute fineness and excellence.

       Prot. Surely.

       Soc. And we also said that truth (*aletheia*) had to be added to them in the blending.   10

Prot. Yes, we did.

Soc. Then if we cannot use just one category to catch the good **65a**
let's take this trio, fineness, commensurability, truth (*aletheia*), and
treating them as a single unit say that this is the element in the
mixture that we should most correctly hold responsible, that it is
because of this as something good that such a mixture becomes good.   5

Prot. We should indeed.

Soc. In that case anyone could judge adequately between
pleasure and intelligence and decide which is more closely related to
the highest good and has a more honourable position among men   **b**
and gods alike.

Prot. Quite. But it would still be better to argue the matter
through.

Soc. Then let's take these three one by one and assess them   5
vis-à-vis pleasure and intelligence; for we have to see to which of
these two we are to assign each as more closely related.

Prot. You mean fineness, truth and measure?

Soc. Yes. And take truth to start with. Take it, and after   10
looking at all three, intelligence, truth (*aletheia*) and pleasure, take **c**
your time, and tell me whether you think pleasure or intelligence is
more closely related to truth (*aletheia*).

Prot. What need is there to take one's time? There's no comparison. There is no greater charlatan than pleasure. In fact, it's   5
always said that in love, which seems the most intense of pleasures,
even the sin of perjury receives divine pardon, on the grounds that
pleasures, like children, haven't an atom of thought. Thought, on the **d**
other hand, if it is not the same thing as truth is the nearest thing,
and certainly the truest (*alethes*).

Soc. The next thing then is to examine measure in the same way.   5
Has pleasure more of this than intelligence, or the other way round?

Prot. That's another easy question you have put. I shouldn't
think you would ever find anything naturally less given to measure
than pleasure and excessive enjoyment, nor more given to it than
thought and knowledge.   10

Soc. Well said. All the same, you must still speak to the third. **e**
Does thought or the pleasure category have a greater share of fineness?

Is thought a finer thing than pleasure, or vice versa?

Prot. Good heavens, Socrates, who ever found anything in any
5   way debased in intelligence or thought?—not even in his dreams; let
alone awake. No one has ever conceived them as becoming, being or
going to be debased in any way.

Soc. I agree.

Prot. But as to pleasures, especially in general the most
intense ones, when we notice anyone indulging in them, and see how
66a they bring absurdity and even utter debasement in their train, we
even experience shame ourselves. Indeed, so far as possible, we try
to keep them out of sight, confining all that sort of thing to the
hours of darkness on the grounds that it is not proper for the light
of day to see them.

Soc. In fact, Protarchus, you are prepared solemnly to declare,
5   either by proxy or in your own person, that pleasure is neither first
*   nor even second among your prized possessions. Rather, the first is
somewhere in the area of measure, moderation, appropriateness,
and everything of that sort.

Prot. That follows from what we are now saying.

b   *Soc.* The second place goes to the area of what is commensurate, fine, complete, adequate, and everything in that category.

Prot. That seems right.

5   *Soc.* And you would not be far from the truth (*aletheia*) if I
am any prophet, if you gave third place to thought and intelligence.

Prot. Possibly.

Soc. As to fourth place, shouldn't we place fourth after those
three those things we reserved to the mind (*psyche*) alone, forms of
c   knowledge, skills, and what we called correct opinions?—if at least, as
we have claimed, they are more closely related than pleasure to what
is good?

Prot. Perhaps so.

Soc. Fifth place should go to those pleasures we marked off as
5   free of distress, the ones we called purified pleasures of the mind
(*psyche*) alone, some attending forms of knowledge, others attaching
to perceptions.

Prot. Possibly.

Soc. As Orpheus says, 'Let the hymn of praise end with the

sixth generation.' So perhaps our discussion will come to an end at   10
the sixth judgement. All that remains after that is to sum up what   d
has been said.

Prot. Then let's do that.

Soc. Come along, then; as a third toast to the deity, let's   5
recapitulate the evidence of the argument.

Prot. What have you in mind?

Soc. Philebus proposed that our good in life consisted of every
conceivable sort of pleasure.

Prot. It looks as though your third toast is going to consist of a   10
complete repetition of the argument, Socrates.

Soc. Yes, but let's hear the rest. The point is that I noted the   e
facts we have just been over, and objected to the thesis propounded
not only by Philebus but countless other people as well; so I put
forward the view that thought was far superior to pleasure and a
preferable choice for a human life.   5

Prot. That's true.

Soc. But I suspected there was far more to it than this, so I
said that if something emerged that was superior to either of these,
I should fight hard for thought against giving pleasure second prize,
and pleasure would lose even that honour.   10

Prot. You did indeed.   67a

Soc. It was then most satisfactorily shown that neither of these
proposed goods was satisfactory.

Prot. Very true.

Soc. So far as this argument is concerned thought and pleasure   5
escape the burden at least of being the good itself, since each
lacks self-sufficiency and the capacity to be satisfying and complete.

Prot. That's true.

Soc. But when a third contestant emerged superior to either of   10
the others, thought was clearly infinitely more closely related to and
more essentially connected with the winning category than was
pleasure.

Prot. Certainly.

Soc. So according to the judgement demonstrated by the present
argument the influence of pleasure would come in fifth place.   15

Prot. Apparently.

b   *Soc.* And not even if every cow and horse and the whole
animal kingdom spoke for it by their pursuit of enjoyment should it
be given first place; although most people put in animals the trust
prophets put in birds, and so think pleasures are the most powerful
5   factors in making a good life for us. They consider the loves of
animals the decisive criterion rather than the loves of arguments
which have constantly prophesied under the inspiration of the
philosophic muse.

Prot. We are now all agreed, Socrates, on the truth of your
position.

10   *Soc.* In that case, you will now let me go?

Prot. There is still a little unfinished business. As I'm sure you
will not flag before we do, I will remind you of what remains to be
done.

NOTES

11b4–c2 'Philebus holds . . .' Strictly the first sentence could mean that pleasure is *a* good thing for all living beings. As in b7, however, the thesis is clearly one about *the* good, and indeed the whole dispute is about rival candidates for a single post. It would be quite possible to hold that both pleasure and intelligence are good. It is only when at least one is proposed as *the* good that dispute arises. Note that Socrates only claims thought etc. are *better*; cf. 22e–23a, 66e.

11d5 '. . . person (*psuche*).' See note on 30a3.

11d6 '. . . the most desirable life.' For 'eudaemon' cf. General Commentary, p.140.

11d11 'Suppose some other . . .' It is total conditions of the soul or person, or complete lives that are in contrast. This remark hints at the admissions of 20–2, and suggests the version of the opposition given in the General Commentary.

12a7 'My view is . . .' Philebus' incursions are very much those of Mr. Loveboy (which is what the name means), repetitively obstinate and immune to argument. They are probably intended as a reminder of the unthought-out status of most unrefined hedonists of this sort. Cf. 22c3–4, 27e7–28b6.

12c6 'Mentioned by itself . . .' Socrates introduces a doubt about the whole hedonistic enterprise, a doubt that is given prominence by Protarchus' resistance and by the introduction of the Heavenly Tradition at 16 to underline the importance of the methodological issue. Hedonist arguments tend to seem simpler than they are because they are conducted in terms of 'pleasure', in the singular. This suggests that when a man talks of the life of pleasure he is putting just one option before us. Socrates wants to say that there are many pleasures, and the importance of this is that it follows that 'a life of pleasure' ranges over a lot of very different alternatives. If Socrates' point is allowed, a hedonist either has to admit that any life is as good as any other in so far as it is pleasant, or look around for a criterion for distinguishing various pleasant lives. Socrates wants to hold that it is a mistake to treat 'pleasure' as indicating a respect in which pleasures resemble each other. Rather, it is like 'colour' or 'figure'. While 'red' or 'triangular' might plausibly be thought to indicate respects in which things resemble one another, 'colour' and 'figure' could just as well be said to indicate respects in which things may be dissimilar. (For evidence that this is an explicit rejection of earlier methods compare the wording here, especially d8—13a5, with *Republic* 435a—b, *Hippias Major* 299d and *Meno* 72—5, esp. 74c.) This suggests that there will be no hope of comparing pleasures as more or less pleasant, any more than of comparing shades as more or less coloured. The only comparison between lives would be something like relative density of occupation by pleasures or relative 'purity' of pleasure (cf. note on 53c1). But there is no reason except idiom for supposing that a dog's life might not be better than Socrates' by that test. In effect, therefore, either some non-hedonistic criterion of goodness is introduced, or a number of lives will be equally good, some of which quite lack intelligence. In other words, this point sharpens the issue as of the form it is given at 20—2: a Phileban is going to have to acknowledge a non-rational life of pleasure as a good life.

The argument is suggestive rather than conclusive. There seem to be two points at issue: (i) whether pleasures differ qualitatively; (ii) whether pleasures are, as Hume seems to hold, even if differing in quality, nevertheless always effects of other activities or experiences. At least the first is claimed by Socrates, but it seems that it can only be said to be argued on the assumption that the Humean position is rejected. But that rejection is not argued. The conclusion that pleasures differ is argued on the grounds that being a rake is different from sobriety, good sense from silliness. But if one holds a Humean view it does not even look like an argument for the required conclusion, for which the only argument could be observation of the pleasures. If, however, Plato is thinking that the pleasures of silliness consist in being silly, those of good sense in acting sensibly, then the obvious contrast between silliness and good sense will be a difference between the pleasures. But in that case the crucial issue is whether one should talk of pleasure as caused by or accompanying activities and experiences or as consisting in them—and that question is not argued. At most an analogy with colour and figure is urged. Until the point is proved it is open to anyone to hold either a Humean or a Protarchan position holding that pleasure is an effect of what gives it. He can even accept the general importance of Socrates' point that not all general words of classification or characterization stand for a respect in which things resemble one another. He only has to say that the point does not hold of 'pleasure'. It may be that Plato thought he had done more than he had because there was no opposing theory of what sort of way we should think of pleasure, as e.g. a certain sort of feeling. Consequently there was no clear interpretation to put on the language of causing and accompanying. Knowledge, success, and so on can all come from varying sources, but this gives rise to no temptation to talk of a single thing produced in all cases. In that case Plato's examples might seem more persuasive and to be revealing the verbal nature of the opposing position.

The refusal to separate pleasure from the activity or experience enjoyed reappears at 36b seq. on false pleasures. It may be that Plato saw no third way between treating pleasure as a simple thing found in all pleasant activities, and thinking of pleasures consisting in the activities or experiences enjoyed. Pleasure, in Greek, gets naturally classified as a *pathos*, or something that happens to one, but there is no terminology of feeling related to it that might tempt one in a Humean direction.

There is a problem about what 'refusing to separate pleasure from the activity or experience enjoyed' amounts to, and similarly about what would count as saying what pleasure is. Clearly, saying that A gets pleasure from ϕ-ing is saying more than either that A is engaged in an activity or that he is engaged in ϕ-ing, and Plato would not, I think, deny this. In this sense, therefore, he would separate pleasure from what is enjoyed. On the other hand, it might be that only experiences and activities can qualify as members of the class of pleasures (i.e. be properly called pleasures), and that 'A gets pleasure from ϕ-ing', while it says more than that 'A is ϕ-ing', does not attribute a further experience or activity over and above ϕ-ing. Consequently, every pleasure will be identical with some experience or activity. This Plato may have thought, but one could only attribute the explicit thesis to him if one could say that he was explicitly interested in the concept of pleasure, or what expressions such as '. . . gets pleasure from . . .' can govern and what they 'say of' their subjects/objects. Unfortunately, this is not so. It does seem that Plato relies on being able to talk of experiences and activities as pleasures, and wants to say that they are the pleasures in a way that seems to rely on a thesis about the meanings of the terms. But when he flirts in the *Republic* (580d–585d) with the view that pleasure is satisfied desire, or in the *Philebus* (43) with the view that some pleasures are perceived restorations of natural balance, these can hardly be views about what we are saying of episodes when we call them pleasures. These are theories giving either a general characterization of conditions for the occurrence of pleasure, or sets of conditions for different pleasures, and are not in any sense conceptual analysis. 'Physical pleasure consists in the perception of the restoration of natural balance' is not a statement about what we mean when we say that someone enjoys quenching his thirst etc.

Indeed, it seems from 16 seq. that when by dialectic we discover the unit, pleasure, we have not either explicated a familiar expression or discovered some general conditions for the occurrence of pleasure, but have devised a science of pleasure on a special interpretation of 'science'. There might be several ways of showing pleasure to be one thing, and so saying what it is, without there being any ambiguity in the term 'pleasure' or change of account of the conditions under which people enjoy themselves. The fact is that Plato just does not distinguish these different ways of interpreting the question 'what is pleasure?', so that if we ask 'what is he doing precisely?' the answer is 'nothing precisely'. He wants to do something called asking what pleasure is, and is prepared to run together considerations from the meaning of 'pleasure', considerations from a theory of the conditions for the occurrence of pleasure and considerations from views about what would constitute a skill of pleasure as though they all obviously bore on the same question. For related points see note on 35a3, General Commentary, pp. 162–171 and 213.

12e5 '. . . as opposite as can be . . .' Plato has no clear doctrine of opposition. Characteristically he thinks of a scale whose opposite ends are, so to speak, in total opposition. But sometimes one characteristic or state is said to be the opposite of another when its description is the contradictory of that of the other. Sometimes it is simple incompatibility that is at issue. In the case of colours it is hard to see what talk of degrees of opposition would amount to, though with figures approximation to a circle as the figure at furthest remove from a triangle might be in mind. Opposition is again a difficult notion with pleasures although if the pleasure of virtue consists in being virtuous it might be considered opposed to that of vice just because virtue is the opposite of vice, either linguistically or in terms of some theory of virtue and vice. Difference and dissimilarity, in what follows, are presumably lesser forms of opposition (cf. *Parmenides* 159a). At 23 seq. the indeterminates are given as pairs of opposites, and it is the function of the determinant in some sense to end the opposition (25d11–e2). The point there is presumably that 'high' and 'low' are related as opposites and it might therefore seem that high and low notes are incompatible, but the determinant introduces commensurability and so allows the combining of the apparently opposed. For some other places where 'opposite' plays an important role cf. *Protagoras* 330–3, *Phaedo* 70d–72d, 104–6, *Republic* 436b–439d, 479, 523 seq., *Sophist* 257b–259b.

13a7 'Because . . .' This may look like a suggestion of a difficulty only. After all, the fact that some pleasures may be opposites of others is no obvious reason for denying that another predicate as well as 'pleasure' can be applied to them all. But Protarchus is wanting to effect some sort of identification of pleasure and goodness. The suggestion (admission?) that *A* and *B* are opposed as pleasures (i.e. in respect of pleasantness) ought, therefore, to be glossable as that they are opposed as goods (i.e. in respect of goodness). The expression 'opposed as goods' is opaque, but can be read so as to suggest that if *A* and *B* are opposed as goods they must be at opposite ends of the 'good' scale, and so at least one of them must be bad. So if two pleasures are opposed as pleasures and so, according to Protarchus as goods, at least one must be bad. In that case in the expressions 'as goods' 'in respect of goodness', 'good' and 'goodness' would have neutrally to denote the scale of comparison rather than one end of it, much as 'weight' and 'velocity' do. But if that is so, of course, 'opposed as pleasures' must be similarly interpreted, in which case at least one of two opposed pleasures might emerge as not a pleasure at all, and the point would be harmless to Protarchus. Alternatively, the talk of opposition simply amounts to saying that two pleasures or goods are mutually incompatible, while retaining the characterization. This better fits the analogy with colour and figure. In that case debauchery and philosophizing might be opposed pleasures in that they are in Plato's view incompatible activities. Similarly, liberty and equality, or democracy and efficiency might be opposed goods in that on a given interpretation any degree of one involves limitation of the other. But now, of course, there is no implication from opposition as pleasures and identification of pleasure and good to some pleasures being bad. Either

1. '*A* and *B* are opposed as pleasures' entails '*A* and *B* are opposed as goods' (because pleasure = good), and this entails 'at least one is bad', in which case at least one is not a pleasure; or
2. The first entailment holds, but '*A* and *B* are opposed as pleasures' entails '*A* and *B* are both pleasures', in which case a similar entailment holds with regard to their being good. For Plato's use of 'opposite' see note on 12e6.

It remains, however, that if pleasures only as much as vary a good deal, and 'good' and 'pleasant' are not synonyms, it is a good question whether all pleasures are good. It may be that they are, but the position no longer has its original simplicity. Granted the association of opposition with dissimilarity, Plato may be thinking of complete opposition as entailing total dissimilarity.

13c5-d1 'Not at all ...' Faced with the argument from opposed pleasures to bad pleasures, Protarchus retreats to the original position. Socrates claims that this is a retrograde step to youthful sophistry. He interprets Protarchus as holding his position only because he thinks that general terms denote respects in which things resemble one another or that all members of a single class must resemble one another. Socrates' objection may be either: (i) I could take two dissimilars such as black and white and argue that as they are both colours they must both closely resemble each other, or more dramatically: (ii) if A and B are both most unlike, then each merits the description 'most unlike'; but that must on Protarchus' thesis indicate a respect in which they are most alike (cf. *Parmenides* 147c–e, and *Protagoras* 331d–e).

13d7 'Hissed off the stage.' Hackforth has 'our discussion would be "stranded and perish". Let us get it back again, then, into the water.' Certainly *ekpiptein* can be used of shipwreck, but is also a common verb for orators or stage-performances being hissed off. With *logos* as subject, one might most naturally take the latter sense. There is no doubt, however, that *anakrouesthai* is a familiar nautical term for backing water. One could, therefore, with Hackforth, preserve the metaphor throughout, or take the hissing as the most natural sense, and take the 'back up' metaphor to be so weak as not to be discordant. In this case the immediate move to a wrestling metaphor would be fairly easy, as both arguments and law-cases were often spoken of in terms of combat.

13e9 'All the forms of knowledge together . . .' It is important to note that the difficulty Protarchus is in is characterized as one of allowing that there are many pleasures, despite the fact that talk of pleasure suggests unity. The plurality that is causing difficulty is the plurality of forms of pleasure, not of instances. It is natural to assume that if two things merit the same description then they share a common feature in respect of which they can be compared. No doubt in so far as one can give an account of why the same description applies to both one can simply mean by saying that they share a common feature that such an account is available. This move is harmless so long as one does not hope to derive much from it, but a prior assumption about the conditions necessary for a term to be usable of a number of things may lead one to take 'common feature' very strongly, and then the appearance of many forms becomes puzzling. The point can be seen very clearly with 'unlike'. If A is unlike B and C is unlike D, A and C share the common feature of being unlike. But there is no guarantee that they can be compared in that respect. There is no such thing as just being unlike, but only being unlike B or unlike *D*. Similarly, one may say that physics and anthropology have it in common that they yield knowledge, but this can be misleading if one fails to realize that the first gives knowledge of the properties of matter, the second of the forms of primitive cultures. What follows the 'of' specifies the form of knowledge, and there is no such thing as just knowledge (cf. *Sophist* 257c–d, *Republic* 438c–d). Socrates wants to hold the same of pleasure, that while sadistic practices and philosophy both give pleasure, it is a mistake to suppose that this is to be analysed as 'There is something that is pleasure, and both sadistic practices and philosophy give it.' In fact there is no more something that is just pleasure than there is something that is just knowledge. There is only the pleasure of causing suffering, or the pleasure of doing philosophy.

It is arguable that the strong insistence on the importance of this point signalizes a realization of a new departure on Plato's part. The requirement of a single adequate definition that seems to underly the procedure of the early dialogues can suggest that it must be possible to specify the features common to all instances of virtue, courage, knowledge, and so on, and in a way that allows us to identify members of the class independently of knowing other members. The repeated failure to reach such a definition might show a failure to reach the truth, but it might also show that we have been pursuing a chimera. Instead of asking 'What is virtue?', 'What is knowledge?', and refusing to examine the various forms of each, we are now to examine the various forms, and then ask why they may all be called virtue or knowledge. Proposed definitions will always be refutable because they suppose a common feature. Meno and Theaetetus were wrong in listing examples in so far as they were asked for a definition. Nevertheless they were right in that that is where one's examination should begin. (See note on 12c6.)

It is not clear just where Plato stood on this question. It seems fairly obvious that 'unlike', 'different', and so on are in fact in a different category from 'knowledge', 'pleasure', and others, despite my 'similarly' earlier in this note. One might have some hope of giving a general account of why the various forms of knowledge acquire the same name, perhaps along the lines suggested at 55 seq. It is quite baffling to think what an account would be like of what entitled all things that are different to be called different. They seem different sorts of terms altogether. Plato's tendency to illustrate the general point by reference to 'unlike' (if that is how we are to take 13d), and to illustrate his view of 'different' by the example of 'knowledge' at *Sophist* 257c suggests he did not see any radical difference. The same is suggested by the use of *physis* (nature) at *Sophist* 255e, 257c, and by his characterizing the difference between difference and change as simply one of degree of pervasiveness (*Sophist* 253–4). On the other hand *Parmenides* 147c–e suggests a clear realization of the peculiarity of any strong interpretation of *phusis* when talking of difference. It seems that he has seen clearly that a certain model for the analysis of terms will not do; it fails indifferently on a number of examples; and the differences between the examples are not clearly spelled out because their main interest is that they show the inadequacy of the false model.

14b1 'In that case let us not . . .' I have translated τοῦ ἀγαθοῦ (*tou agathou*: the good), excluded by Burnet following Bury. It seems hard to read λόγου (*logou*) in Protarchus' speech as meaning anything so precise as 'definition', but on any less precise rendering (e.g. 'position') it is an unacceptable antecedent for 'mine and yours'. Consequently it would be necessary to read ἐλεγχομένω (*elengchomenō*: under examination) the dual, with Grovius, to agree with the supplied τὸ ἐμὸν καὶ τὸ σόν ἀγαθόν (*to emon kai to son agathon*: both my good and yours).

14c4–5 '. . . glad to receive . . .' See note on 22b6–8, for an explanation of the Greek word '*hekon*' translated here as 'glad'.

14c11–e4 'You mean . . .' Two one/many problems are mentioned and dismissed. With the first, as Striker points out, there is an ambiguity. The point may be (i) that Protarchus, while a unit, becomes many hims, even opposed to each other, or (ii) that Protarchus becomes many and opposed hims. (For a similar ambiguity see 13e9–10.) If (i) then the point is presumably that Protarchus is a plurality in virtue of having many predicates true of him (cf. *Sophist* 251–2). But the point is made in terms of opposites only, which suggests (ii). Anyone holding that the applicability of many predicates shows plurality would presumably be holding that something different in reality corresponds to each predicate, so that our units turn out to be collections. Someone holding (ii), on the other hand, could accept that many predicates may be true of the same thing without affecting its unity, but feel that opposite predicates cannot simultaneously be true of the same subject, since the same thing cannot be *F* and the opposite of *F*. Plato himself in the *Republic* (436 seq.) uses a refined relative of this consideration to show that there must be different parts of the soul. How the problem is to be resolved depends upon what is substituted for '*F*' (cf. *Parmenides* 129 for possibilities). In that passage in the *Parmenides* it is suggested that the problem is childish as applied to physical objects, but would become critical if applied to Forms. In the *Philebus* the difficult problem is also held to concern Forms.

The second problem concerns the unity of things with physical parts, as a human body is made up of various limbs. Thus in both cases the childish problems concern physical objects, and are contrasted with the serious ones which concern monads such as Man, Good, and so on.

If it is right that the first problem relies on the paradox of saying one thing has two opposite properties, then it bears a superficial resemblance to the problem we are in. For this arose (12c–13b, 13e–14a) from the discovery that certain apparent units contained opposites, and that general description fits Protarchus' example. So it was not utterly foolish of him. Yet the problems come from opposite directions. Protarchus' example generates a paradox on the ground that (i) X is F and G, (ii) 'F' and 'G' are opposites, but (iii), if (ii) then X is F only if X is not G, and conversely. Therefore X is not F and G, but there must be two things X, Y, one of which is F, the other G. How one gets out of the paradox depends on what is substituted for F and G. If 'black' and 'white' are substituted, then different parts will be black or white, and the paradox will collapse into the second one, which Socrates mentions. If 'like', 'unlike' are substituted, or 'large', 'small' (cf. *Phaedo* 102 seq.), then X will be like and unlike different things, or small and large relative to different things. But this sort of solution will not help with Socrates' and Protarchus' problem. This does not arise from seeing that Pleasure is F and G, but from seeing that X and Y are Pleasures. Thus the difficulty is: (i) X and Y are F, (ii) F is one thing, (iii) X and Y are opposites in respect of being F. Therefore F cannot be one thing.

This is not, of course, the problem of the *Parmenides*. (See General Commentary, pp. 143–5). There, too, there is a problem of how certain units, Forms, can be one and many, but there the problem is how one can consistently talk of Forms as units while holding that particular objects partake in them. As Striker brings out (pp. 13 seq.), the terminology of that problem is noticeably absent from this section of the *Philebus*. The problem may be alluded to in 15b, but its solution is not relevant to Socrates' present problem, and the best that could be done would be to claim that Socrates brings to our attention units whose existence as units we all admit and which are vulnerable to the *Parmenides* objection. This might serve to cool our enthusiasm for the objection without spelling out just how it is to be met. Even this much, however, requires an interpretation of the following passage which is not free from objection (see General Commentary: The Heavenly Tradition, The Determinant and Indeterminate).

15a–b   See General Commentary: The One and the Many pp.

143 seq.

15b1–2 '... units in the strict sense.' Cf. General Commentary, pp. 143 seq.

15b4 '... it is nevertheless unshakeably one ...' See General Commentary, pp. 144 seq.

15b5 'scattered abroad.' Cf. 25a1–4, 23e5.

15d4 '... the identification of one and many ...' This seems the strict rendering, the one and many becoming the same, the participle 'becoming' (*gignomena*) agreeing with the plural 'many'. It may, however, as Badham takes it, be agreeing by attraction, in which case the sentence should run 'In my view, the same thing becoming one and many crops up ...' cf. General Commentary, p.153.

15d8 '... our statements.' The word is *'logoi'* and so could mean 'words', 'definitions', 'accounts', 'arguments', 'discourse'.

15e2–3 '... rolling it one way ...' There is uncertainty as to the metaphor. I have followed Bury, who discusses it in his note. The image may, however, be of a man putting his treasure into a pile and then spreading it out, or rolling up his manuscript and then unrolling it.

16b5–7 'There could be no finer way ...' It may be as well to query the implications of this statement. Hackforth, for instance, takes it for granted that the method mentioned here is a method of collection and division first advocated in *Phaedrus* (265 seq.) and illustrated in *Sophist* and *Politicus*. This may be true, but the proof of it will be in examining what is said in the various dialogues and seeing if they tally. There is no reason to suppose that Plato thought there was simply one method for all problems. Socrates could love this method while loving others too, but think some more appropriate to some problems than others. It is true that Plato has a tendency to use 'dialectic' as though it were the name of a single procedure. But as Robinson has argued (*Plato's Earlier Dialectic*), it is more accurate to say that it is his name for proper philosophical procedure, whatever he may think that to be at the time, and proper philosophical procedure might involve the application of various methods. It is beyond the scope of a work like the present to undertake the detailed comparison with other dialogues required for arguing the question. I simply want to deploy the defensive argument that this opening sentence cannot be used to argue that if an interpretation of the *Philebus* method makes it different from the method of the *Phaedrus* then the interpretation must be wrong. Even if collection and division is referred to, what follows will affect what one takes that method to be. What is said in 16–19 should be compared with 23e–25a. It should be noted that the description 'dialectic' comes from the tradition, not Socrates (cf. 17a). For further remarks, see General Commentary, pp. 202–4.

16c2 '. . . any skill.' For 'skill' as a translation see General Commentary, p. 153–4.

16c5 'As I see it . . .' What follows must be a reference to Pythagoras (cf. also *Laws* 715e7 seq.) One and Many, determinant and indeterminate were well-known Pythagorean pairs,—and the Pythagoreans had a notoriously mathematical view of reality which Plato found sympathetic. Thus the present insistence on number and the elucidation of the notion of determinant in mathematical terms has a strong Pythagorean ring, and the description of the Indeterminate at 31a9 as that which has neither beginning, middle, nor end is again Pythagorean. While other philosophers before Plato used one or both of the terms, reports of Pythagorean philosophers suggest that they were the immediate ancestors (cf. Diels-Kranz, i. 398 *ad fin.*) According to Aristotle (*Nicomachean Ethics* 1106b29–30) they made a similar connection with good and bad. For a later discussion of earlier views on the Indeterminate, cf. Aristotle, *Physics* Γ 4 *ad fin.*

16c9 '. . . those things which are from time to time said to be.' Or: '. . . which are from time to time said to exist.' The introduction of 'said' suggests a reminder that the problem is to do with speech (cf. 15d4–8), and that the point is about the way we—necessarily—talk. The point is not that individual pleasures are a combination of determinant and indeterminacy, one and many, nor even, at least primarily, that the Form of Pleasure is, but that 'pleasure' is a term that unifies an indeterminate range, and it is our business to find the unity in finding the 'number'. 'From time to time' probably indicates that it is the familiar items of which, in the dialogues, we are often asked to agree that 'there is such a thing as . . .', even in cases where Forms are not in question. It is the context that determines the coverage of the expression. It would be possible (cf. Striker, pp. 18–22) to translate as 'that those things which exist eternally are made up of one and many . . .' This would make Forms the subject-matter of the passage, and exclude any embarrassment ensuing on the possibly wide coverage of 'the things said to be' (cf. 53e1 where it is clearly covering perceptible phenomena). It would also fit well the interpretation of 15b—c given by Professor Anscombe (see General Commentary, pp. 146 seq.). It would, however, be strange to attribute to Pythagoras a doctrine about Forms if he is the Promethus. Granted that the Forms are alluded to at 15a—c, it seems that at 15d Socrates proposes a way into the one/many problem which no one can avoid since the route is an inescapable feature of language. We can all be faced with the problem, whether or not we accept the Theory of Forms, and one would expect the introduction of Pythagoras to help us tackle the problem at that level without reference to a disputed theory. The section that follows illustrates how in the Pythagorean tradition one can account for a plurality constituting a unity without the bafflement that comes if with Protarchus we suppose that similarity is required. It is that supposition that makes variety a problem.

16c10 '. . . determinant and indeterminacy.' This translates *'peras'* and *'apeirian'*. 'Indeterminate' and 'indeterminacy' come also as translations of *'apeiron'* and *'to apeiron'* used adjectivally or as a noun. The translation is governed largely by the interpretation. Other words that have been popular, and variously better fit other interpretations, are 'limit', 'unlimited', 'finite', 'infinite', 'determinate', 'determinable'. That should suffice to give some idea of what further pairs might stand a chance of being acceptable. Strictly, *'apeirian'* and *'apeiron'* suggest unlimitedness, determinability, or whatever, and *peras* limit, determinant. So that 'determinate', 'finite' should be given a slightly 'active' sense, as against the suggestion of indicating things characterized by those adjectives.

16d1—3 '. . . we should always posit . . .' On the first interpretation mentioned in the General Commentary this amounts to saying that for every individual object we should suppose some genus under which it will fall, and look for it with confidence. The encouragement to search and the confidence in success both seem intelligible.

On the second interpretation the sentence is more obscure. For we start, supposedly, with a genus, which, by some amazing feat of absent-mindedness, we then misplace, and have to posit its existence and search for it all over again. Confidence in success is perhaps justified by the memory of original possession, but ought equally to be undermined by the memory of later stupidity. Alternatively, Plato is thinking of starting with species, or something less than *summa genera.* In that case we always posit a *summum genus* and proceed from there. This would make sense of the sentence, but can hardly claim to be suggested in either what precedes or what follows. It is only discerned after much interpretation, and in particular after the realization that if we started with a *summum genus* we could not proceed. It might be better to interpret 'posit a single form' as supposing that what we start with *really is* a single genus; searching for it and finding it will be the process of making clear the bounds of the genus and so establishing its unity.

On the third interpretation we start with something like pleasure, knowledge, good, man, ox. Positing a unit is supposing them to form a single subject-matter of inquiry, and finding the unit will be finding a way in which they can be brought under one. On both this and the last account of the previous interpretation confidence in success has to be seen as a confidence without which progress would not be made and which so far has paid dividends. It may be that Plato had a stronger faith than that, though his putting it as a tradition makes the matter uncertain. Clearly, to proceed without at least the provisional assumption of possible success would be to abandon inquiry. On the other hand, it seems possible that in any given case (e.g. pleasure?) the subject-matter should not be amenable to such treatment. There is no sign of whether Plato thought this or not, but he might have pointed out that it was hard to prove that the subject matter was not amenable rather than that we were still failing. The most obvious way would be to prove ambiguity of the original expression, but that does not get mentioned as a possibility in the *Philebus.*

It is possible that the participle '*enousan*' ('being in it') has conditional force. In that case there would be no claim that there always is a unit to find, but only that all units are findable.

16d7 '... quantity ...' *hoposa* ('how many'). I have retained the same translation for this and '*to poson*'. cf. 17b7, c11, 19b3, 24c3, 6, 7, d3, 5.

17a1−3 '... too quick and too slow.' Too quick in that they should pause for the many and not pass immediately to the indeterminate. Too slow in that the things between thereby escape from them, i.e. slip through their fingers, and so no progress is made. More haste less speed. This is the explanation that seems to be given in the text. There is no call for the emendation of βραδύτερον (too slow) to βραχύτερον (too short). Bury's explanation of 'too slow' is that it indicates an unscientific roundabout route. But Socrates is quite clear that because these men move directly to the indeterminate the intermediates get away, so that for all their speed they are too slow to catch them.

17b4 '... indeterminate variety.' Literally 'indeterminate in number'. The translation is determined by the interpretation. It is possible to take 'sound' so that sounds are individuated by quality or by occasion. In the first way the same sound can occur on two occasions from different sources, but not in the second. On the first an indefinite number of sounds is an indefinite variety, but not on the second. Cf. General Commentary, p. 170–3.

17b8 '... their properties.' This is not a numerical notion, but is inserted here, and at d1, and picked up by Protarchus at 19b3, and seems to reflect a wish either to modify the numerical suggestion of the passage, or at least the suggestion of counting. The properties might be the ratios of points on a scale to others. For further discussion see General Commentary, pp. 165 seq., esp. p. 173.

17c1–2 The text is uncertain. I have translated a version that omits the τό (*to: the*) and an ἐν αὐτῇ (*en autei*: in itself) of the Oxford text. Ἐν αὐτῇ may well be a corruption from '*en tautei*' (in this) which in turn might have been added in an attempt to make something of a corrupt sentence. Possibly we should read 'Φωνὴ μέν που κατὰ τοῦτο (sc. τὸ μουσικὸν ποιοῦν) καὶ κατ ἐκείνην . . .' and leave out ἐν αὐτῇ. It would translate: 'You will grant that vocal sound both in this case (music) and in that skill (letters) is one.' This would give a possible beginning of the present remnants, and the sentence would be either making the point translated, or possibly asserting that there is one *phone* that is the subject-matter of both *technai*. Cf. General Commentary, pp. 163 seq. for the translation of '*phone*'.

17e6 '... can never give account . . .' The Greek has a pun. The word translated 'of no account' is formed from the word for number, meaning 'not to be numbered (among the distinguished)',— and this because he cannot reduce anything to number. I have tried to catch this by 'account' which is audibly indistinguishable from 'a count' though, as I have remarked, there is more, for Plato, to numbering than counting.

18b1 I have omitted ἐπί (*epi*) in front of ἀριθμόν (*arithmon*: number). It seems to make no sense, and probably is a thoughtless echo from 'ἐπί τινα ἀριθμόν' ('for some number') two lines earlier and ἐπὶ τὸ ἕν ('at the one') immediately preceding.

18b–d Strictly this example is not one of going through the many to the one if that means starting at the lowest many and working up in order. Theuth notices the indefinite variety, then some main divisions which still contain variety, then he gets that systematised and finally establishes that letters constitute a unity. But we start with the indeterminate and end with the one.

It is perhaps worth noting that at least Philebus thinks this illustration very illuminating.

18c6 '... element...' See General Commentary: The Heavenly Tradition, p. 164—5.

18e Note that Socrates declares all this relevant to the One/Many problem we began with, and as part of the question whether to choose a life of intelligence or pleasure.

20c4—6 'In my view, then,...' It is a good question why this change should release one from the need to 'distinguish the various forms of pleasure'. What happens, after all, from 31b onwards? See General Commentary, pp. 208 seq.

The world translated 'distinguish' is in noun form, and is the word often translated 'division' in contexts where Plato seems to have a special method in mind, sometimes referred to as Collection and Division. An interpretation of the Heavenly Tradition that makes that an exhortation to this method will attach significance to the term. But there is no reason why the term must carry such reference, and if it turned out that the Heavenly Tradition method were different it would still be a perfectly natural word to use. If it turned out that there was no single method deserving the title 'the method of division' there would be even less cause for worry.

20d1 '... perfect.' The Greek word '*teleon*' is difficult to translate. It is the adjective from '*telos*', meaning 'limit', 'goal', 'completion'. It can be translated 'perfect' and possibly has in context the suggestion that what it describes is a genuine goal. See Aristotle, *Nicomachean Ethics* 1097a15—b21.

20d7 'One thing about it...' For the use of this principle and problems concerning it see General Commentary, pp. 181 seq., 166—7. See Aristotle, *Nicomachean Ethics* X 2: this is the *sort* of consideration adduced by Eudoxus to support his view on pleasure. What Plato adds to 'what everything pursues' is the notion of 'knowing'. He gets somewhat confusing when talking of animals, when he is inclined to suggest (cf. 22b, 60c) that the mixed life is good for animals too. But at least he shares with Eudoxus the view, at least for present purposes, that the good life for something of type X is the life that things of type X pursue. The admission is extracted that things of an intelligent type will pursue a mixed life and therefore, on

Eudoxus' principle, pleasure cannot be their good. It is not clear whether Socrates is saying that everything capable of knowledge pursues the good or that everything that knows the good pursues it. The text is ambiguous.

20e4–21a2 'Intelligence must form . . .' This argument is mentioned approvingly by Aristotle, *Nicomachean Ethics* X, 1172b26 seq. (and seems first to have been used by Eudoxus), and G. E. Moore, *Ethics* ch. 7. The notion of needing nothing else or sufficiency, while perhaps clear enough for the purpose of the argument, becomes obscure if pressed. If we are talking of human beings, would sustenance and sleep, even if pleasureless, count as things needed in addition to intellectual activity? One is tempted to say no, because though necessary, their inclusion is required only for intellectual activity to take place, they have no independent value. In that case, pleasure counts because we should want that even if its inclusion were no help to our intellectual exercises. But as remarked elsewhere, that is not quite how the argument for including intelligence is developed (see General Commentary: Victory to the Mixed Life).

21b3 '. . . you would be glad . . .' See Addendum p. 231.

21b6–d1 'But if you lacked . . .' It is not clear whether Socrates is envisaging removing from a dog's life both memory and expectation of pleasure, or whether a dog's life, even with canine memory and expectation, is one that lacks intelligence in the relevant sense. The choice of jelly-fish and shellfish might simply be for purposes of abusive description, granted that the contrast is between human and animal intelligence simply. On the other hand they may have been chosen because while alive their lives have an air of drift and passivity that contrasts with the evidence of memory and intelligent pursuit in higher animals, so that they are examples of things lacking intelligence. Probably, however, the contrast is meant to be between human and animal intelligence in general. The words translated 'knowledge', 'judge', 'true judgement', 'predict' ('*logizesthai*', 'calculate', the same root as '*logos*') tend in Plato to have suggestions of operations conducted by language users (cf. *Theaetetus* 184–7, 190 and *Sophist* 263–4 for judgement); then the constructions tend to be 'knowing that', 'remembering that' one enjoyed oneself. In the particular case of realizing at the time that one is enjoying oneself, it is hard to know how to interpret this except on the supposition that Plato means that an animal, lacking the power of conceptual judgement, cannot recognize the truth or falsity of 'I am enjoying myself', since it is incapable of justified true judgement and so of knowledge. It does not follow that Plato thought that human beings, in possession of language, could fail to know whether they were enjoying themselves. For this see notes on 36e5–10, 43d7–9.

21d9–e2 'The supposed case of ...' Speusippus (cf. Aristotle, *Nicomachean Ethics* 1153b1–7, 1173a5–13) may at some time have put forward the view that the good life is free of both pain and pleasure. The position mentioned here is a possible version of such a view. There is no certainty on the date of his formulating the position, but it is possible that the opposition between pleasure and pleasureless/painless intellection is intended to recall some Eudoxus/Speusippus opposition. (See M. Schofield, *Museum Helveticum*, 1971.)

22b4–6 'For it would have to be adequate ...' The reference to 'plant or animal' recalls the universal criterion of Eudoxus, but 'capable of so living throughout its life' so modifies it as to remove reliance on observation of actual pursuits. It is not clear why a cabbage should be thought to benefit, at least in the way of being a better cabbage, by a capacity for calculation. Further, lacking legs it could not put its calculation of cutting time to any use. Plato seems simply to be expression the view that thinking is a 'better thing' than vegetating. Alternatively it is no benefit to them because they are unable to reason, in which case, why mention them?

22b6–8 '... In defiance of the nature of the good.' The language strongly suggests that the real nature of the good can, in principle, be known, and judged independently of what people choose. The appeal to Protarchus must be to elicit what he would choose on reflection, but the present passage suggests that 'on reflection' means more than 'after a pause'; the reflection must be based on knowing what the options are (20d8), and 'knowing', presumably, means 'knowing the nature of ...'

'Against his will.' The two Greek words '*hekon*' and '*akon*' are often translated 'voluntarily', 'involuntarily', or 'willingly', 'unwillingly'. Their precise sense can only be caught cumbersomely in English. A person acts *hekon* if he does what he wants to do and does it because he wants to; he acts *akon* if he does something it distresses him to have done and does not do it because he wants to. (Cf. Aristotle, *Nicomachean Ethics* 1109b30–1111b3 for an extended discussion. Plato's two possible explanations of 'unwilling' behaviour—ignorance and necessity—receive some refinement at Aristotle's hands.) The dictum that a man chooses anything but good only against his will is notorious Platonic doctrine. It is a direct result of justifying and/or giving the rationale of morality by reference to what people want. It would be possible to try to give the rationale of morality simply by indicating a purpose which moral norms in general serve, and which seems to govern arguments concerning their alteration or modification. One might, for instance, argue that moral norms are distinguished from others as being geared to the greatest happiness of the greatest number. But this might well be accepted as the rationale and then rejected as a justification or acceptable reason for adopting such norms. There is now a temptation for a moralist to try to strengthen the position by arguing that the end or goal which is the rationale of morality is also one that we all really want. The history of philosophy contains numerous attempts to push home such a claim. One might for instance take it as truistic that every man must always and only want to do what he wants. A life containing unsatisfied desire is in at least some respect not really what he wants—because it fails to meet some want. If one can now establish, perhaps by observation, that there are certain desires that people have, even, perhaps, without realizing it, one might hope to argue that only a moral life meets all the desires a man has, and so only a man living such a life is doing, without any qualification, what he wants. A man who says he wants another sort of life may be right about what he is actually pursuing, but is wrong about his desires. Some such line Plato seems to try in the *Republic* (Book IX, esp. 577e, 579d–e). It will now seem natural to claim that if a man does not do what is right, then either he is incapacitated or ignorant of what he really wants. For it seems in general that if A wants X, but his behaviour is quite unrelated to the achievement of X, then either he must also want, and want more, something else, or he is mistaken about the identification or means of getting X, or he is in some way under some necessity so that he cannot be said to be acting as he is because he wants to. The first option is ruled out in the present argument by the premiss that a man *only* wants to do what he wants. So either he is wrong about what he wants or under some necessity to act as he does. In the *Philebus* Plato seems to be moving towards a different way of producing a similar conclusion, but one also adumbrated in the *Republic* (cf. Book VI, 505d–e). The basic premiss now is that everyone wants the best sort of life possible. It is plausible to think that most people would agree to that form of words. If some teeth can now be given to 'best' in the form of a reliable way of deciding what is really good, then again we might hope to argue that a moral life is the only form that is good, and so is what everyone really wants. Pursuit of other forms of life shows the influence of ignorance or necessity. There is no wanting any other life than the best possible, for whatever life we pursue we pursue in the belief that it is the best possible. This approach *seems* to be implicit in the way in which the appeal to desire operates (see General Commentary, pp. 181 seq.).

If the appeal to what all men really want can be made good in either form, then we have not simply a rationale, but a demonstration that the moral life must seem desirable to all reasonable men. Immorality shows ignorance or incompetence. In the context of the arguments in which Plato was involved these would be pleasing charges to bring home—a point not, of course, peculiar to Plato's day. For a more extended treatment by Plato cf. *Laws* 860 seq.

23a1–2   Cf. 11b9–Socrates' candidate is only claimed as better.

23e3–6   'First, then, let's . . .' Here and at 25a1–3, 25d6–8 the verb used ('round up', *sunagein*) is the one used in the *Phaedrus* (265d etc.) to describe one stage in the application of the method of Collection and Division. For the relation of this method to the Heavenly Tradition see General Commentary, pp. 202–4. Two points are worth noting: (i) this term does not occur in the description of the Heavenly Tradition, not even in the account of Theuth, and there is only one occurrence of the word used to describe 'division', without any indication that the use is technical, so the description of the Heavenly Tradition does not explicitly allude to Collection and Division; (ii) it is hard to match what is done here to the recommendations of the Heavenly Tradition.

The expression 'scattered abroad', used here to refer to the different *sorts* of *apeiron* is that used at 15b5–6 to describe the one/many problem there.

24a2   '. . . the determinant.' Plato uses two expressions: '*peras*' and '*peras echon*'. Literally, the first means 'limit', the second 'having a limit'. Some commentators try to see a distinction in the difference of expression. In the present paragraph the second expression is used twice, the second time picking up the first. The first, however, is supposed to be mentioning one of the 'elements' supposedly used in the Heavenly Tradition, and there is no option for it but to pick up the '*peras*' of 23c10. This is a very bad way of making a distinction, and I have not tried to allow for one in the translation. For those interested to pursue the matter '*peras*' is used at 23c10; 25b1, d3; 26a3, b8, c6, d4; 27b8, d9; 30a10, c4, and *peras echon* at 24a2, 3–4; 26b2, 10. A third term '*peratoeides*'—Literally 'limit-like'—occurs at 25d6, once again picking up '*peras*', and so apparently used for stylistic rather than philosophical reasons.

24c3   '. . . quantity.' The word is the one used at 17b7 and other parts of the Heavenly Tradition.

25a3 '. . . scattered abroad . . .' Cf. 15b5–6, 23e4–5.

25a7–b1 '. . . and every proportion of . . .' Literally either (i) 'and everything which is a number in relation to a number or measure in relation to a measure', or (ii) 'and everything which a number in relation to a number or a measure in relation to a measure is'. The first suggests that equal and double consist in a relation of number to number, and are examples of this general category. The second suggests that equal and double are examples of relations that numbers and measures may have to each other. The translation is intended to be ambiguous, but the second seems to me preferable. For a discussion see Striker (pp. 58–60). Roughly, the first encourages us to include in *peras* everything that can be characterized by numerical predicates, and these are all envisaged as, as it were, rational numbers; the second suggests that the predicates concerned ('equal', 'double', etc.) are predicates of numbers, and so ensures that numbers only are covered by *peras*. While Plato might be prepared (see General Commentary pp. 192–4, 198–201) to characterize as *perata* phenomena described in terms of order etc., they would more likely feature as *meikta*, and certainly in the present passage where the terms are being formally introduced he is unlikely to envisage anything but numbers—though one should remember Plato's conception of number (see General Commentary: The Heavenly Tradition, pp. 165 seq., The Determinant and the Indeterminate, pp. 196 seq.).

25d5 'The one we should have rounded up . . .' What Socrates had failed to do is give what constitutes the examples listed as a single class. He has just talked of equal, double, etc. (25a–b). It is fairly clear, moreover, that no simple characterization in terms of number will do, because not all quantities or measures are in order, and what determines which ones are is not given by mathematics, but by the particular *techne*. Plato may therefore have felt the difficulty of a general characterization of *peras*, though the sort of thing he had in mind would be clear from a consideration of the various proper mixtures that *technai* cover. But see next note.

25d7 'Perhaps it will do as well . . .' The sentence is less than clear. 'That one' must, in the context, refer to the class of determinants (25d10–e2). In that case 'these two' refers to the indeterminate and the mixture, since there is a presumed refusal to round up the determinant and we are relying on rounding up other things to become clear on it. On the other hand, we get no proper rounding up of the mixed class. Either we get a list, or its unity is given in the characterization as mixture, in which case it depends for success on the rounding up of determinants, which is just what Socrates declined to do. Further, from 25b5 onwards the problem class is really the mixed one, which is still giving trouble at 25e3—7, 31c2—11, so that one might naturally expect Socrates' point to be that the *third* class will become clearer from a mixing of the other two—and certainly he proceeds to introduce his examples as the effects of imposing determinants on the indeterminate. The simplest solution is probably Bury's transposition with 'συμμισγομένων' (*summisgomenōn*: mixed together) for 'συναγομένων' (*sunagomenōn*: rounded up) at d8. The whole would read: '*Soc.* The one we should have rounded up just now, the class of determining elements, as we rounded up the indeterminate into a single class—but didn't. *Prot.* What class? what are you talking about? *Soc.* That of equal and double and whatever puts an end to opposites being at odds with each other and by the introduction of number makes them commensurate and harmonious. But perhaps it will have that same effect now: with these two mixed together, that other will emerge clearly.'

25e1—3 'Commensurate.' I have translated the Greek '*summetra*' by 'commensurate' because the word and its opposite were common in discussions of irrationals. Granted the Pythagorean air of the *Philebus* the word would have this suggestion strongly.

26b6 '... fine ...' The adjective *kalos* and the noun *kallos* are usually translated 'beautiful' and 'beauty'. Beauty is too readily taken to be in the eye of the beholder, and when we speak of a beautiful horse we are primarily considering looks. Calling a horse *kalos* would at least as much suggest that it was an admirable specimen. While 'fine' and its noun are not always the most natural words to use in English they come nearer to catching the ambivalence of the Greek words than the usual 'beauty', 'beautiful', and their occurrence in the translation reflects the occurrence of *kalos*, *kallos* in the Greek.

'... (*psuche*). See note on 30a3.

26b9—10 '... law and order as determinants.' Here, as with the study of letters at 18 and again with the good life, it is not clear whether Plato hopes that everything could be expressed mathematically, or simply looked upon the cases where things could be so expressed as paradigms, or whether he is stretching notions like 'number' so that they are applicable, as the English 'proportion', 'measure', to non-mathematical examples. The mathematical language at 25a and 25d11–e2 seems too strong for the last, but it has to be recognized that there was a tendency to take terms from a technical context and apply them somewhat recklessly elsewhere without always asking what effect the change of context has on the term's sense, or the extent to which the original context is just a useful model for the new rather than the new a further instance somehow of the old. For later varied applications of the terms 'peras' and 'apeiron' it is instructive to read Proclus' commentary on the First Book of Euclid's Elements, for instance G 30 (B62), G 40 (B83). Striker suggests adopting the reading of B, ἐχόντων for ἐχοντ(α). Her reason is that Plato must have realized that law and order do not admit of double or half or proportion of number to number (25a–b), but at best bring them with them. The alternative reading would say that the goddess introduced the law and order belonging to determinants. The reading is certainly possible, but the ground offered is that at 25a–b determinants are what allow of double and half and every proportion of number to number, measure to measure, and so are presumably numbers and measures. For these, but not law, can be described as double etc. One has to accept a degree of precision on Plato's part in the use of the expression for 'allow of', to take this point (see General Commentary, pp. 192 seq. for doubts). Also, I think, one is helped if one supposes that while Plato might hold that good order implies measure he would hardly hold the converse. But this (see General Commentary, pp. 199 seq.) would be a mistake.

26d4–5 'Again, with the determinant . . .' The MSS, and the Oxford text give the following sense: 'Again, the determinant did not exhibit many forms, nor did we complain that it was not one in nature.' The difficulty is that 25a makes it clear that peras does exhibit many forms just as apeiron does. Then at 25d7 (see note) we are told that we ought to have rounded up the class in question, which is that of peras, but did not. This implies that the task is feasible. But you cannot round up a unit, but only a plurality into a unit. So this sentence would be blatantly untrue. I have followed Bury in inserting 'ὅτι' (hoti: that) after the first οὔτε (oute: neither).

26d8–9 '. . . comes into being.' The terms conjoined, 'genesis' and 'ousia', are standardly contrasted in Plato (e.g. Republic 534a, Timaeus 28–9). The first indicates the condition of physical particulars, subject, in Plato's view, to constant change, the second the condition of Forms which just are what they are eternally and unchangingly. This distinction marks the contrast between Forms and particulars so that it is impossible that either should share the other's condition. The present passage has been taken as indicating a preparedness on Plato's part to recant his earlier exclusive dichotomy (cf. G. E. Owen, 'The Place of the *Timaeus* in Plato's Dialogues'), in line with *Sophist* 248—9. This is not the place to argue that issue. That would necessitate a detailed examination of what the contrast amounts to and of the typical ways of expressing it, and then a comparison with the purpose and wording of the present passage. The simple fact that Plato uses the two terms together in this way is not enough, as Plato is not given to constant technical usage; nor is the fact that e.g. at 27b8—9 the language looks like deliberate paradox of great weight unless one can establish the implausible thesis that Plato would only use such a paradox to signalize a change of view.

26e3—4 '. . . there must be something responsible for its becoming that thing?' This looks like a statement of 'Every event has a cause', but needs reading with caution. The word translated 'responsible' (*aitia*) can be translated 'cause' or 'explanation'. In the present philosophical climate the latter is preferable of these two for its relative neutrality. Aristotle (cf. *Physics* 194b16—195b30) distinguishes various forms of explanation, or forms of answer to the question 'Why is *X F*?', but there is no sign that Plato had got so far. He had, indeed, realized that there were different views as to what constitutes an adequate explanation (cf. the famous passage *Phaedo* 97—9), but did not have a systematic account. The present passage might suggest a failure to develop the hints of the *Phaedo*, as it seems (26e6—7) to equate explanans with producer and (27a1—2) explanandum with product. The passage is, however, limited by its context: it is the explanation of how good mixtures come into being that is in question, and the expression into which the word for 'explanation' enters at 26e3 suggests that the producer is what is sought (and cf. 23d7—8). So the equation of explanans and producer need only be an equation of the explanans of the genesis of a good mixture with its producer. For his awareness of other 'causes' cf. 22d6—7 and 64d3—5. More important in connection with 'Every event has a cause' are two further points: (i) the events in question are limited to good mixtures (cf. 27a11—12 'the things that come into being' are said with their elements to be the three classes mentioned earlier; but the mixtures there are only good ones); (ii) it seems that not just anything will count as a producer. Already at 27b1 we have the notion of something that fashions the mixtures, which prepares one for the view of 28c seq. that only intelligence can produce good mixtures. So all that we can be sure is taken as obvious here is that the generation of a good mixture requires an (intelligent) producer. (See note on 28c6.)

27a5-6   '. . . natural priority.' The image here is of more than temporal priority, suggesting control and dependence. Intelligence is going to be given a controlling role, pleasure an insignificant part in the dependent product.

27b1   See note on 26e3-4.

27d1-10   Now begins the application of the previous distinctions to the issue of prize-giving. The good life belongs to the class of good mixtures. At 27e pleasure is classed as an indeterminate and from 28a there is an 'argument' for classing intelligence as producer.

27e1-2   '. . . the life you advocate.' Strictly it is not now lives that are in competition for second prize, but elements in the good life. At 27e5-6 the question seems, properly, not to be about lives. The whole of 27e, involving the shift to Philebus rather than Protarchus, is argumentatively unsatisfactory. It looks as though the mention of the pleasant life is there to lead Philebus on. For of course he will say that it has to be a life of unlimited (*apeiron*) pleasure, and so the pleasure has to be unlimited. For obviously, in his view, a life of unlimited pleasure is better than one of limited pleasure. That is not to the point—a life of knowledge might be viewed as the unlimited exercise of intelligence and the more the better. For the previous analysis it is admission of degrees of pleasure that is important, not anything about lives. The passage serves to emphasize Philebus' lack of grip on the conversation, and to obtain an easy admission that pleasure is in the indeterminate category. For discussion of the latter see General Commentary, pp. 208 seq.; pp. 226-7.

27e8-28a1   '. . . completely good . . . completely evil.' The MSS. have πᾶν ἀγαθόν (*pan agathon*: everything (whole) good) at e8 and πᾶν κακόν (*pan kakon*: everything (whole) evil) at a1. Philebus in that case presumably says either: pleasure would not be the whole good, or everything good; or: not every good would be pleasure. Similar possibilities hold for Socrates' rejoinder. It is hard to see how the fact that there is a limit on pleasure would make Philebus think either of these things. As, however, he thinks that pleasure is the good and the more the better, it is very natural for him to suppose that any limit on it will bring about something less than the complete good (πανάγαθον: *panagathon*). Only unlimited (*apeiron*) pleasure can be *the* good. The translation 'unlimited' would better make the point here. Socrates is trading on the ambiguity of '*apeiron*' and of the notion of limitation. I have therefore translated πανάγαθον (*panagathon*: completely good) at e8 and πάγκακον (*pankakon*: completely evil) at a1.

28a3 'But you can leave . . .' The MSS. have τούτων δή σοι τῶν ἀπεράντων γεγονὸς ἔστω which seems untranslatable. At best it might mean 'Let it be among these points not yet determined.' The Oxford text reads τούτω δή τοι τῶν ἀπεράντων γε γένους ἔστω, meaning 'Then let these two be among the undetermined things.' 'These two' might be supposed to refer to pleasure and pain, and 'undetermined' to the fact that they are *apeira*. Alternatively 'these two' indicates the two questions about the good and evil of pleasure and pain, and 'undetermined' the fact that they are not yet settled. I have translated Bury's reading, as being closer to the MSS. viz. τοῦτο δή σοι τῶν ἀπεράντων γεγονὸς ἔστω.

28c6 'All men . . .' It is perhaps worth noting for the record Plato's use of 'all'. According to *Phaedo* 97–9, it would seem that Anaxagoras was alone in thinking that intelligence was effective ruler of the universe, and even he failed to give it much of a role. Plato could, of course, say the rest had no claim to intelligence. Alternatively he could resort to a selection of theologizing poets or we may take the *Phaedo* remarks as exaggerated, since the *Philebus* comment seems true, on the whole. No great weight can be put on the use of 'all' (cf. 15d5, 16d1, 26b7).

28d5 'Should we say . . .?' Cf. *Laws* 889–99.

28e1 'Heavens, Socrates, . . .?' Commentators have queried the text. As it stands the literal meaning is 'it is nothing of the same things'. Badham and Bury consider the reference of 'it' too vague, and feel that if we read ἀλύτων (*alutōn*: insoluble) for αὐτῶν (*autōn*: same) the 'it' would naturally refer to Socrates' question: 'it is nothing insoluble'. Hackforth retains the text and translates: 'A very different matter'. The difference is between the question as put at 28a, in a way that puzzles Protarchus at 28b, and as put at 28c–d when Protarchus finds answering it a different (and easier) matter. It strikes me as slightly more natural to take the expression as taking up the obvious difference between the proposals just put forward by Socrates, with 'O amazing Socrates' (here rendered by 'Heavens, Socrates') indicating surprise at his audacity in mentioning both, since the obvious difference is in the impiety of the one as against the obvious acceptability of the other.

30a3 '. . . the body we have has life (*psuche*).' The word '*psuche*' is difficult to translate. 'Soul' has connotations of intelligence and the possession of moral capacities, whereas the Greek word is often used for the principle of life, and the adjective from it (*'empsuchos'*, cf. 30a6) means 'living'. Any intelligent thing must be alive (c9–10), living an intelligent form of life, and so in many contexts where intelligent life is in question *'psuche'* is more naturally translated 'mind' (or perhaps 'soul') or even 'person'. Thus at 32c4 following the discussion is about pleasures with no special physical cause, and they are attributed to *psuche* alone. There and predominantly in the following passages the nearest translation is 'mind'. But at 48e8–10, where people who consider themselves to have assets they lack are under discussion, we are told that most people are in error about the class of things in their *psuchai* (plural). In context this clearly refers to the quality of their lives considered as human lives. That is, it is not health that is in question, nor perceptual faculties, but the excellence of their lives where, in characteristic Greek fashion, this includes excellence in all capacities supposedly peculiar to human as against other animals. I have there translated 'the class of things in their *psuchai*' as 'their moral and intellectual equipment' (cf. also 26b6) which comes nearer to what is meant than 'their lives', 'their minds', or 'their souls'. At 11d5 it seemed more appropriate to give 'condition of a person' rather than 'of a soul', 'of a mind' etc.

30a9–b7 'Otherwise we should have . . .' This is a cumbersome sentence, the end of which I have translated in a slightly different sense from Hackforth. His rendering makes Socrates' point that it is incredible that the cause at work in the universe should have failed to supply the finest of natures, viz. an intelligent soul, for the universe. The difficulty, as he recognizes, is that either this involves two intelligences, or the intelligent cause is spoken of as obviously fashioning itself. The trouble starts at 30a10–b2. Here Hackforth's translation suggests that he takes 'cause' as a single element, which puts a soul in each of us. Then at 30b4, *sophia* is translated 'Wisdom' with a capital W. I have taken 30a10–b2 as saying that the class of causes can be observed to be present in the world, and that in us it supplies souls/life, and (in consequence) various forms of skill and intelligence. What is incredible is that no such cause should be operative in the universe at large, since there the finest works are to be seen, and so one would expect the finest intelligence to be at work. This, I think, better fits the drift of the argument.

Striker would omit the expression ψυχήν τε παρέχον (*psuchēn te parechon*: supplying with a soul or life). For it cannot be the function of human reason (cause) to supply the body with a soul. since that, like all reason (30c9–10), requires a soul as a condition of its existence. Therefore it must be the function of either the world soul or the divine soul. But that reference would spoil the argument since the whole point is to argue that there is such a thing as a Divine or World reason and soul, and the conclusion is not established until 30c–d. It would be absurd to argue that if the world/divine reason has given us souls it must be responsible for the world order and so there must be a divine/world reason and so soul. This objection hinges on taking 'supply' in a causal way, and this seems to me unnecessary. One could say that in us the category of determinant supplies order, that of mixtures good health, and similarly it is the category of cause that supplies life, and 'supplies' simply indicates that these things are to be sought in these categories. If we consider life, exercise, cure of illness, these are functions of the class of causes, and so of intelligence, and if this set of functions and the concomitant wisdom (*sophia*) are assigned to the class of causes, are we to refuse to posit a cause when we note similar but grander functions in the universe at large? Taken this way the passage does not seem particularly awkward, and so there is no special reason to drop the offending expression, although the passage will doubtless run equally well without it.

30d10–e2 'But also it supplies...' Omitting τῆς (*tēs*: 'of the') after γένους (*genous*: 'category') and excising τῶν τεττάρων ... τοῦτο. The text is corrupt, but it is doubtful whether it is worth struggling with for present purposes as the alternatives make no important difference to the general sense. There is no need to supply a pun (Stallbaum) or a Homeric allusion (Bury) as the reference for 'this fooling about' below. The answer to the question has been given in the long section about the world soul, and it is there that it has escaped Protarchus' notice. The fooling about is done in the unargumentative extravaganza on the relation between individuals and the universe.

31a9 '... beginning, middle or end.' A traditional Pythagorean characterization of the indeterminate.

31b2–4 'Next we must...' It is not made clear why we must discuss the area in which each occurs and how it comes about. This is not obviously 'listing kinds' or imposing a *peras* on an *apeiron*. It is, however, an enquiry relevant to bringing out what Philebus is wanting us to spend our lives on.

31b5–6 'But we could never...' This is the first time pain is directly linked with pleasure in this way (though cf. 28a). The point is clarified at 31d seq., that they are movements in opposite directions, and so come under a common account. But this is not a general point about pleasure, but only about physical ones (32b6–7, c3–5). (Cf. *Republic*, Book IX, 585a.)

31c2–3 '... distress and pleasure ...' Pleasures are in the joint category in that the understanding of the nature of these physical pleasures involves understanding about the proper constitution of the body. As emerges at 43b, these are necessary, not sufficient conditions of pleasure and pain. The perception of these changes needs to be added. The changes are part of the ordinary functioning of the organism righting itself, and such pleasures are those that are necessary, in that the organism, in order to preserve its nature, has to counter deprivations. The discussion is of conditions for the occurrence of pleasure, not of what is being said when it is said that *X* is a pleasure. Cf. *Timaeus* 64 seq.

31e10 'Again, thirst ...' Here thirst is considered as the perception which is in fact a perception of deprivation. At 34d10 it is said to be a desire. The Greek allows, as English, for the term to cover both feeling thirst, and thirsting for. It may be true that what I feel is thirst, though not having that interpretation of my sensation I am not thirsting for anything. It is the unpleasant feelings in throat or stomach that 'thirst' and 'hunger' refer to in this passage, with no connotations of desire.

32a9 '... of indeterminate ...' Reading τοῦ (τou: 'of the' neuter) for τῆς (tēs: 'of the' feminine) before ἀπείρου.

32b6 'Then can we agree ...' Anyone who wishes to hold that Plato intends to 'count kinds' of pleasure should take heart at this sentence.

32b9–c2 Pleasures of the mind 'by itself'. The point is: not as a a result of certain physical changes, or, if 43b is already in mind, not sensory pleasures. Cf. *Phaedo* 79–80, where Plato shows a tendency to talk of perception as a function of the body, judgement being necessary to justify talk of the mind. While there are times (e.g. *Philebus* 33d, *Timaeus* 43) when Plato talks of physical operations as only sometimes penetrating the body so as to be perceived, and so of the body as a condition for certain experiences, more typically (e.g. 46b–50d) he talks of the body in contrast with the mind as the seat or possessor of certain pleasures. For the translation of *'psuche'* (mind) see note on 30a3.

In view of what is to be said about anticipation, it is worth noting that hope and fear are here spoken of as pleasant and painful expectations, and as being *of* pleasure and distress. They both seem to belong to the class mentioned at 50b7−c3, d1, as mixed pleasures.

32c6−d1 'And if I am right . . .' As the text stands, this is an obscure sentence. There ought to be a reference to the two forms of pleasure and pain, those resultant on deformation or restoration of the normal condition of the body and those of expectation. Alternatively it may be, as Hackforth takes it, marginally less naturally, a reference to the two forms of expectation. In either case, it is worth asking how Plato is hoping to consider them, and why he thinks that by so doing his question will be answered.

If we suppose a reference to the two forms of pleasure and pain, we have to interpret 32c8 not as 'without admixture of pleasure and pain' (for, as Badham remarks, they must have some admixture of one or other), but as 'not a mixture of pleasure and pain'. In that case, we consider painless restorations of physical harmony, and hopes without admixture of fear. Considering these will lead us to understand whether all pleasures are to be espoused.

If we suppose a reference to the hopeful and fearful forms of expectation, then the point is that by examining each in pure form—utterly fearless hope and utterly hopeless fear—we shall be able to judge whether all pleasures are welcome.

In either case, it is difficult to see how considering each in pure form will help answer the question. It is certainly not what he proceeds to do. The discussion that follows is largely taken up with mixed examples. It looks as though on the first interpretation the point must be that we must try to isolate unmixed cases because (cf. 61d seq.) only these are clearly admissible, and once isolated, and so distinguished from the others, the undesirability of the others will clearly emerge. If this is Socrates' thought, it can hardly be said to emerge clearly from the sentence. On the second interpretation it has to be a study of unmixed examples of anticipation that will settle the question. Yet Plato seems to go out of his way (cf. 35e seq.) to confuse the point by insisting on the presence of distress in situations of anticipation. Suppose we waive that, and take it that we are to concentrate on examples of hope that are without a trace of fear, and prescinding from the present distress that stimulates the hope. In that case, the question of whether all pleasures are desirable has to be settled by the discussion of falsity at 36 seq. But in fact it is not. Indeed the precise bearing of the discussion of falsity is never brought out clearly. The conclusion that some pleasures are to be rejected is not based on the discussion of anticipatory pleasures specifically, but on that of mixed ones generally. The most that can be done for the discussion of false expectations is to suppose that 63d–e is taking up the discussion of 41b seq. and accusing deluded anticipations of interrupting thought, but it is more natural to take the reference as to 47a, and to refer to 65c–d where it might indeed be false pleasures of anticipation that he has in mind.

Possibly the answer is as follows: the importance of false anticipatory pleasures is threefold. First, it leads to the statement of 39d seq. that such pleasures are characteristic of the wicked, and so, of course, not desirable, so helping answer 32c. Secondly, through equivocation on the notion of truth, it leads into the discussion of mixed pleasures, which are, because mixed, 'false'. Thirdly, they are repugnant to the intellect, and so lead to the rejection of pleasure at 65c–d. It would be nice to be able to dismiss 'pleasure and pain' as a scribal insertion. In that case the important thing would be to discuss each class separately, i.e. the classes of physical and mental pleasures, and that is both done and considered important.

32e3 '... what is the state?' Cf. 42e–43c, where Protarchus is made to jib at such an intermediary state, and there is a more careful statement. The important point for Socrates is not that there should be a state of physical quiescence, but that there should be a state with no experience of pleasure. For the intermediate state, and a possible life consisting of it cf. 43, and for the possible life spent in physical pleasures, implied here, cf. 35d–e, 43d, 47b, 54e seq.

33a3–5 '... it is important...' It is important to note this declaration of importance, together with the passages mentioned in the last note. The point cannot be important in that Plato thinks there is a desirable life of this intermediate sort. Nor should it be that he thinks that someone who is 'in between' is therefore not enjoying himself. The present analysis covers physical pleasures only. The point is to draw our attention to the possibility of a life predominantly or totally without physical pleasures. This would not be pleasureless, but without Phileban pleasures, and might well be what Philebus might call an intellectual life merely.

It seems (cf. Aristotle, *Nicomachean Ethics* 1153b5 and 1173a6) that Speusippus held the ideal life to be free of both pleasure and distress. No doubt when Eudoxus was putting forward his hedonist views this not only lent encouragement to those of a Phileban turn of mind, but also led others who thought of pleasure in physical terms to devise views that rejected pleasure along with distress. In refusing to talk of pleasure in the singular and refusing to give an overall 'similarity' account, Plato is able to clarify and develop the dispute, and take a position which, while oddly intellectual to many modern ears, is in structure more balanced than that of either the hedonists or anti-hedonists to whom he is reacting.

33b6—c2 '. . . the most divine . . .' Cf. 22c5—6, and the microcosm/ macrocosm argument of 28c seq. It is worth comparing especially 66b. While some base their arguments on animals, and make them the basis of the contention that pleasure is the good, Socrates appeals to a notion of divine intelligence. Granted the impropriety of attributing pleasure or an interest in pleasure to such intelligence, and especially physical pleasure, we get the suggestion that pleasure is only part of the good for *man*, and only because man is an inferior sort of being. It would be better to be a god, and so better to be able to live a perfect life without pleasure. For contrast cf. Aristotle, *Nicomachean Ethics* 1154b26.

33c—34a *Perception.* For other treatments of perception cf. *Timaeus* 43—4, and *Theaetetus* especially 156—7, 184—6. It is worth noting that in the *Philebus* perception does not include judgement (cf. 38b—c). In fact, the point made at *Theaetetus* 184—6 is accepted. The words translated 'aroused' and 'arousal' at 34a3—4 are the verb and noun for 'motion', and doubtless Aristotle's criticisms of the view that pleasure is motion (*Nicomachean Ethics* X, 1174a13 seq.) could be adapted to this treatment of perception. While Plato is quite prepared to use the word strictly (cf. *Republic* 436c—e), he also (cf. *Theaetetus* 181d, *Cratylus* 439e) uses it as a more general word for change, and also, as here and perhaps at *Republic* IX, 583e, even more extendedly to indicate that something is actually going on.

34b2 'And surely . . .' For memory cf. *Cratylus* 437b, *Theaetetus* 163d, 191—2. For recollection cf. *Phaedo* 73—4, *Meno* 85d. The 'retention of sensation' referred to in the definition of memory at 10—11 refers presumably not to, or not merely to, the capacity to know what we have been perceiving in preceding moments. According to b10—c2 it is possible to regain memory. It seems that 'memory' refers to the capacity to recall, 'recollection' to the occasions of recall. But it is not clear whether it is sufficient, for recall, to be able correctly and from memory to describe the earlier experiences, or whether it is also necessary as it were to re-experience them. The language of b6—8 suggests the latter. The presence of 'piece of knowledge' at b11 suggests the former.

34c10–d1 '... all the forms in which it does so.' Literally, 'all the forms of it'. 'It' could refer to 'pleasure' or the noun *'genesis'* translated here by 'how ... comes about'. Hackforth's translation retains the ambiguity. I have taken 'it' as referring back to *'genesis'* because it seems to me that that is what he primarily proceeds to do (and cf. 31b8 seq.).

34d2 *Desire:* The general account of desire should be compared with *Republic* IX, 580–6. In the *Republic* the word here translated 'desire' is used generally for any case of wanting, and not contrasted with other terms (but cf. IV, 436a–b). When Plato in the *Philebus* appeals to Protarchus to say whether pleasure or whatever is desirable, the question tends to use other words. Either he is asked whether anything is lacking (*prosdei* 21a11), or whether the life is chooseable (*hairetos* 21d3) or pleasures welcome (*aspasteon* 32d4). or the question is about what men or animals pursue (*diokein* 67b2). The word for 'desire' (*epithumia*) is restricted to cases where what is wanted is the replenishment of some felt lack. It won't, for present purposes, cover a child's spontaneous desire to paint a blank wall. While this is not necessarily restricted to physical desires like thirst, (for cf. 51e–52a), these are the obvious examples. It seems that there was some bias in the ordinary use of the word that made it a natural one for singling out felt physical wants. An adjective from it is chosen to hive off physical desires in the *Republic* (cf. IV, 436), and cf. Aristotle *Nicomachean Ethics*, 1118b18–19, 1103b17–19. One thing is fairly clear from the present passage, and that is that what one desires is not thereby what one pursues, nor do we have any general analysis of the notion of wanting. There is no reason to think it is intended to apply to more than the cases under discussion.

34d10–e1 'Just now we spoke ...' This must refer to 31e6 seq. (see note there). In fact, thirst was not spoken of earlier as a desire, but simply, and for that context rightly, as the distress resultant on lack of moisture.

34e11 'In fact this means ...' Cf. *Gorgias* 496, *Republic* IX, 585–6, *Timaeus* 64–6, for analyses in terms of deprivation and replenishment.

35a3 seq. 'So it seems ...' The conclusion of this argument is that desire is a psychic function. This is what it is to establish that these pleasures are really 'of the mind alone'. Anticipations and hopes are at least desires, and desires are mental operations. The argument is that the first experience of deprivation is just that, with no apprehension of replenishment. But desire is for replenishment not for the state of deprivation. So something about the desirer apprehends replenishment. The body has no such apprehension, and, so far from having any contact with replenishment, is in a state of deprivation, the very same state experienced by the man who first feels thirst, where it has been agreed there is no desire. So a full description of the physical state has no bearing on statements about desire; for that we need reference to memory, knowledge, etc. It is not clear, however, that sensation or thirst as the first experience of deprivation is hereby shown not to be mental. 34a–b seems in fact already to have made the point for sensation, but then the question arises, why the special argument for desire? The point is that to be a function of the mind for the purposes of the present passage it is not enough to be mental or psychic in the sense in which sensations are. The important sentence here is 35d1–3. The issue is whether the body or the mind is responsible for the initiation of activity and so on, which of them is the *arche* (initiator). In sensation it is physical occurrences that affect the mind, and so could be spoken of as the *arche* of the sensation, which is itself a *pathema*, something undergone by the mind. The analysis of desire is, then, not intended merely to show that no description of the physical state entails any conclusion about desire. It is rather intended to show that the physical conditions which are at least necessary for sensation, are neither necessary nor sufficient for desire. To desire the quenching of thirst a man must (i) have retained the earlier perception of quenching, (ii) recall it—both mental operations–, and (iii) move towards replenishment. No particular present physical state is needed, nor is any enough. It is true that Plato is only going to consider anticipations which are stimulated by the perception of a present lack, but *present* physical lacks play no part in the general explanation of the occurrence of desire, and certainly do not initiate the movement of the agent.

One may now want to ask precisely what Plato is arguing. He could be arguing that 'X is thirsty' means 'X is experiencing a state of physiological lack'. Consequently we can infer from the sense of 'X is thirsty' that if he is then X is affected by some physiological condition. By contrast 'X desires Y' carries no such entailments. It does, however, entail that X has experienced some lack, has experienced its removal, remembers these experiences, and now initiates a movement towards redressing the physiological balance. So while 'X is thirsty' attributes an active role to physiological factors, 'X desires Y' does not attribute any role to physiological factors but an active role to psychological ones geared to producing certain physiological conditions. Such an argument is about the (current) senses of certain types of sentence. It leaves it an open question whether there are physiological conditions that determine the occurrence of desire(s). Alternatively, Plato might be arguing that whereas thirst is caused by a physiological condition desire is not, but is, by contrast, a non-physical cause of changes in one's physiological condition. Asking which Plato is doing is, of course, anachronistic. For while the theses are in fact independent such distinctions are not generally made by Plato, so that actual arguments will sometimes fit one, sometimes the other, though apparently conceived of as yielding conclusions about the nature of desire, pleasure, or whatever it may be.

35a7 '. . . contact.' What the body is in contact with in the circumstances under discussion is deprivation. If it were in contact with replenishment, there would simply be no thirst felt.

35e7 '. . . falls between these two.' This is not to be confused with the state of experiencing neither pleasure nor pain spoken of at 33a–b and 42–3. The analysis of 31–2 makes the processes of depletion and replenishment the conditions of pain and pleasure. The man who is thirsty but looks forward to quenching his thirst is in between, not in that he is somehow already on the way out of thirst, but because he is not simply in distress (one end) nor simply enjoying himself (the other end) but in between. Later (cf. 46–7 and 48 seq.) it will be argued that a person can be in distress while experiencing pleasure both when the pleasure/distress is simply physically conditioned, and when neither is. The present is a less surprising example of mixture of the two in that while the agent undergoes both at once, the distress and the pleasure can be independently described, and can occur independently, neither of which holds of the later examples.

36c6–11 'Are we to say . . .' The question is introduced abruptly, so fixing attention on it. For the significance of this section in the general dispute see General Commentary pp. 212 seq., and notes on 32c6 and 37e8.

36d6 '. . . your master's pupil . . .' Either Gorgias (cf. 58a7) or just possibly Philebus (cf. 18a1–2. d3–8).

36e5–10 'So on your view . . .' The question was whether anticipatory pleasures can be true or false. Socrates now asks whether it never happens that someone considers himself sometimes to be enjoying himself when he is not. What is puzzling is the utter irrelevance of the question. Suppose we admit that if I dream I am enjoying a Christmas pudding, I mistakenly think I am enjoying one. From this we could not infer that any anticipatory pleasure was false, only that the judgement that I was enjoying something was false. That is the first puzzle. The second is to know what Protarchus' response amounts to. As I have translated it, he is acknowledging that these mistakes do occur. But so far as I can see, the Greek could be construed as 'we all take it that all these things are so', i.e. we all agree that no one ever . . . In that case we have a further problem that it is then agreed that we must discuss whether we are right about this, and immediately proceed not to discuss these questions at all, but the falsity of admittedly genuine anticipatory pleasures.

It seems easiest to admit the strict irrelevance of Socrates' question, and take it as softening up Protarchus. If Socrates takes Protarchus as generally, but as yet confusedly, rejecting the mixing up of pleasure and falsity, he might hope to bring him round at least to discussing the matter by taking him as rejecting the possibility of a class of familiar situations. This would involve translating Protarchus' answer as I have. Then he accepts these examples, which Socrates ('on your view') takes him as having rejected in the refusal to attribute falsity to pleasure, and so must be prepared to reconsider the rejection (examine the view). The portrayal of Protarchus as not yet having a precise view either on what he wants to say or what he is asked to accept serves to arouse attention to the argument and, with the later Protarchan opposition, underline that Plato does want to say of some pleasures that they can be literally true or false.

37a1–b3 The argument is even more obscure in the Greek than the English. I have given the translation 'is pleased' because I think that as Plato has in mind anticipations and wants to talk of the relevant pleasures as hopes, 'is pleased' is an English expression that most readily lends itself to the development, and does not sound too peculiar in conjunction with 'correctness'. If the pleasure we have in mind is my being pleased about something that never happened, then it is easy to talk of my pleasure as unfounded, misconceived, and other terms suggesting incorrectness. But then we cannot have 'enjoy' as the relevant verb. In Greek, however, the one verb has to cover being pleased and enjoying. So 37a9 does not in the Greek carry the limitation of the translation 'being pleased'. It would seem obvious just as much because 'there is something that a person who enjoys himself enjoys'. In this situation the talk of correctness would not be so readily interpretable. On the other hand, just because the one verb covers being pleased and enjoying, talk of correctness is less baffling than it would be if the verb were equivalent to the English 'enjoy'. Even so, 'be pleased' is too broad for Plato's purposes (see General Commentary, pp. 217–8).

It is important to establish that the genuineness of the pleasure is unaffected by its falsity if the analogy with belief, and so the literal attribution of falsity, is to hold. This raises the question of whether perhaps Plato was well aware of the equivocation on 'true' later— though it is not always welcome to be defended from stupidity via a charge of dishonesty. The fact that the genuineness of belief is unaffected by its falsity may seem obvious to us, but that beliefs could only be true, and that false beliefs were not beliefs, were argued in Plato's day (cf. *Cratylus* 429–30, *Theaetetus* 167, 188–9, *Sophist* 237–40), and while Plato may have thought such views obviously wrong, he also took trouble to refute them.

Arguments of the form 'there is something that is judged' (37a7) and so on are common in Plato (cf. *Republic* V, 478b, *Theaetetus* 189, *Sophist* 237c–d) and it is not always easy to see what the admission amounts to. As the present context envisages false belief and pleasure, it can hardly be the admission of the existence of what we believe or are pleased about. It must at least be an admission that there must be answers to the questions 'what do you believe?', 'what are you pleased about?', for if there are not, it seems clear that there is nothing we believe or are pleased about. Plato seems to have in mind e.g. the situations which, we believe, will be pleasurable.

37b6 '. . . while pleasure is only true.' This picks up 36c8–9 where Protarchus only questions the possibility of pleasures being false. Nothing seems to be made of the point. Protarchus' objection as developed is not that pleasure can only be true, but that it is judgements not pleasures that are false, and there is no indication that he would not accept the same about truth. The point is simply a dig at Protarchus who is portrayed at seizing on falsity, which would be a criticism of pleasure, instead of the general nature of the question at 36c6–7 which mentions both truth and falsity. This polemical blindness to the main point is characteristic of Protarchus, and may have seemed to Plato typical of an orator's pupil.

37c4–6 '. . . but pleasure and distress . . .' One possible reason for rejecting the attribution of falsity could be that pleasures are just pleasures and cannot be qualified, an extreme position easily rejected. But it may be that this section is directed to the position mentioned in the last note, that pleasure can only be true. For it looks as though Plato may be taking the thesis that pleasure and distress just are what they are and not of such and such a quality as denying not that nothing can be said of them, but that they cannot *vary* in quality. In other words, to say that pleasure has no qualities is to suppose that all that we can do with pleasure is recount those truths that hold definitionally or at best invariably, i.e., say what pleasure is. If some pleasures are F, some G, then what 'F' and 'G' indicate cannot be part of what a pleasure is, only of what it is like. (For this contrast cf. e.g. *Meno* 86d–e.) Consequently someone who said pleasures are only true would be claiming that 'true' is part of an account of what pleasure is, not a description of what any pleasure is like. The proof that there are some qualities of pleasures thus appeals to the fact of incompatible adjectives being applied; for their incompatibility is enough to establish that they are not part of an account of all pleasures at all stages, i.e. they will hold of some pleasures sometimes, of others at others. In this connection it is worth noting a fact concealed by the translation. Where the translation says 'but pleasure and distress just are what they are, and do not allow of qualities' the Greek, more literally, says, 'but pleasure and distress just are what they are and do not become of such and such qualities'. The word 'become', which recurs in Socrates' next sentence, may well be significant, for the possibility of talking of change brings with it the need to be able to talk of some qualities as lost or acquired, and so not invariably holding of their subject.

37c9–10 'Some time ago....' Cf. 21b and 27e with the implications of calling pleasure indeterminate (and cf. 24).

37e1 '... object of judgement...' Literally: 'that about which a judgement is made'. There is no technical notion of object involved. See note on 37a1–b3 and General Commentary: False Pleasures, pp. 214–18.

37e12–38a2 'Of course ...' It is interesting that it is at the point of attributing falsity that Protarchus finally objects. There is no demur about talking of correctness at 37d6–7; when it comes to talk of mistakes, Protarchus shows suspicion (37e8–9); the last straw is falsity. It looks as though just as in English it is acceptable to talk of being rightly pleased with one's progress, slightly odd to talk of being mistakenly pleased, and unacceptable to talk of being falsely pleased, so in Greek some adjectives in the 'error' area applied naturally and others not. Socrates is trying to edge from the natural to the unnatural but Protarchus will not accept the extension of 'true' and 'false' to pleasures until after the analysis of these pleasures that follows.

38b2 'Then let's examine...' It turns out to be the difference between pictures based on true and on false statements.

38b12–13 'And in every case . . .' This picks up the analysis of 32c seq. It is not a statement out of the blue, in which role it would be hard to interpret, but a reminder connecting the present passage with the earlier analysis of desire. The context of the discussion of falsity is anticipatory pleasures and the judgements in question, judgements that, e.g., quenching one's thirst will be pleasant. The discussion of sensation, memory, and desire included the element of recalling as necessary for desire, and as supposing sensation and memory. But recalling was making judgements which, in Protarchus' language, might give rise to pleasure of anticipation. It is highly improbable that the statement is meant, as Ryle (*Plato's Progress*, p. 251) treats it, as a general definition of 'judgement' (*doxa*). It is not uncommon for Plato to make a statement in similar unqualified form while apparently intending it to fit only the immediate context (cf. e.g., 32a8–b4, 42d5–7, the analysis of desire at 34d seq.). It may be objected that these two examples purport not to define pleasure and desire respectively, but only to give conditions of their occurrence—but the same is true of the sentence on *doxa*. The context invites discussion of judgements like those that occur in anticipatory pleasure, but not a general discussion of the nature of judgement.

38e1–6 For other examples of the relation between judgement and statement see *Theaetetus* 189e–190a, *Sophist* 263d–264a.

39a1–6 I have preserved τοῦτο τὸ πάθημα in a4. I have translated πάθημα (*pathema*) as 'what is undergone'. Hackforth translates the first occurrence 'feelings', the second 'experience'. While feelings are considered by Plato and Aristotle as *pathe* or *pathemata* these words do not *mean* 'feeling'. They indicate something that happens to a subject in contrast to something it does (cf. 33d2, *Parmenides* 157b3–4, *Sophist* 248). Hackforth takes the first occurrence here to refer to the feelings of fear etc., but this seems to me improbable. Fear, hope, and the rest are, like anticipatory pleasures, pictures, and the picturing is based on the *logoi*—it is not the stimulus for them. The reference is back to 34–5 where we get an account of the interplay of perception and memory in the genesis of desire. It is clear from that account that two *pathemata* are important. There is the present condition of lack undergone and the previous undergoing of replenishment. The first, the lack, is undergone by the body, and is its *pathema*. It has no contact with replenishment. That is contacted by memory of a previous *pathema* of replenishment. Perception and memory and the related *pathemata* of present lack and previous replenishment band together to write the judgement. The constan. use of the verb (*paschein*) and nouns *pathos* and *pathema* in the earlier passage discussing the interplay of perception and memory make it certain that that is the reference of '*pathemata*' here. τοῦτο τὸ πάθημα (39a4) (*touto to pathema*) is certainly awkward, partly because it refers to a different *pathema* (i.e. what is undergone as a result of the interplay of the others with memory and perception) and partly because it is to be picked up by 'scribe'. Yet the verb needs a singular subject, unless we go in for considerable rewriting, or suppose that 'this, as it were internal scribe of ours' got moved from its proper place here and τοῦτο τὸ πάθημα was later inserted as a bumbling attempt to supply a subject. Memory should not strictly be the subject since it is not alone responsible for the writing (a2), though this is not a serious objection.

39b3–7 'Then I want you to . . .' The Painter is established as a distinct operator whose role comes *after* judgement. Plato's account does not cover pleasant imaginings, nor cases where people start by thinking how nice something would be and picturing having it to themselves until finally they come to believe it—which would fit Hackforth's translation of the previous paragraph. The judgements are of the form 'such and such will be pleasant' (cf. 35, but also 32c where the anticipatory pleasure is hope of pleasure, and 40a6–7 where hopes are said to be judgements; it is on such a judgement that the picture of 40a9–12 is based).

39d7–e1 'Now take the writings . . .' The hopes/anticipatory pleasures all concern the future. So far nothing has been said to suggest that either Scribe or Painter is concerned particularly with the future, so in order to bring that analysis to bear on anticipatory pleasures it has to be allowed that they are not confined to past and present.

39e8–40c2 'Well now, I want you . . .' These remarks about the wicked being beset by false pleasures come as a surprise. We have almost reached the end of some careful argument for the conclusion that pleasures can be true and false, and suddenly there comes this moralistic digression. Worse, it is not at all obvious why wicked men have also to be so inept as characteristically to experience false hopes.
  On the first point, one has to remember 32c–d (see note there). The aim is not simply to establish that pleasures can be false, but that false pleasures are undesirable. They are so because characteristic of the wicked. But this seems to beg the important question.

For how do we tell who is indeed wicked? We need an account of virtue, which as yet we lack. Without it we cannot say that false pleasures do not play a large part in a virtuous life, or that they are characteristic of wickedness. There is no justification yet for any notion of truth operating as a criterion of worth.

One possibility is that the important expression is 'sure of the gods' blessing'. The point might be not that those whom we know, by other criteria, to be just are also sure of every blessing, but that the words for excellence should be given to those the gods favour. But clearly, the gods will not let their favourites be in a regular condition of false hope—that is no blessing. This is a point that a hedonist might well accept. After all, he will count it a misfortune or defect to be bad at predicting pleasure. Ideally one should be good at it quite apart from the disappointments of bad prediction. So the undesirability of false pleasures might seem acceptable even to a hedonist.

The difficulty with this suggestion is the words translated 'just' and 'pious' at 39e10. They carry too strong a connotation of well-recognized and approved forms of conduct. It may still be that reliance is being put on the fact that even a hedonist might be expected to admit that the gods' favourites will not be affected with many false hopes, while at the same time Plato is relying on normal piety to insert a point in favour of justice. Alternatively, Plato is taking it that he can show ordinary virtues to be part of a man in good working order, and clearly a man in constant error is not in good working order (cf. *Republic* 413 and *Laws* 663c).

40a9 'And especially the painted images . . .' Literally 'painted phantasms (or appearances)'. For the interpretation of 'painted' here and at b6 see General Commentary, pp. 217 seq.

40b6 '. . . painted pleasures.' See previous note.

40c5—6 '. . . caricatures of the true ones . . .' It is not clear why they are thought to caricature them. This would fit the relation between expectation and final pleasure discussed as the second type of false pleasure. In the present case, either my present expectation must caricature the true one, or my present false pleasure caricature some other true one. The first does not seem right, since it is false *pleasures* that are said to caricature true *pleasures*. Since the man at 40a9—12 is not going to have any pleasure there is not a possible true pleasure to caricature. The second alternative, on the other hand, seems bizarre. A possibility is that Plato is still thinking primarily not of individual pleasures but of the typical habitat of true or false ones. In that case the wicked man's anticipations are a caricature of the good man's—a caricature in that while the good man sensibly anticipates with pleasure occasions with which he will be pleased when they arrive, the wicked man imitates the anticipation, but with ludicrous wishful thinking, and regularly falls flat on his face.

40e2–4 'The same would hold...' Cf. 47e1–48a6, 50b–c: It seems Plato is levelling a two-point attack on the emotions, here on the ground of falsity strictly speaking, secondly on the ground of their being mixed forms of pleasure and distress.

40e9–10 'Nor, I take it...' Presumably a hint of 52–3.

41b1–2 'We might find...' Possibly a reference forward to 63d–e. See General Commentary, pp. 219–20.

41e2–6 'Just whether...' This suggests that Plato considers the typical anticipatory situation as one of thinking that something else will be pleasanter than what we have, so involving a comparison between the present and possible future states. This may hold of the particular examples he has in mind, but is clearly not an account generally applicable to all anticipatory pleasures. My present enjoyment of a holiday may be enhanced by the pleasurable anticipation of still more pleasures to come. If, say, the holiday programme is fixed, I may never raise these, in the circumstances, fruitless questions of how the next treat compares with the present one. These cases serve to underline the limitations of the discussion of anticipation (cf. 41c–d, 35e–36c).

42b2 seq. 'But now, from being viewed...' See General Commentary, pp. 219.

43a2 '... what the experts say...' e.g. Heracleitus. Cf. *Theaetetus* 179–83, *Cratylus* 439–40.

43b1–3 In relation to the question of whether Plato thinks that pleasure is a feeling, it is interesting that here, where pleasure (i.e. physical pleasure) is treated as a perception, it is not a perception of a feeling that comes from a given bodily change, but a perception of that change. So the general account of physical pleasure implicit here is not that pleasure is a feeling or set of feelings resultant on other experiences, but that it is the perception of the organism's return to harmony. Even when it is conceded that this gives the conditions for the occurrence of pleasure, not a definition of the concept of pleasure, it remains that only the large changes are said at 43c4–6 to cause the pleasures and pains, picking up the point made in the present sentence that only the large ones are perceived. There is no hint of the *perceptions* giving rise to pleasure or pain. That Plato might himself accept this view of these pleasures is suggested by *Timaeus* 64–5.

43c4–6 'By saying that . . .' The explanatory role of 'big changes' is largely illusory. The criterion of size can hardly be physiological. Although anaesthetics were not available, sleep, swoons, and sickness were known to the Greeks, and it should not have taken long to discover that some 'large', even violent, physiological changes go unperceived. The alternative, that the changes are constituted as big by being perceived, makes 'big' another, perhaps more colourful, way of saying 'perceived'. It looks like a common-sense promissory note of explanation that is not intended to be taken up. For similar terminology cf. *Timaeus* 64.

43d7–9 'So when you hear . . .' The mistake, here and in what follows, is obscure. One might have someone who put forward the life free of pain or distress as the good, but he is hardly likely then to declare that life one of pleasure, let alone the pleasantest. The point must be, then, that there is in fact a state that is neither pleasant nor painful and people say of it, falsely, that it is pleasant. But that does not seem quite right, because people are not described as saying '*X* is pleasant' when in fact it is not. Their mistake is to say 'how pleasant to live free of distress', which may be true, but is not truistic. So their mistake is to fail to distinguish the descriptions 'pleasant' and 'free from distress', and to suppose one can pass analytically from 'free of distress' to 'pleasant'. In that case, they might in fact be right about the situation that counts as being free of distress, i.e. that it would in fact be pleasant. So their mistake is not about the condition of life they are calling pleasant, but consists in supposing that the description they give to it is equivalent to 'pleasant'. But 44a4–10 suggests that their mistake is to say of a pleasureless condition 'it is pleasant'. If we take Plato's account of judgement as making statements to oneself, there is no distinction between (i) they falsely say 'pleasure and freedom from distress are the same thing', and (ii) they falsely say, of something which is in fact only a state of freedom from distress, 'that is a condition of pleasure': they are both mistakenly saying to themselves (judging) that freedom from distress is pleasure. For similar conflation elsewhere cf. *Theaetetus* 189–93, *Sophist* 237–40.

44b10 '. . . that they are pleasures.' See Addendum p. 231.

44c5 'No . . .' Cf. 51a. The digression is less of a digression, and less irrelevant to the argument, if we suppose that Plato's objection is to the view as a general account of pleasure. But he might well think that what these thinkers say is (largely) true of the sorts of pleasure that figure largely in Phileban hedonism, and so they are worth considering in an examination of Philebus' candidates.

44c6 '... difficulty...' From here to 46a the Greek has verbs, nouns and adjectives from a single root. It reads like deliberate allusion. For its possible significance see M. Schofield.

44d7—e4 'Their argument goes...' It is not easy to see just what Plato's position would be in face of this principle. 53b8—c2 suggests that he might agree that the 'truest' pleasure was also pleasantest. In that case his quarrel with these scientists would be over their equation of 'most intensely pleasant' with 'pleasantest'. Even so, he might agree that with physical pleasures of release from pain, 'most pleasant' and 'most intensely pleasant' came to the same thing, and that the nature of *these* pleasures, but not of pleasure, was revealed in these examples. This seems a dubious principle unless it is assumed that it is somehow in the nature of this sort of pleasure to tend towards the extreme of intensity. In that case, something that might be called the power of physical pleasure is best revealed by seeing them uncurbed. But the assumption, while arguably underlying Plato's treatment of physical desire in the *Republic*, and apparently being generally attractive, seems highly questionable. It assumes that the excitements of an obsessional glutton are revealing of the nature of the normal pleasures of eating. But most people manage to enjoy their meals without the slavering quivers of gluttony, and to anticipate them with equanimity. If the extremes are in any firm sense to reveal the nature of the normal moderate pleasures it must be because indulgence of the moderate ones leads to the extremes. Now a glutton indulges immoderately pleasures that a temperate man indulges moderately; but this only amounts to saying he eats more. In so far as the temperate man's pleasure comes from satisfying his hunger, it is not true that a glutton indulges that immoderately—a glutton does not have to be hungrier than an ordinary man, and so satisfy his hunger more often, despite 54e. The whole trouble is that his pleasure is simply in eating, not in satisfying hunger, and hunger and its satisfaction have no obvious tendency towards gluttony. The trouble comes from lumping together physical pleasures, obsessive pleasures, and highly exciting pleasures. There is some plausibility in holding that some of these last, involving release of tension, as sexual pleasure, rather than fillings of gaps, are such that once experienced they generate an itch for reptition. It is simply false that the experience of satisfying extreme hunger or thirst generates an itch to recreate the conditions. Yet Plato is not alone. Either because of his influence, or because of some natural attractiveness in the thesis, or because of its suitability in supporting conclusions, this undiscriminating treatment of 'physical' pleasures has proved popular in moralizing circles. The suggestion of the *Philebus* is that physical pleasures involving felt desire are suspect and only to be admitted as strictly necessary, since their natural tendency is turbulent (cf. 45b, 63d–e).

45b3–4 'And yet, surely the pleasures...' Strength of desire is presumably thought of in terms of insistence as e.g. in craving. Plato seems to think (i) physical disharmonies typically give rise to insistent desires in proportion to the felt disharmony, once the release has been experienced. (ii) The release is intense in proportion to the intensity of the desire. (iii) Both the desire and the pleasure are hostile to the exercise of rational faculties. (iv) Such intensity only arises where felt lack is intrinsic to the desire. Consequently those physical pleasures related to physical desires are anti-rational. But physical desire can be (a) desire for some physically perceptible condition, (b) physically stimulated pursuit of some physically perceptible condition. Hunger would count as (b), most people's daily interest in food as (a). Further, many a lover of the good things of life would only count as 'suffering' from (a), and it is doubtful whether a glutton, for all the insistence of his desire, is perceiving a natural lack as Plato would use that expression. In short, the account of physical desire is too crude, the examples it has to cover too varied.

45b9 Reading ἀποπληρούμενοι (*apoplēroumenoi*: from replenishment) with Hackforth. The Oxford text must mean that the sick get greater pleasures than those who are replenished, which is clearly not Socrates' point.

45c8 '... really is pleasure.' See note on 44b10.

45d3 'Tell me: if you...' The insistence here, and above at c4, that it is intensity not number of pleasures that is at issue, is significant. Socrates never suggests that the good life will be short on pleasure. The implication of the talk of pleasures of health, virtue, and knowledge (63e, 66c5) is that the life will be full of moderate pleasures, and (cf. 53b–c, 63d–e) by Plato's criterion, pleasanter. He probably still holds the view propounded in *Republic* IX, that the intelligent, virtuous man does better than the professed hedonist for pleasure (and cf. *Laws* 732 seq., where the distinction between intensity and number is developed; see also *Protagoras* 355 seq.).

45e3 '. . . roaring about.' See Addendum p. 232.

45e6 '. . . degenerate states . . .' The word *'poneria'* and its adjective can be used with moral overtones to mean 'wicked' or 'depraved', but can also be used in other contexts wherever what is described is in a bad way. As has been remarked (see note on 30a3) *'psyche'*, translated throughout as 'mind', can also mean 'soul' and on occasion could be rendered 'person' or 'personality'. In this sentence 'mind' is becoming awkward.

46a12–13 'This seems clearly . . .' Hackforth suggests reading πάθος (*pathos*: experience) for κακόν (*kakon*: bad), and translating 'this is a mixed experience', but then the point of the following sentence is weakened. Hackforth's objection is that σύμμεικτον κακόν (*summeikton kakon*) must mean 'mixed evil'. But (i) σύμμεικτον and κακόν appear as first and last words, each therefore in an emphatic position, making it difficult to accept the weak 'a mixed evil'; (ii) σύμμεικτον clearly immediately answers (or refuses to answer) Socrates' query as to whether the experience is a form of pleasure or distress; (iii) τι (*ti*: something) presumably goes with σύμμεικτον, so that the whole is: 'this certainly seems to be something mixed evil', where this means not 'mixed-evil' but mixed, evil (an evil thing).

46b1 'Well, I didn't . . .' This must, I think, mean 'for Philebus' sake', not Hackforth's 'with any reference to Philebus'. This would be the natural reading, and I have translated it 'to please Philebus' because there seems a double possible point: (i) Protarchus' 'a bad affliction' is taken as said with a wrinkle of the nose, and this sentence refers to a possible similar reaction from Philebus; (ii) Socrates is insinuating that it is (argumentatively) a bad affliction, in that this is the clear revelation of the nature of the *type* of pleasure Philebus advocates—but then he didn't produce the point to help Philebus.

46b8–c4 'Well, some of these . . .' The talk of mixtures might suggest that Plato thinks of pleasure and distress as separately identifiable feelings that sometimes occur simultaneously—i.e. mixed. But on such a view no pleasure is in any strict sense mixed—it is always just a pure pleasure accompanied, sometimes or occasionally, by pure distress, each aroused by some other experience. On such a view there is no interest in, or even *prima facie* puzzle about, mixed pleasures. Having my toes tickled while I have toothache, learning I have won the game just after I have barked my shin, and so on would be cases in point, and not distinguished in type from quenching one's thirst. If, however, the relevant experience is in some sense to be identified with the pleasure, mixtures become more interesting and more problematic. Plato's position seems to be that the pleasure is, say, the experience of quenching one's thirst. But the full description of that experience includes mention of thirst, and so the relevant experience could as well be described as a form of distress as of pleasure. The pleasure of learning that I have won a game does not require in its description mention of barking my shin. cf. 51e—52b for a similar point on learning itself. The particular form of *pleasure* that is quenching one's thirst is also necessarily a particular form of distress. This indicates that Plato is not thinking of pleasure as a feeling aroused by experiences. If anything is the pleasure it is quenching one's thirst, and for that reason it is not a pure or true pleasure.

46d7—47a1 'Do you agree, then, . . .' The paragraph is obscure and has been subject to emendation. I have accepted the Oxford text ἐν τοῖς (*en tois*: in the) before ἐντός (*entos*: within, inner) in d9. If ἐντός alone is accepted it must mean the same as the amended text, which seems to give the sense more easily, and the loss of ἐν τοῖς is readily explained. At e1 I have read τὰ δ᾽ ἐπιπολῆς (*ta d'epipolēs*: the surface parts) to have a plural antecedent for αὐτά at the end of the line. At e2 the Oxford text has πυρίαις (*puriais*: vapour baths, and generally any means of external application of heat), a reading accepted by Hackforth. I have translated the MSS. ἀπορίας (*aporiais*: distress) as there seems no necessity to change it. The topic is mixed sensations where distress predominates as e.g. some internal itch, which cannot be relieved by surface scratching. The sufferer takes measures to relieve it. First he exposes himself to a fire and, if we read πυρίαις, tries by heat application to change to the opposed condition. This leaves it obscure in what way the condition is an opposite one. There is no reason to suppose that the internal itching is cold, or congealing, though it may be that by heating the skin the inner part becomes relatively cool. It seems more likely that the sufferer exposes himself to the fire and then, by changing to the other extreme, i.e. cooling down, produces great pleasure. The coolness soothes after the sensation 'of heat, and heating will bring pleasure after the feeling of cold. The effects of heat and cold are to relax and congeal (i.e. disperse and unite elements), which are mentioned as the causes of pleasure and distress below. The point of exposing oneself to the fire is not, as many commentators take it, simply to set up a change on the surface to contrast with the internal sensation. The point of heat treatment is that surface treatment, e.g. scratching, has been found not to work because it only disperses the surface area (not, as Hackforth has it, tears the skin). Heat treatment is presumably better because it will disperse not only the surface, but the internal area. But the dispersal works from the surface inwards. So the subject exposes himself to the fire. This disperses what is united first at the surface and then further in. But as it penetrates internally it violently separates the external area, causing pain, and the subject transfers to the cooling operation, setting up a condition opposed to what is now happening internally. The cooling also operates from the surface inwards with similar results, and so it goes on. We start with a predominantly distressing mixed internal sensation. As it gets relieved and becomes a pleasant (if still perhaps mixed) sensation there is a predominantly painful sensation in the surface areas, and so the total is still clearly mixed. Relief of the surface distress beings coolness penetrating internally, with the same mixed result. According to the direction in which they (the outer parts) veer there is an opposition in respect of pleasure and distress between them and the inner parts, and so, by the process of dispersing and uniting, the sufferers always produce mixtures of pleasure and distress. As they start with something predominantly distressing they start on a course of relief. This course sets up a see-saw of violent pleasure and distress producing the reactions of the next paragraph.

I have retained the final ὁμοῦ λύπας ἡδοναῖς παρατιθέναι (*homou lupas hedonais paratithenai*: and so these cases serve up distress alongside pleasure) omitting καί. The whole sentence is involved. These could, as Hackforth says, be a foolish gloss, and certainly it would not be without precedent to have τὰς μὲν ... (*tas men*: with some ...) of the opening sentence left hanging—but these last words save one from supposing this.

Finally a word about ἀπορίαις (*aporiais*: distress). This is the best-supported reading, but while accepted by some commentators has usually been amended, and even if accepted usually conceded as strange. Difficulty may be felt at various points: (i) it might be felt that ἀπορία (*aporia*) cannot mean what is required. But this would be a mistake. The word in the first instance refers to difficulties, particularly arising from some lack. It then connotes the distress relevant to such difficulties that comes with not knowing how to cope, and medically to physical distress or discomfort. This is precisely what is needed in this context. (ii) The plural might seem odd. This is Bury's reason. In that case emending to the singular ἀπορία is simplest, but it is worth questioning the need. It cannot simply be because of the sense: the word is used again at 51a9 in this connection. So it must be that there seems only *one* form of discomfort here, whereas a plural suggests more than one. But on the interpretation offered the picture, somewhat compressed, is one of a person caught between discomforts and constantly changing because of them, so that the plural seems appropriate. (iii) It might be the dative that gives trouble, but if so, I cannot see why. Granted that ἐν ἀπορίᾳ (*en aporiā̦*) is a common phrase, it would not do in the present context as it usually means 'in difficulty', whether the difficulty be intellectual or of other circumstances. In the present context the word is used, as in medicine, of a tossing and turning condition of discomfort (cf. *Theaetetus* 151a5—8), and the dative construction seems unproblematic.

47e1 'Take anger, fear . . .' Cf. 50b—d. The treatment of 'malice' is intended to cover a whole range of feelings. It is noticeable that in particular the pleasures of artistic pursuits are all covered, i.e. the pleasures of the cultured man (cf. *Republic* X, also II—III). The translation 'malice' is awkward, but so is any other, and so was the Greek word, for the purposes to which Plato is to put it.

48b8—9 Malice is presumably called a form of distress simply because a malicious person is described as being distressed about . . . Whatever may generally be true of φθόνος (*phthonos*: malice, envy, spite), it is hardly plausible of the reaction Plato goes on to describe.

48b11 '. . . misfortunes.' No English will catch the Greek (*kakon*) which covers defects of character, wickedness, and misfortune indifferently.

48c2 '. . . ignorance.' Reading ἄγνοια (*agnoia*: ignorance) here, as in 49c2, 49d9, 49e6 instead of 'ἄνοια' (*anoia*: folly), since it is opposed to a form of γνῶσις (*gnōsis*: knowledge, c10), and it is clear that what is in question is a form of ignorance about oneself (48d8 seq.). It is this state of false belief that is said to be ridiculous in weak people, dangerous in the strong. 'Folly' is not an apt word for summing up what is said except perhaps in the case of the weak, but 'ignorance' does precisely. 'Misfortune'. '*Kakon*' again.

48c6 '. . . failing . . .' '*Poneria*' again; cf. note on 45e6, there translated 'degenerate state'.

48e9 '. . . moral and intellectual equipment . . .' See note on 30a3.

49b9 'As for those strong enough . . .' The MSS. have 'As for those able to stand up for themselves . . . if you describe them as frightening, powerful, and enemies;' (φοβερούς καὶ ἰσχυρούς καὶ ἐχθρούς: *phoberous kai ischurous kai echthrous*). This is possible, though the insertion of 'powerful' between 'frightening' and 'enemies' is odd, as the other two adjectives primarily indicate the attitude these people arouse. Further, there is a contrast with those mentioned in the previous sentence who are weak and unable (*adunatoi*) and the Oxford text reading supplies the expected 'able and strong', or 'strong enough to...' I have therefore kept to the Oxford text.

49d1 '...unjustifiable.' Literally 'unjust' or 'wrong'.

49d3 'But it is...' See *Republic* I, 332b−d, *Meno* 71e.

51a5 '...real.' Or possibly 'true'. Commonly the participle 'being', especially when, as here, contrasting with appearing, connotes not existence but genuineness, and so gets interchanged with '*alethes*' (true). The treatment of true pleasures here is entirely in terms of lack of mixture, according to the equation worked out in 53. Hackforth suggests that the notion of purity ('*katharos*', a word I have translated 'purified' rather than 'pure') has connotations of the mystery religions. Certainly the *Philebus* shows Pythagorean influence, and it may be that the connotations of purification are intended to carry some persuasive load, though purity in relation to pleasures is not made a function of freedom from the body or the senses. It seems fairly clear from 53 and the use of the notion in relation to knowledge at 55 seq., that an example of F is 'more purified' to the extent that it can be said without any qualification to be an example of F (rather than its opposite, or rather than not). The intention seems to be to isolate examples of each candidate that manifest its character in undiluted and unadulterated form, so that we can be clear as to what we are admitting.

51c6 '...beautiful in a relative way.' Literally: 'beautiful in relation to something (or: relatively)'. Hackforth takes this as follows: 'They are, that is to say, relatively beautiful in the sense that they come at some point on a scale of greater and less aesthetic satisfaction'. Certainly the point cannot be that they are beautiful in relation to what they imitate, i.e. their beauty is judged in terms of their success in measuring up to some original, for animals are excluded along with pictures, and straight lines (which are not relatively beautiful) are as much or as little to be judged by relation to some original standard as are animals. But the expressions 'in themselves' and 'in relation to something', 'in relation to something else' do not at least clearly suggest the kind of scale Hackforth envisages nor a general contrast between Forms (which are in themselves) and particular objects which are in relation to Forms. 51d6−9 suggests a contrast between visual and audible objects that give pleasure in themselves and in simple form, and those (not necessarily an exclusive set) that are beautiful as part of an arrangement. But this leaves the problem that Hackforth also has, of why Plato should single out these only as pure pleasures. Why cannot complexes also be pure? They would be less divine, no doubt, but smells are allowed (51e) although they suffer from that defect.

The clue probably is that Plato wishes to isolate pleasures connected with visual beauty, but not as understood by most people. It is worth considering then how he thinks most people would understand it. If we remember the account of various arts in *Republic* II—III and X, it seems likely that Plato thought that the average persons' appreciation of beautiful sounds, for instance, would always be in the context of a piece of music in the Doric or Lydian modes, and so as arousing martial or effeminate emotions. Similarly paintings would be beautiful as bringing out the triumph of victory or feminine grace. But pictures and music imitate real life, and the form appreciation takes there indicates the form it takes in real life. Appreciation of physical beauty sees it in relation to sexual passion; a beautiful voice is being judged as such as a sign of courage or trustworthiness. In no case is the shape, colour, or sound isolated for appreciation—it always has an emotional context, and so (cf. 47e, 50b—d) the pleasure will be mixed and the beauty relative to a context. Similarly the appreciation of animals is tied to various emotions, the lion to courage or strength etc. Perhaps the 'pure tune' of d7 is meant in this way as appreciated for its musical rather than emotional properties.

51e1 '. . . a more earthy set.' Literally: '. . . a less divine set.' For the connotations of divinity cf. 22c5—6, 28 seq. and 33b. Both straight lines and single notes (and *pure* tunes) are good starting-points for mathematics, and delight in them the beginning of delight in numbers, whereas smells lead nowhere.

51e7—52b8 'Then we have still to add . . .' Cf. *Republic* IX, 585—6. As Plato is inclined to talk of a desire for knowledge it is clearly important in the context of the present polemic to establish the 'purity' of the pleasure of satisfying the desire. While he acknowledges the existence of pleasures that are not replenishments of lacks (the pleasure of anticipation is not a replenishment, nor, for anything that is said, is malice) we get no treatment of the pleasure of exercising knowledge. Talk of the pleasures of health (63e4) suggests that even at the physical level the replenishment-of-gaps picture is not enough, and that the image of *Republic* IX, 584d seq. might still be operative.

The reference to the pleasures of learning being the prerogative of the few (b6—8) recalls *Republic* IV, 441a—b and *Epinomis* 973c. Obviously the account we have been given will fit just as well the satisfaction of a child's curiosity about a piece of machinery which is not typically preceded by an agonizing intellectual thirst either. It is not confined to the desires of the learned. Probably Plato has shifted to thinking of the pleasures as forming the main pursuit in life, as he might well in the context of the *Philebus*. In that case he might well think that a life of intellectual curiosity is one for the few, and so its peculiar pleasures those of the few. This does not, however, justify the restriction. Nor is the intellectual labour of an intellectual life much emphasized. 52a7–b1 makes it clear that it is *types* of pleasure that are under discussion. But cf. note on 44d7–e4, for this point might hold for types of pleasures of eating.

52c   The criterion for admission to the indeterminate category is here no longer whether it makes sense to talk of degrees of *F*, but whether certain types of instance of *F* are liable in fact to show variation in degree. Those types that are are indeterminate. Further, they show variation of degree in a particular way. The pleasure of philosophizing would remain ordered however exquisite, presumably, and the reason would be that that pleasure consists in philosophizing, which is an ordered activity. It is, in fact, a paradigm of ordered activity because it consists in precise reasoning. The disordered pleasures either concentrate attention on the sensations experienced, or arouse overpowering desire. In either case a person's capacity to reason matters out and order his activity is to some extent impaired. The point is not that *every* pleasure of the disordered type is disordered, but that being of that type it is liable to develop to disordered states. It seems essential to Plato's position that either there is no inherent tendency to any distracting thrill of discovery in philosophy, or any such thrill is not the pleasure of philosophizing. That academic interests can also be inordinate is not envisaged.

52c1   '. . . purified . . .' See note on 51a5.

52c4–d2   'Those that admit of . . .' The text is in a chaotic state, though it seems clear what the point is. I have attempted to translate the following: καὶ τὰς τὸ μέγα καὶ τὸ σφοδρὸν αὖ δεχομένας, καὶ πολλάκις καὶ ὀλιγάκις γιγνομένας τοιαύτας, τοῦ ἀπείρου τε ἐκείνου καὶ ἧττον καὶ μᾶλλον διά τε σώματος καὶ ψυχῆς φερομένου θῶμεν αὐτὰς εἶναι γένους, τὰς δὲ μὴ τῶν ἐμμέτρων.

52d6–8   'How should we say . . .?' Reading ἱκανόν (*hikanon*: adequate) with B and T, but, following Bury, placing it after εἰλικρινές (*eilikrines*: unadulterated) to make two trios. The Oxford text translates: 'Are the purified and unadulterated cases better off, or the intense, large, extreme, and vigorous ones?'

53b1 '. . . finest of all whites . . .' This is picked up at b5 and c2. In the last it is transferred to pleasure. Perhaps the point is simply that the unadulterated whites/pleasures are the finest specimens of whiteness, that is to say they stand out as paradigms of their class, on which one should pick to indicate the class meant. It is hard to avoid the suspicion, however, that the word is intended to carry the sense of 'more admirable' that it has at 65a, so that some propaganda is insinuated here in favour of unadulterated pleasures that is not justified by the point being made.

53c1 '. . . is pleasanter.' This is the only place in the *Philebus* where we get any indication of how Plato would interpret the notion of degrees of pleasure as between particular pleasures or types of pleasure. Perhaps the model of whiteness has helped, in that an unmixed instance of white is certainly whiter. But it is not clear that the analogy with 'pleasant'/'pleasanter' holds, at any rate as those terms are usually used, though Plato is of course entitled to give this as the sense in which he will use the terms. On occasion Plato wishes to argue that the philosopher's life, the virtuous life, is in fact pleasanter than its alternatives, so that a correctly pursued hedonism would come out with the same result as himself (though it would involve use of more sophisticated criteria than just pleasantness). For these purposes it is important to have means of comparing activities/lives for degrees of pleasantness. On either side of the *Philebus* in *Republic* IX, *Laws* 732 seq., there are different attempts at this. The *Philebus* contains, but does not develop, the scale of relative lack of adulteration. It is an unattractive one by itself at least in that it is unlikely to strike opponents as being the scale they are interested in, or indeed what is usually meant by describing one activity as pleasanter than another, where what is envisaged by talk of 'greater' earlier in the dialogue might be more to the point. It is of interest, however, that while Plato might hope to use this way of deciding degrees of pleasantness to show that the good life is pleasanter than any rivals actually in the field, he can still say that assessment of degrees of pleasure cannot be used to determine the form of the good life. For there are many possible descriptions of lives containing only pure pleasures, and so pleasanter than political or sybaritic lives, which are not descriptions of the good life because they either do not contain the right pure pleasures, or not the right proportions. Plato's account of degrees of pleasantness does not allow for assessment of relative degrees between pure pleasures.

53c4–5 'On pleasure, haven't we heard . . .' The physicists of 44b seq. concentrated on the analysis of Phileban pleasure as a release from pain, and the denial of positive reality relied on the notion that pain and normality were definite states, while 'pleasure' has to be explicated in terms of departure from a definite state. The present theorists look upon pleasure as a return to a proper state, and 'with pleasure there is no such thing as being' means that any given pleasure has to be described in terms of the end-state to which it is tending, just as any bit of building has to be described in terms of the end product at which it is aimed: he is building a yacht, or whatever. When the yacht is complete, the building is over.

53d10 'Virile.' Literally 'brave' or 'manly'.

54c9–11 'Well, that to which anything . . .' Cf. Aristotle *Nicomachean Ethics* 1152b12 seq., 1173a29 seq. It is at this point that the importance of the language at 53e4–7, and of the examples, becomes clear. In the case of shipbuilding we have a purposive activity, and the goal serves as a criterion for judging whether the performance is good or bad. Judging the performance as good or bad involves, at least provisionally, taking a building as a good thing. In these contexts it also makes sense to talk of something happening for the sake of something else. But any deterioration in health is a process of becoming—becoming ill—and has to be explicated in terms of the form of illness towards which it is a deterioration. It looks as though the view under consideration would have to consider illness as a failure to be something. In other words, it embodies a notion like that of harmony, balance, or nature at 31d seq. In this case, a process is not simply a process of becoming X for any value of X. X can only range over certain proper states in relation to which other conditions are judged good or bad, and any condition of being on the way to X cannot be in the category of a good, but at best assessed as good according to its success in approaching X. Cf. 55a2–3. Becoming is in contrast with destruction (55a) and is a matter of approaching the condition of having a nature.

This principle need only be part of the view being considered, not Plato's own, but when interpreted so as to sound plausible it echoes remarks in e.g. *Republic* 353 seq., 608e seq., *Timaeus* 28–30, *Phaedrus* 270, and is in keeping with the widespread and sometimes puzzling teleology found in Aristotle (cf. *Physics* 197a36–199b33). See also 23d and 26 seq. where coming to be does not include coming to be destroyed.

54e8 '... without hunger and thirst ...' Note that hunger and thirst are taken as what a sybarite goes in for. It may of course be that Plato is only wanting us to think of their desires as analogous, but that itself would be significant. See note on 44d7−e4.

55b This paragraph does not seem integrated into the argument. Only later (60a9−10) is Philebus accused of anything approaching identifying 'good' and 'pleasant', unless 13a7−b5 is taken to do it implicitly. But the first passage only clearly attributes to Philebus the view that they are two names for the same thing, not that they have the same sense, while the second only expresses surprise that if pleasures are different there is another word that can be applied truly to them all—though admittedly there is the suggestion that of course no problem would arise if 'all pleasant things are good' meant 'all pleasant things are pleasant'. Of course, Plato might not distinguish between saying '"A" and "B" are two names for the same thing' and '"A" and "B" mean the same', but even so the present argument appears as a refutation of a thesis only attributed to Philebus with any clarity some pages later. For if the present argument is to be taken at all seriously it only tells against a view that says that 'pleasure' can be substituted for 'good' in all uses without loss of truth. It is only on this interpretation that it is clear that the hedonist cannot say 'courage is good'. For this means, now, 'courage is a pleasure', which as it stands, a general statement, is false. Similarly to call someone good might be construed as attributing pleasure to him. Even so, it needs more careful statement. But if the hedonist is holding that pleasure is *the* good he has no need to get into these difficulties, since he can allow of instrumental uses of 'good' say, without being committed to instrumental uses of 'pleasure' and so on. Compare the argument of *Gorgias* 495−7.

55e1−56a1 'Suppose for instance ...' Cf. *Republic* VIII, 522c, *Epinomis* 977c−e.

56a3−7 '... and lyre-playing ...' Reading καὶ κιθαριστική (*kai kitharistikē*: and lyre-playing) after αὐλητική (*auletikē*: flute-playing) since few flutes have strings, and φθεγγομένης (*pthengomenēs*: sounding) for φερομένης (*pheromenēs*) whose translation would be a problem. It is possible that 'φερομένης' should be excised rather than emended, but Plato might be thinking that even when a player gets the right note, it is always an aural judgement and he is ready to adjust his fingering in search of the right one. The search is governed by the ear. When the right note is struck, the search is just very short.

56d1–e3 For 'philosophers' units cf. *Republic* VII, 525c–526a. The word translated 'academic' is literally 'of the philosophers'. The word for 'philosopher' tended to be used to cover those who pursued knowledge academically rather than practically. In the *Republic* however, expecially Books VI–VII, there seems to be a distinction between the ways philosophers and mathematicians approach mathematical hypotheses which *might* suggest special connotations of 'philosophical mathematics'. But it seems fairly clear that what is here called philosophical mathematics corresponds to the non-applied mathematics of the *Republic*, and is not identical with dialectic (cf. 57d–e).

56e6–57a1 'Well, then. Comparing . . .' As it stands the Greek starts as if there were to be a sentence declaring one sort of calculation and measurement different from the other, which goes appropriately into the genitive. But instead it turns into a question as to whether they are one or two. There is no call to supply a word for 'different'. On the contrary, if we supply it we have to suppose it already said that they are different, and then the question whether they are one or two becomes inappropriate. It is not uncommon, in either real life or Platonic conversations, for a sentence to start one way and finish another. Strictly, no doubt, the result is senseless, though the meaning is usually clear enough.

57a10–11 '. . . to have thrown up . . .' Reading προβεβληκέναι (*probeblēkenai*: to have thrown up) with the MSS. and taking it that the object understood is 'these considerations' from Socrates' last speech six lines earlier. Others follow Schleiermacher in reading προβεβηκέναι (*probebēkenai*: to have reached), in which case the sense is: 'It seems to me that in its search for an analogue to the pleasures the discussion has reached this point of enquiring whether . . .' The change, however, seems unnecessary. If it is felt that 'these considerations' harks too far back, there are still two possibilities: (i) one could with Stallbaum cite *Hippias Major* 293d1–4, and claim it as an example of προβάλλειν without an object. (ii) One could cite the same passage, claiming that προβάλλειν as well as ἐλεήσας (*eleēsas*: pitying) takes 'inexperience and lack of education' as object, and say that in the present passage it, as well as ζητῶν (*zētōn*: seeking) takes ἀντίστροφον (*antistrophon*: analogue) as its object. For (i) the translation would be: 'It seems to me that the argument, in its search for an analogue to the pleasures, puts forward a proposal by enquiring whether . . .' For (ii) it would read 'It seems to me that the argument, in its search for an analogue to the pleasures puts one forward by enquiring . . .' I have preferred to go back to 'these considerations' as the object because I think the word in 57a5, προηνεγκάμεθα (*proēnenkametha*: we have brought forward) is probably being picked up by προβεβληκέναι— Socrates brings before the meeting what the argument throws before the meeting.

57b6   '. . .less precise.' Plato has two words, one (used here) '*saphes*' literally meaning 'clear', and one used at c3 (*akribes*) meaning something like precise or accurate. He does not put any weight on any distinction between them. I have not used the English 'clearer' here because it does not seem to me to suggest any definite point. The Greek word seems, when used of subject-matter, to have suggested being more clearly laid out to view, when of branches of knowledge bringing things into clearer focus, and so in both cases related to the possibility of determining precise relationships. For other examples cf. *Republic* V, 478c10–11, VI, 509d, 511c.

57d2   '. . . accuracy.' Literally 'truth' (*aletheia*). The roots of this word suggest the property of not escaping one's notice, not slipping past one. The notion of some techniques being superior to others in respect of things not escaping notice but being catered for, is not so odd as that of some being truer. In addition, the English 'true' is habitually used of particular statements, propositions, beliefs, and when knowledge is said to be of the truth it is knowledge of a particular fact that is envisaged. The Greek word '*episteme*' means (roughly, but see General Commentary, pp. 153–4) a branch of knowledge, which in English is not naturally thought of as being true or false. Two techniques for approaching the same subject-matter, or using the same concepts, might be compared with respect to the accuracy with which they tackle the subject-matter or use the concepts, and so 'accuracy' seems a more apt translation.

57d4   '. . . experts in ambiguity.' It is not clear that Plato has any clear conception of ambiguity, and the expression will cover people who play fast and loose in argument in whatever way. It just happens that in the context it might be described as ambiguity, though just as well in terms of their being two sorts of . . .

58a1   Reading δῆλον ὅτι ἢ πᾶσαν ἂν τήν γε νῦν λεγομένην γνοίη, adding ἂν with Bury. The Oxford text would mean 'It is obvious that everyone would know the one now mentioned at least.' It involves, however, reading ὁτιή (*hotiē*). This is rare anywhere meaning 'that' rather than 'because', but so far as I can discover it occurs nowhere else in Plato in either sense, so that one might well hesitate over it. On the Oxford reading what is referred to as now mentioned is dialectic, on the other reading it is all the preceding branches of knowledge, and the 'at least' may indicate that this is not all that comes within the scope of dialectic.

58a2 '... the final truth.' The expression cannot mean simply 'the truth'. It could mean 'that which exists' or 'existence' or 'reality' (for a fuller list see Crombie, *An Examination of Plato's Doctrines*, (i. 42–3). The issue is complex, but it seems to me that Plato's use of the expression is most readily understood if one starts with the rendering 'the truth'. In the context of his view of the conditions for knowledge/understanding in the unqualified sense this gets confined to the truth about certain questions such as 'What is justice?', 'What is unity?', and so on. The reason for this is that Plato is interested in branches of knowledge, not knowledge, and for reasons well beyond the scope of this book seems to have taken as paradigms those which involved mathematical techniques among other things. Mathematicians, however, while they might reach true and eternally true conclusions, showed themselves (cf. *Republic* VII, 533b–c) unable to explain, e.g., what the units were that they were talking about. So while they may have truths, they do not have the whole truth about what they are talking about, for if they had they would be able to explain themselves. This final or complete truth is what 'philosophical' understanding supplies. The greater degree of 'truth' does not imply that the answer is truer in the English sense, but more comprehensively explanatory.

58a4 'Most genuine.' Or 'truest' (*alethestaten*). The dialogues show a persistent hostility to rhetoric and sensitivity to its power and glamour in contrast with philosophy (cf. e.g., *Apology passim*, *Gorgias passim*, *Theaetetus* 172–7, *Republic* VI–VII). A recurrent *éminence grise* is Gorgias, a famous sophist and writer of speeches who trained people in rhetoric, and whose follower Isocrates ran an academy in Athens teaching rhetoric. As Ryle argues (*Plato's Progress*) these passages should probably be seen in the context of an educational dispute between the academies. Hackforth detects a change of attitude to rhetoric here from that shown in the *Gorgias*, and takes Socrates to be admitting the lack of usefulness of dialectic as against the practical value of rhetoric. As a general rule, however, Socrates' politeness is more hostile than most people's abuse. There are at least two reasons from within the dialogue for not taking these remarks at face value. First, a dialectical approach as welcomed by the pleasures at 63b–c would seem to be potentially of the greatest practical value, and of course (cf. 59d–e) this high point of intellectual achievement seems to be Socrates' main candidate, which he is arguing to be of the greatest value to men after the good itself, and according to the macrocosm/microcosm argument of 28 seq. is a sharing in the directing power of the universe. In this context the praise of rhetoric sounds a little thin. But also at 62d1–3 Protarchus is made to judge his own point by making the value, not to say safety, for a man of the other forms of knowledge conditional on possession of the first. The first, in context, (cf. 62a) is knowledge of what justice is etc. This is just the subject on which Gorgias would claim expertise, but the description clearly envisages philosophical knowledge, not rhetorical know-how, and so the passage puts rhetoric in its proper place. Within the passage itself it is worth noting the pairing of prestige with profit.

58c7 '. . . what I said earlier about white.' It will be remembered that at 53a–b greater purity of whiteness went with a finer or more admirable white.

58d4–5 '. . . but whether there is not innate . . .' This is in fact the first mention of an inherent love of the truth for its own sake. As remarked elsewhere (see General Commentary, pp. 183 seq.) the way in which the mixed life is agreed to be the good would allow of the view that the sole function of the intellect was to discover how to have an enjoyable life. It is clear that Socrates has always had more in mind than this, but hitherto we have only heard of the intellect's important and noble role (26e–27c, 28c–31a) and the possible high point of its achievement in the section preceding (and following) the present sentence. This is the first time the claim is explicitly made that there is a desire for the complete truth (i.e. with truth, not pleasure as its objective) that may dominate a man's life. This recalls the highest division of the soul in the *Republic* (cf. IV, 431a–d, 442–4; VI, 485; IX, 580) and the intellectual passion of the *Symposium* (211–12). Other practical uses of the intellect fall under the description of *Republic* VII, 533b–c, but Plato seems to have felt that all other forms of knowledge could be shown to be either unable to deal with paradoxes, or unable to solve puzzlements about themselves, and that as a matter of fact the mind considers paradox and obscurity as things to be removed, thus showing the presence of a desire whose full satisfaction will lead to philosophy.

59a1–5 '. . . common opinions . . .' Cf. *Republic* V, 476 *ad fin*; VI-VII *passim*. Plato is inclined to use the word translated 'common opinions' (*doxai*) in a semi-technical way sometimes, recalling Parmenides' relegation of 'opinion' (*doxa*) to the degree of knowledge one can hope for from reliance on empirical observation. Such a use may be present in this passage. But *Republic* VI (493) suggests that one common fault of *doxai*, especially on certain topics such as justice, beauty, and so on, is that they are founded on and pander to 'common opinions'. If we consider other 'skills' mentioned earlier, such as building, shipbuilding, medicine, and the like, the complaint might be that they are aimed at what are commonly taken to be goods, without broader inquiry into the physical and psychological nature of the beings they are supposed to serve. Even when people do purport to examine nature they are interested only in the processes of nature, not in questions about the nature of what they are studying. For Plato's objections to this way of doing science cf. *Phaedo* 96–100, and for a possible sketch of the preferred way cf. *Timaeus*. But this last presupposes the possibility of not just studying how things are related, but of determining the natures of the various sorts of things in the universe, which determine the best sort of arrangement. If '*doxa*' is being used technically, some tanslation such as 'empirical judgement' might suit.

59b4–5 'How in fact . . .' There is difficulty in determining just why this should be so. It is not that Plato believes in evolution and so thinks that nature is constantly putting our generalizations in jeopardy. Yet the very statement is presumably one statement that always holds of any member of the material world, viz. that it has no stability, so the point cannot be that no universal truths hold of things in process. There seem various possibilities, and the truth is probably that they are all right.
(i) It is possible to give a complete account of what it is to be a man, shuttle, unit, an account quite unaffected by changes in the world (for it is the degree to which they measure up to the account of 'shuttle' that entitles them to be called one; they do not determine what it is to be a shuttle); it is not possible to give a complete description of actual men once and for all, because the individuals are always changing, and so must the description.
(ii) The same as (i) to begin with, then: it is not possible to make any universal statements that are specific to men and true of all men at any time. Even those truths embodied in the account of the nature of man will not, for these will specify either a stage of full development, or a form of growth. The first will be instantiated by few, and only a part of the second instantiated by any given man, and a different part by different men and by the same men at different times.
(iii) The same as in (i) to begin with, and then: a generalization such as 'food keeps men alive' is only true for the most part. Waiving the frets about old men, even apparently fit young ones are in a

constant state of change such that with some on occasion some food is fatal. This fact both renders such generalizations always for the most part true only, and results in a recognized liability to error in practical pursuits based on them, for it is not possible prior to the event to be sure that the relevant change will not occur.

59c1—6 (i) The notion of 'least tainted' or 'least adulterated' applied to truth ought, in strict analogy with pleasure and whiteness, to imply not mixed with error. If the note on 58a2 is right the opposite of truth is a little more complex than 'error' suggests. In the case of knowledge 'unmixed with ignorance' would catch the point. (ii) By parity of argument pleasures other than the pure ones are only in a secondary sense to be called pleasures. In earlier dialogues Plato shows a tendency to tighten the criteria for applying a description, and claim, e.g., that only philosophy really gives knowledge. Aristotle, by contrast, regularly discusses, as a preliminary, the many ways a term is used, and in particular for some terms distinguishes between primary and secondary uses (e.g. *Nicomachean Ethics* 1115a9 seq. on courage, 1148b4 seq. on incontinence). Whether this treatment of knowledge is intended as an example of dealing with a one in many, or as something different, the *Philebus* shows signs of explicit attention to ways of dealing with troublesome concepts which get more systematic elaboration in Aristotle. That such methods of treatment received attention from the Academy is suggested by Aristotle's *On Ideas* (cf. G. E. L. Owen, 'A Proof in the *Peri Ideon*').

59d7—8 'Yet these . . .' These were the names. But only an argument that the organizing intelligence needs to know the eternal truths would show that the intelligence spoken of here is in some sense the same as that of 26e seq. For this a development of the central books of the *Republic* would be needed.

60a9 '. . . two names . . .' For the question whether Plato distinguished between 'two names for the same thing' and 'two synonymous names' cf. e.g. 26e—27a, *Theaetetus* 204b10—c6, *Sophist* 243—5, 250—5, *Protagoras* 349b, 355b.

61a4—5 'We need, then . . .' What we get is a sketch. 'The good' is not the *Republic* Form of the Good, but the good for man. On the other hand it could be held that Socrates is interested in that which in the good life makes it good. The expression 'looking for the good in the mixed life' at b4—6 is ambiguous as regards 'in' as between the 'in' of 'Plato found in philosophy the answer to his discontent' and

'Plato discerned the structure in his *Philebus* even if his readers didn't'. The first seems more likely right. Generally in the dialogue, and immediately preceding this passage 'the good' refers to the goal in human life, and this has been found in (i.e. been admitted to be) a life of intelligence and pleasure. What we next get is a sketch of the combination (= a sketch of the good) as a preliminary to the prize-giving.

61e6—9 'Suppose then we . . .' As remarked elsewhere (cf. General Commentary, pp. 183 seq.) this is not a principle obviously acceptable to the opposition. It looks as though Plato is interpreting the talk of mixed, qualified cases of pleasure and knowledge as being ones that contain an element of their opposites: distress and ignorance. But we have no warrant for including either of these in the good life. The admissions of 20 seq. only entitle us to include pleasure and knowledge. Therefore only the 'true', pure forms can safely be admitted. The move serves, however, as a convenient way of introducing the application of the examination of pleasure and knowledge. In fact, it is the examination of pleasure that becomes important, and one suspects that the picture of intelligence that has been built up through the dialogue has made that clearly indispensable, and that the real test for admission is of pleasures at 63d seq.

62a3 'Let us then . . .' This is the first mention of justice as something known by the highest form of knowledge. Cf. General Commentary, pp. 222 seq. for its significance.

62a4 '. . . powers of reasoning . . .' Or: 'and with an account of it suitable to (or consequential on) his understanding.' (*Logon echōn* may mean either possessing reason, or having an explanation or account.)

62b8—c4 'We shall have to . . .' Literally: 'It is necessary'. Presumably the first are necessary if we are to live at all. But the 'necessity' for music is far weaker. It is as weak as 'necessary for a tolerable life'. But when at e9 necessary pleasures are admitted a similar appeal to what Protarchus would consider necessary for a tolerable life would be in danger of letting in too much. The necessary pleasures there are presumably those that are necessary to life, such as quenching thirst and satisfying hunger—though it is not clear that one has to be hungry in order to live. It is eating that is necessary, not either hunger or pleasure.

62c2 '. . . imitation . . .' It has nowhere been said that music is full of imitation, certainly not where it is referred to as a skill (55e—56a), nor even in discussing pure pleasures of sound (51d). Plato did, however, tend to think that ordinary music was in some sense imitative (cf. *Republic* II–III *passim*, X; *Laws* II, 668), and it may be that the word slipped in either from his or a copyist's association of ideas.

62d1–3 See General Commentary, pp. 222 seq.

62e8–9 '. . . necessary.' See note on 62b8–c4.

63b7–c3 'What was said earlier . . .' The preference for knowledge of everything else but especially full understanding of each pleasure, comes because the knowledge in question is not, or not simply, knowing how to define 'pleasure', but knowing all about pleasure. This 'philosophical' knowledge is vital from the point of view of getting the pleasantest life (cf. *Republic* IX, *Laws* 732 seq.). In general Plato did not think philosophical knowledge to be useless, but vital for conducting matters properly. His discussions of the impracticality of philosophers (e.g. *Republic* VII, *Gorgias* 508–10), portray them not as ignorant about how to live, but as inept in contemporary public life. The ineptness is at joining in the confusion of actual politics. Plato did not think that men in public life really knew what they are about.

63c8 'What sorts of pleasure?' The word used ($\pi o \iota \omega \nu$ (*poiōn*: what sort of ?)) probably picks up the same word at 17b8, d1, 19b3.

63e9 '. . . most harmonious . . .' Literally: 'With least (civil) discord'. Cf. *Republic* VIII–IX where great use is made with the image of civil discord. The protrayal of physical desire in that dialogue matches the view of physical pleasures in this. See notes on 44d7–e4, 45b3–4. See also *Phaedo* 65–7.

64b2 '. . . truth . . .' See General Commentary, pp. 212 seq. A further complication is that the word can mean a capacity for attaining the truth (cf. Plato *Definitiones* 413c6–7. This is not by Plato, but probably records a sense current in Academic circles.) Usually (e.g. Hackforth, A. E. Taylor) the word here is rendered 'genuineness' or some equivalent, and it is then puzzling what the point is. Genuine examples of pleasure and knowledge have been included, so it cannot be genuine items that are lacking. If it means genuineness must be added to the mixture, i.e. it must be a genuine mixture, the point of this is highly obscure. Any mixture is genuinely one, unless those with mutually antagonistic ingredients are nongenuine. But we have already ensured compatibility of the ingredients, and so on this count genuineness.

Socrates' previous sentence says that what he is going to mention is necessary for anything coming into being, and the context might limit this to any mixture coming into being. The talk of coming into being is repeated in the present sentence. This might be intended to recall 26e seq., where intelligence is responsible for coming into being, and *aletheia* here might mean 'capacity for the truth' (intelligence). This would make Protarchus' assertion at 65d2—3 nearer to being obvious. It would also help another puzzle. At 65a1—5 Socrates lays down three marks of whatever for tying down the good: fineness, measure, and truth; and this is summing up 64a—e. These are applied in reverse order in 65c—e, with a change of name for the middle one (cf. 64e5—7 for general interchangeability). 66a—b seems to give the first three prizes to these three. At least that is what one expects, and the first two, while there is further mixing of names, seem to correspond to measure and fineness. But the third is intelligence. If 'truth' has meant 'capacity for truth' previously, the introduction of 'intelligence' here is not an abrupt change of topic but only a change in term in line with the changes rung on the other items. It must be admitted, however, that this is hardly a common Platonic use of the word. Otherwise, the abruptness involved here is certainly no more, though perhaps of a different sort, than that involved on any other interpretation. For occurrences where *aletheia* need or must not mean either 'true' or 'genuine' cf. *Republic* 331c2 where it means truthfulness, *Gorgias* 526d where the phrase might mean 'exercising (or training) my capacity for the truth', and cf. *Laws* 730c where it means capacity for and/or devotion to the truth.

64c5—d5 'In that case, which . . .' Cf. 22d, 26e. The 'cause' here is clearly not the efficient cause, but the *peras* of 23 seq. (cf. 25b1, d11—e2, 26a8 for the notions of measure, balance and so on; 26b1, 6—7 for fineness).

64d9—e3 'Simply that . . .' It is noticeable that Plato acknowledges the possibility of bad mixtures. But if the previous note is right their trouble is that they lack *peras* (cf. General Commentary, p. 187 seq., 197 seq.) and so are not mixtures of the sort discussed at 23 seq. 'They cease to be a blend of anything.'

64e5—10 'So now it looks . . .' In what follows there is considerable interchange of the terms for measure, harmony, fineness, and they do not seem to be seen as seriously different (cf. note on 64b2). It may be that Plato wishes to indicate a difference between susceptibility to measurement and possession of good order, but if so the readiness to interchange the terms seems equally to indicate that he does not want to mark a sharp contrast. It is perhaps worth noting that *'aletheia'* is never interchanged with 'measure', 'fineness', 'commensurability', though on any plausible interpretation of the 'genuine' rendering it is hard to see why. On the interpretation suggested in the note on 64b2 this, with the substitution of 'intelligence' at 66b5–6, seems more understandable. The cause is not to be confused with what it imposes.

65a1–5 '... because of this, as something good ...' See General Commentary, pp. 224 seq. Nowhere does Socrates call pleasure 'something good'. He only allows that a life without it is not the good life for man.

65b2 Note 'and gods alike', and cf. General Commentary, pp. 224–5.

65c5 'There is no greater charlatan.' Cf. note on 32c1–2 for the possible significance of this, though as Protarchus elaborates the point the reason is not that they lead us astray in prognostication, but are generally admitted to make people commit perjury. Pleasure is being judged by reference to its disorderly rather than orderly species (cf. 52c) as also in the application of the tests of measure and fineness to follow. This illustrates the anti-Phileban bias.

65d9–10 '... nor more given to it ...' Intelligence is ordered in the sense that to understand something is to find order in it, but there is no obvious reason why a person should not have an inordinate interest in the truth, a rabid don leaving his family to starve while he extends his knowledge. Plato never seems to envisage such a man. Probably this is because no search for knowledge below the level of philosophy counts, without serious qualification, as knowledge, and it is the highest kind that is at issue (cf. 59d). At this level it is a love of good ordering, searching out the harmonious arrangement of the universal mind, with the sympathy of a similar mind recoiling from the idea of bringing discord into such an arrangement. Vicious action is discordant. It remains that someone less than a philosopher could have an inordinate love of the pursuits of 58e4–59a4. It is simply not clear why these pleasures should be deemed 'measured' (52c).

65e1–66a3 Cf. General Commentary, p. 224.

66a8   'Rather, the first . . .' The text is uncertain. πρῶτον (*prōton*: first) must be taking up the 'neither first nor even second' of the previous sentence. What follows must mean 'Instead, the first (is) somewhere in the region of measure, the moderate. The problem is with what follows. There is no MS. consensus on the text. The word for 'eternal' occurs, preceded by a feminine accusative article. Some MSS. then have nothing meaningful, or the infinitive 'ᾑρῆσθαι', (*hēirēsthai*, a middle or passive perfect of the verb for 'to take') sometimes followed by φύσιν (*phusin*: nature) or the infinitive εἰρῆσθαι (*eirēsthai*, a past perfect of a verb for 'to say') followed by φάσιν (*phasin*: they say). There are various possibilities. First, one might try to recover something from the remnants, without supposing interpolation. In that case it is probably best to take φύσιν as a corruption of φάσιν and preserve ᾑρῆσθαι. The above translation would then proceed either (i) 'and all things of that sort which one must suppose to have acquired the eternal nature', or (ii) 'and all things of that sort which one must suppose the eternal nature to have acquired', or (iii) it would have to be altered entirely to read: 'but first of all the eternal nature is captured somewhere in the region of measure, the moderate, the appropriate, and all things that one must consider of that sort.' The last may be slightly modified if one thinks that 'one must consider' governs 'that the eternal nature is captured' rather than 'to be of the sort'. On (i) it is presumably being said that the members of this first category are Forms. On (ii) it is somewhat obscure what the reference of 'the eternal nature' is—on (iii) the word 'captured' presumably takes up the searching/ hunting language of 64c and 65a. In that case 'the eternal nature' presumably refers to the good. But as the good is in this case the good life, not the Form of the Good, it becomes obscure what the role of 'eternal' is. It would, I suppose, have to refer to the eternal, blueprint, element. On any account the sudden mention of the eternal nature is surprising and can only be defended by fairly elaborate expansion of what is there. It would be hard to gather these expansions from the text. It becomes tempting, therefore, to suppose that 'nature' was inserted by someone who, because of his general interpretation of the dialogue, wished to gloss 'measure etc.' as referring to Forms. In that case one might take Hackforth's suggestion that with 'the eternal . . .' we supply a cognate accusative of the verb 'to take', and render the infinitive as passive, reading: 'rather, the first has been secured for everlasting tenure somewhere in the region of measure . . .' This is possible, but is hardly an obvious sense. It seems more likely that the whole is an interpolated comment. The talk of measure here would naturally, and rightly, recall the language used of *peras* earlier, and it has from early times been a popular view that *'peras'* is either a new name for the class of Forms, or for the mathematical element in their analysis. So it would be natural to add a note to the effect that the eternal nature is referred to. We may have lost this note beyond recovery, or it may be that those MSS. that put χρή (*chrē*: one must) after τοιαῦτα (*toiauta*: of that sort) are right. In that case the jotting was: 'one has to suppose the eternal nature has been captured', giving a reader's view that here the form of the Good has been run to earth. In that case one simply understands 'is' as the main verb of the original sentence. I have translated on this last assumption.

66b5–6 '. . . not far from the truth . . .' While this is a perfectly natural phrase, if the interpretation of *'aletheia'* offered in the note on 64b2 is right, this may be intended as a play on the words–'not far from the truth we mentioned earlier'. Cf. Badham's note.

66d7–8 '. . . every conceivable sort of pleasure.' Note the undiscriminating form of thesis attributed to Philebus. In effect, once it is shown that in talking of pleasure we are talking of a great variety of things, someone who says pleasure is the good, without bothering about the 'number' of pleasures, is saying that every pleasure without discrimination is good, and by the time we have been through the various false and mixed pleasures the view looks less attractive.

67b11 'There is still . . .' This presumably refers back to 50d8–e2.

GENERAL COMMENTARY

OPENING SKIRMISH, 11b–14

In this section we are introduced to the dispute that has been going on between Philebus and Protarchus, as to whether pleasure or intelligence is the good. The dispute is familiar (cf. *Republic* VI, 505) but is nowhere given such detailed, nor, it must be admitted, such baffling treatment as in the *Philebus*. Even the nature of the dispute is unclear. In particular, questions arise about the expression 'the good'. (i) Eudoxus (cf. Aristotle, *Nicomachean Ethics* 1172b9 seq.) seems to have held that all animals desire pleasure and only pleasure, and that that shows it to be the good. On such a view to say it is the good is just to say that it is the one goal that in the last resort all things pursue. Since no living being can conceivably pursue anything else the question of whether they ought to want it, whether it is desirable in that sense, will not arise. So saying pleasure is the good will be saying not that it ought to be desired, but that it in fact determines all answers on what ought to be desired. For we can only raise those questions of other things than pleasure, and the only sense we can give them is 'Is this something that leads to more pleasure than any alternatives?' Any decision that we ought to want *X* is in effect a decision that *X* is what best leads to what we want (viz. pleasure). (ii) The generalization to all animals (and cf. 22b, 60a) certainly echoes the Aristotelian report of Eudoxus. The account of Philebus' thesis is, however, very brief. It is just as possible that he is advocating pleasure as the goal, and holding that while it may be that some beings ignore it, the mark of a successful life is successful pursuit of pleasure. This would break the tie between what is in the last resort wanted and what is good or pleasant, and would make pleasure not what is desired, but what ought to be desired, and similarly the good. This certainly corresponds better with the way Socrates uses the expression 'the good' (or, strictly, 'the better', cf. 11b9). Intelligence and the rest are not billed as what everything desires, at least by any observational criterion for desire, but as what would be the greatest benefit to anything capable of them. We can presumably infer that these beings ought to want them, but no interest is taken in whether they do.

Saying that intelligence and the rest confer the greatest gift a man could receive might be construed hedonistically, as underlining the value of intelligence for organizing the pleasantest life. This is clearly not Socrates' thought. Pleasure and intelligence are rival candidates for the role of constituting a life that is *eudaemon* (11d). *'Eudaemon'* is a hard word to translate, but the traditional 'happy' is probably a worse translation than most. Originally it was a word for remarking on what a good guardian spirit a man was blessed with. It leaves open how we should judge the worth of guardian spirits. Their ability to supply us with happy or pleasant lives is obviously one possible criterion, but for that very reason 'happiness' cannot be the meaning. Thus Socrates is holding that a guardian spirit has done his work as well as can be hoped if he supplies us with intellectual gifts and a life spent in their exercise, and certainly better than if he just supplies us with pleasure. I would not suggest that Plato clings to a belief in guardian spirits, any more than a person who describes a man as gifted must believe in a creator who lavishes gifts. But sometimes the more primitive roots of a word can throw light on its later operation. Socrates, then, is wanting to advocate the intellectual life as what ought to be pursued, and is not claiming that it is pursued. As will emerge later, however, appeal to desire of a sort is used to buttress the advocacy. (iii) It is unclear whether the claim that pleasure or intelligence is the good amounts to the claim that nothing is desirable except to be enjoying oneself (or thinking), or that what determines the constituents of the good life is pleasure or thought, though of course the good life must contain many elements that are not pleasures or pieces of thinking. Further, it is not clear whether the claim is that there are some pleasures or pieces of thinking that have this status, or that the simple fact of applicability of the description 'pleasure' or 'thought' is enough to confer the status.   •

Of course, this is only the introductory phase. On the other hand, it is probably right to claim a bias in favour of the interpretation that says that the positions are: (a) a life is good to the extent that it is pleasant, and (b) a life is good to the extent that it is taken up in intellectual activities. Each position allows factors espoused by the other to be present in any given version of the good life, but declares them irrelevant to its goodness except, perhaps, as means. Consequently a life without them could theoretically be as good as a life with them. The view that this is the bias is justified at least to this extent, that when the major shift occurs at 20–2 it is the candidates interpreted in this way that are rejected. It must be admitted that of themselves the admissions at 20–2 would only entail that both pleasure and intelligence are necessary for the good life and so only entail rejection of a hedonism that claimed pleasure to be sufficient. They would allow of the position that the reason why intelligence is necessary is that it enables us to secure the best balance of pleasures and/or itself supplies some of the greatest ones.

This would leave pleasure as the criterion of what is good and bad. The earlier argument, however, on the multiformity of pleasure tells against that position. For until someone produces a 'science' of pleasure we are left without an operable criterion. So both these versions of hedonism (that the best life is one of pleasant activities only or that it is pleasure that determines what constituents are needed in the good life) are directly attacked in the first ten pages of the dialogue. The sybaritic version, on the other hand (cf. Introduction, p. 3) is alluded to, but not directly treated in the early part of the dialogue. There is nothing comparable to the *Gorgias* or *Republic* attacks. Even later in the section up to 31 its rejection could only be a consequence of the view of the place of pleasure in the good life, rather than of an analysis of sybaritism. But in fact at 32d it is recognized still to be an open question whether all or only some pleasures are desirable, and the some could be the sybarite's.

Some light may be thrown on the matter if we remember that Eudoxus visited Athens and was a member of the Academy in the mid-360s. According to Aristotle (*Nicomachean Ethics* 1172b) he held that it is clear that pleasure is the good because all living things pursue it, and his views won credence not so much because of the cogency of his arguments as because of his sobriety of character. As we have seen, there are signs of the grounds for this position in the description of Philebus' thesis. Aristotle seems to be suggesting that Eudoxus' character was taken as showing that he did not have a special axe to grind, and that therefore, as he was a very clever man, he must have good arguments. This suggests that people supposed the conclusion to be that of the vulgar hedonist, a position whose advocacy was usually suspect because of the advocate's addiction to the pleasures he sponsored. Eudoxus' sobriety freed him of the suspicion of special pleading. It is likely, therefore, that Eudoxus' position was commonly taken as supporting sybaritic hedonism. As he was influential Plato would have to assess his own position on pleasure *vis-à-vis* Eudoxus, and would be concerned to do so at least in part because of the way in which Eudoxus' thesis was likely to be interpreted. So while Philebus (Mr. Loveboy) hardly represents Eudoxus, he does represent the repercussions of Eudoxus (cf. 12b7: Aphrodite is Philebus' goddess, and cf. 65c–66a; see also 44b–c: Philebus' enemies are hostile to physical pleasures). Consequently we have someone who appeals to the general fact that all animals pursue pleasure and interprets this as showing that certain pleasures ('animal' ones) are the good. Throughout, taking pleasure (or intelligence) as the good is not simply taking it as that whose presence will make a life good, but as something that we can use as a criterion in the organization of our lives for deciding between courses of action. Clearly, one possible way to counter Philebus would be to say that all beings want the most pleasant life, and that his pleasures do not give it. Plato does not take this line. From the start the attack is on the idea that pleasures are comparable. If they differ widely as pleasures and are even opposites, then a question mark is put over the interpretation of 'all living things want pleasure'. It has been taken as meaning 'There is one thing that all living things want'. Now it would have to read 'For each (kind of) living thing there is one thing it wants'. But the matter is worse, because the examples purport to give dissimilar or opposed *human* pleasures, so that the thesis has to read either 'For each man there is some pleasure that is what he wants' or 'For each desire of each man there is some pleasure that is the object of that desire'. If the first is accepted, then there is no possibility of general argument about the best life for man. If the second goes through, then it is not even the case that an individual can use pleasure as a life-organizing criterion for himself, since his various pleasures differ, and 'pleasure' does not give a means of comparison. Different courses leading to different pleasures do just that. There is no answer to 'Which pleasures are pleasantest?' Any decision to favour some pleasures is either an arbitrary option, or a decision that they are best, where 'best' cannot be interpreted in terms of pleasure. While it is true that Plato himself has (53b—c) a rather weird criterion for degrees of pleasure, it is not (see note to 53c1) one that allows degrees of pleasure to be usable for deciding what is the pleasantest life.

The opening section, then, begins an attack on the possibility of using pleasure as a criterion for choosing between ways of life, on the grounds that 'pleasure' does not in the required way denote a single thing. The importance attached to this is underlined in the following section on the one and many, and by 31 we should be convinced of the unsuitability of pleasure for the required role. It will need an expert with knowledge of proper measures to decide what pleasures to include. This would not, however, suffice to show that certain pleasures or all were not the good (i.e. did not constitute the goal to be aimed at), even if it removed one intellectual defence of that position. From 31 onwards the examination of pleasure is almost entirely an examination of the sorts of pleasure Philebus might be expected to espouse, with a view to showing their unsuitability for the good life. If the section up to 31 develops difficulties for Eudoxus' supposition that pleasure is a single thing and what all want, 31 to the end deals with the repercussions of Eudoxus.

THE ONE AND THE MANY, 14–16

One and Many. It has become clear that the problem about pleasure and knowledge is one of seeing how the plurality of forms of either can be said to constitute a unity. There are various puzzles about one and many, and Socrates wishes to isolate the one in question. For the others mentioned it is interesting to compare *Parmenides* 129b and *Sophist* 251. (See note on 14c11.) The facts in the first puzzle are used, but not for purposes of puzzlement, at *Phaedo* 102–3 and *Republic* VII, 523–4.

The important problem concerns not particulars but things like man, beauty, good. If we claim that not only can we speak of individual men, good things, and so on, but can also ask what man is and what good is, we imply that in each case we have a single subject-matter, that there is something called man and something else called good to examine.

There is, however, a problem as to just what this problem is. A number of considerations seem to govern the interpretation: 1. the problem ought to be the one we have just got into, the one at 13e–14b; 2. it should be the one dealt with in the Heavenly Tradition passage at 16c seq.; 3. it has to be the one described in 15b; and 4. 15d–e should be a way into it.

The Heavenly Tradition I shall leave aside for the present. What then of point 3, the description of the problem in 15b? This paragraph is difficult to interpret. First there is a problem of relevance and secondly of punctuation. Roughly, the first is that it looks as though, whatever the details of interpretation, the problem is about how, if man (as distinct from men) constitutes a unit, there can be many men. This can be a problem if we take 'man' as denoting either mankind or the property of being human. In the first case we seem able to examine mankind, but mankind is found wherever there are men, and so is 'split up while remaining one'. In the second the problem is how we can talk of a single property of being a man, when it is found in numberless instances. Surely if it occurs in many places it is only in some Pickwickian sense that we have a single thing? This latter sounds very like the problem of *Parmenides* 131 seq., which the present passage verbally recalls (or conversely), cf. *Parmenides* 131a8–b2 and *Philebus* 15b5–8 (cf. Hackforth). But if this is the problem, then it is a different one/many problem from the one we started with. For that was a problem of how pleasure/knowledge/good could still be spoken of as units if they have many forms, whereas the present problem is how they can still be units if they have many instances. It is hard to see how the solution to the second would be relevant to the first.

There seem to be three possibilities: (i) Hackforth is right, in

143

which case we have moved to a quite different and irrelevant problem. If that is so, then either Plato is being deliberately irrelevant for no obvious purpose, or he has failed to notice the shift. (ii) We should forget the verbal reminiscence of the *Parmenides*. Such reminiscences should not be allowed to weigh against considerations of the relevance of what is said to the argument in which it occurs. The passage should be translated so as directly to state that the problem is one about the compatibility of unity and plurality of form. The difficulty is that the problem seems to be one of how good or pleasure can retain its unity if scattered abroad among things in a process of change. It is hard to read 15b4 seq. so as to exclude all reference to the fact of the 'occurrence' of good and the rest in changing particulars. (iii) The problem is one about the multiformity of units, but the multiformity becomes obvious in and even perhaps arises from the occurrence of those features in the changing world of instances. If we think of pleasure we consider it as a unit, but if we turn our attention to instances we are struck by not, or not just, their multiplicity, but their variety (cf. *Republic* V, 476 for possibly the same point). Participation by particulars produces the appearance of scatter and separation of the unit from itself, but the point is not the *Parmenides* one. Rather the point is that we either have to talk of the unit as scattered in the dramatic sense that it seems to disappear in the multiplicity of forms (cf. 25a where the terminology of 'scatter' is used, apparently recalling this passage, but where the scatter is not among particulars), or else we must speak of each form of pleasure, say, manifesting pleasure in its entirety, in which case the dissimilarity and even mutual opposition of the forms means that the unit is over against itself, and 'separated from itself'.

Plato, on this view, may simply have thought that as a matter of fact as manifested in the observable changing world these units show multiformity. It is just possible that the insistence on the units not admitting of change, in contrast to the instances, is to be given some significance. In that case it may be that he felt that while there are eternal truths to be enunciated about pleasure, or man, it is a necessary feature of instances of pleasure or man that they should be processes of change. The pleasure of philosophizing consists in the process of doing dialectic, and every man, to be a man, must grow, age, and die. While the statement of the general conditions of what it is to be good or man will be unchanging, any instance of X may be at a different stage from any other, manifesting opposing properties, and so a problem of multiformity is raised. This would be speculative, and does not yield the brand of multiformity from which we started. It suggests not a problem between forms of pleasure, but within each form, and introduces, as important, factors that play no part in developing the problem either before or after this passage. On the other hand, Plato may have felt there are various problems of multiformity, and while this is not the main one here it would accommodate man, ox, etc.

It seems simplest to take an interpretation on the lines of (iii) above even though that means giving weight to the context within which the passage occurs and allowing it to influence one's reading. It seems enough to suppose that Plato thought that as manifested in changing particulars things such as good and pleasure showed a variety of forms, without supposing that he goes into every form of possible variety.

One small point that makes it attractive to read this passage as something like the *Parmenides* problem is the first sentence, which on most translations (e.g. Hackforth) seems to be raising the question of the real existence of these units. Literally the sentence reads: 'First, whether one should suppose that there are some such units truly (or genuinely) (*alethōs*) being.' The 'truly (or genuinely) being' is usually taken to be raising the question of their real existence, but could just as well, if not more naturally, be taken as raising the question of their truly being units (cf. *Politicus* 293e, *Sophist* 236a). In that case the question is first whether we should consider them as genuine units, and then, if so, how we can in face of certain facts. What is envisaged then is not the possible non-existence of them, but the possibility of their being psuedo-units (e.g. 'barbarian', cf. *Politicus* 262) or of its not being possible to find a unit (see note on 16d1−3 and note the word for 'posit' at both 15a5 and 16d2). In fact this gives a more unified translation, and removes what would be the intrusion of a quite irrelevant question. The translation given is supposed to be neutral.

There is still the problem of punctuation. The Oxford text inserts a question mark so that from 'then how . . .' it reads: 'then how can they be such that while each is a unit and remains unchanged, admitting neither of generation nor destruction, it is nevertheless unshakeably one? Further, as found in the indeterminate number of perishable things, does one have to say that it has been scattered abroad and become many . . .?' This gives three questions instead of two. It also avoids having a rather clumsy sentence. The difficulty is to see what the second problem is. If one adopts Hackforth's translation of the first sentence then one would have a question as to whether the units really existed, a question as to how they could be units, and a question as to how to talk of them as found partaken of by particulars. That at least looks like three questions, which is more than would be true on the other translation. It is still obscure just what the second problem is supposed to be. The 'nevertheless' suggests that what has gone before would create some difficulty about the unit's being a unit. It is hard to see how the fact that they are unchanging and do not admit of generation or destruction would call in question their unitary status. Yet Hackforth is surely right to reject the suggestion of Archer-Hind (*J. of Ph.* xxvii) that the problem is how the various monads while remaining monads can form a systematic unity, so that we can speak of *the* one system of forms. If that is the point then Plato has obscured it by inserting the red herring about not admitting of generation or destruction; and even if he had omitted that the point would have been well concealed in what remained. The only way to have three questions is to adopt the suggestion of Badham (2nd edition) and insert 'not' before 'unshakeably one'. But 'not' is a philosophically large word to insert.

In *Monist* 1966 Professor Anscombe suggests that there are indeed three questions. The first is whether the monads should be judged to exist, the third is how they are related to the infinitude of becoming. She admits that the second point is obscure and takes philosophical acuteness to notice. The point is that early in his life Plato was inclined to contrast physical particulars, which could both change their properties and have many, with Forms, which just were what they were called. Both change and multiplicity of properties and also their multiplicity as holders of one property, show physical particulars not simply to be what they are called. In contrast Forms are simple. The Form of the beautiful just *is* beautiful—it cannot be separated from beauty, nor is it anything but beauty (cf. *Symposium* 210–11). But this generates problems. For Plato also wants to say of each Form that it *is* what it is, and that it is a *unit*. So while Forms may not exhibit change, it does seem necessary to say that the Beautiful is not *just* beautiful, and so not simple. Consequently, if it is a unit—which is essential to its being a Form—then it is also a multiplicity, which raises a problem as to how it can be a monad. This is the problem of the later dialogues, of the second part of the *Parmenides*, the intercommunion of kinds in the *Sophist*, and so on. It is this that forms the second problem here: how each monad can be a monad.

I do not wish to dispute the general account of Plato's problems, but granted it is right the problem is not difficult to appreciate. When it comes to finding the problem in the present text what is needed is not philosophical acuteness, but a high degree of clairvoyance. Professor Anscombe's article gives a fair indication of what one has to supply. Nor is it any help to claim that this interpretation stays close to the text. For unless we claim the Oxford text question mark to be part of the text it is a matter of option whether one translates the passage, as it appears in the manuscripts, as giving two or three problems. Even where manuscripts contain punctuation it carries no authority. It is already someone's interpretation, and does not, as the lettering does, carry weight. There is no evidence of a Greek question mark in Plato's day, and the dots found in manuscripts do no more than suggest the need to pause for breath. I have not checked the MS. for presence or absence of such a dot, because it is of no significance either way. That one needs in this sentence to pause for breath is beyond doubt. It is a cumbersome passage on any count, only marginally less so if we suppose three questions. Plato is, unfortunately, given to cumbersome sentences at times (cf. 30a9–b7, 46d7–e6, 58c–d, *Sophist* 258e7–259b6, *Symposium* 210a4–e1). One gets carried along by the flow of language and it is only examination that reveals the difficulty of precise interpretation.

It seems preferable, therefore, to drop the question mark at b4 unless one accepts Badham's interpolation. In that case there are two problems mentioned. The first is either whether such monads really exist or whether we can posit genuine units of the sort in question. The second is how we are to reconcile calling them units with attributing to them the plurality (of form) that afflicts them as a result of involvement with changing particulars. Possibly part of the problem here is that the instances of pleasure and the rest have to be processes; that means that in some sense pleasure is caught up in a process of change which seems to conflict with the unchanging unity claimed for it.

The passage that follows (15d1 seq.) is supposed to be a starting point for coming to grips with the dispute about one and many which (cf. 15c1–3) is the important one whose solution leads to progress and which at 14c we are told we have become involved in. It is significant that the starting-point is a consideration of discourse (15d4–5); apparently there the identification of one and many occurs constantly, and is a source of much sophistry. So even if there is in 15b a problem about the relation of universals to particulars of an ontological sort, the best place to start for the problem in hand is a fact about the way we talk.

It is not, unfortunately, immediately obvious what this fact is. Hackforth, taking 15b as primarily concerned with the problem of how one form can be manifested in many particulars takes it that the paradoxical fact is that of predication, since every subject-predicate statement asserts the fact of participation found puzzling at 15b. Yet as it stands this is false of Hackforth's interpretation. 'Justice is good' asserts participation all right, but not of a particular in a Form. The problem of 15b is supposed to be specially related to the division of forms among particulars and only some statements, such as 'Theaetetus is sitting down' imply that. Even in these cases

'identifying the one and the many' is not a pellucid way of characterizing what is done, as it might be of characterizing 'Many people are
sitting down'. Further, to repeat, it is not clear how solving the
problem of how many particulars can be described by a single
predicate will help solve the problem about pleasure and knowledge
having many forms, to which it is supposed to be relevant.

Another possibility is that Plato has in mind the kind of puzzle
mentioned in *Sophist* 251, which is also said to be a favourite of
logic-choppers. The thesis there is that the predicate 'man' can
only be applied to man, the predicate 'good' to good, and so on.
Even to use the word 'is' in 'Man is man' is apparently forbidden, as
only 'man' can be used of man. To use two words 'man' and 'good'
or 'man' and 'is' one needs two things. Otherwise one is in effect
saying that two things 'man' and 'good' are the same, or one. In
short one can only name. Forming names into sentences is forbidden
because it is tantamount to claiming that two (or more) things are one.

This interpretation has the advantage that it would justify the
assertion of d4–5 that *everything* that is said (for the distinction of
saying and naming cf. *Sophist* 261d seq.) gives an example of many
and one becoming the same. For on this view any sentence is of
some general form $P(a)$, and therefore can be accused either of
saying of one thing (e.g. man) that it is two or more (e.g. man and
good), or of saying that two things (man and good) are but one.
It is a paradox that might well delight the young, and certainly
would put an end to philosophical discussion. Further, it is possible
to see it as in some sense a good starting-point for tackling the
problem of 15b, as expounded by Hackforth. For that problem is
essentially: how *can* the one be many, and Plato may have thought
that the assumption behind this question is '"good" can be used of
good, but how can it be used of many particulars which are of a
different nature altogether from good, for they are subject to
change?' But as the *Sophist* shows, if we take that assumption
seriously no discourse is possible, not even the elaboration of the
paradox. Talk of participation has to be allowed if we are to allow
discourse at all. Such an argument may not elucidate the requisite
concept of participation, but it tackles the problem at least to the
extent of showing that the alternative to allowing participation is
silence.

There are four main difficulties with this interpretation. The first
is that it seems to suppose that Plato expects his reader to read the
Philebus with the *Sophist* open before him, and to know that that is
where to look for clues. It is no doubt possible to put this rendering
into 15d–e, but short of supposing the above, or inserting sections
of the *Sophist* into the *Philebus*, it is a good deal to expect of the

reader to get it out. This is aggravated by the second difficulty. On a first reading 15d–e describes in dramatic terms the turmoil produced by young men who delight in this paradox. At 16a Protarchus warns Socrates not to be rude about youth, but asks him nevertheless to save them from the upsets. The natural way of taking 'upsets' is as referring to the turmoil produced by the paradox-mongers. Socrates then proposes a means for doing this which, to be successful, should bear on the paradox viz. the one that assumes sentences to be calling one many. But no interpretation of the proposed method succeeds in doing this. Consequently 'upsets' has to be taken as referring back to the problems of 15b or earlier, to which the proposals of the Heavenly Tradition might be construed as relevant.

Quite apart from any awkwardness in throwing the reference so far back, this serves to isolate this passage from what follows, so that we cannot glean from there any support for the interpretation. Socrates has to be taken as side-stepping the problem and trying a quite new approach. This might be suggested by the wording of Protarchus' request at 16a8–b2–but as that could just as well be taken as asking for a better way than that followed by the paradox-mongers, it only counts as a possible interpretation, not as positive evidence.

A third difficulty is that the interpretation supposes that the identification of one and many is a consequence of a *false* theory (and one presumably, because of the *Sophist*, held by Plato to be false), whereas the text suggests (15d) that it is an acknowledged and important fact that can be abused.

The fourth difficulty is that while a case can be made out for this interpretation as giving a good way of starting tackling the problem of participation of forms by particulars, it seems to have no bearing on the main problem about pleasure. According to 18e, what follows, the Heavenly Tradition, is supposed to be relevant to that problem. So on this interpretation, as on Hackforth's, we have here a curiously irrelevant interlude heralded as vital to the issue in hand.

It would obviously be preferable if one could find an interpretation which left one with something like a developing discussion, as the wording of the text tends to suggest it is meant to be. If we take the third interpretation proposed for 15b (p. 114) we are saved one irrelevance. Can one, then, find a rendering of 15d–e that ties that in too with the main argument?

The sentences at 15d4–8 affirm that it is an inherent feature of our language that in what we say one and many become identified. The problem about pleasure was that talking of pleasure we seem to be talking of a single thing–pleasure seems to be a unit–but any pleasure must in fact be a particular form of pleasure. The predicate 'is a pleasure' treats indifferently the many forms of pleasure as the same. This fact, which Socrates considers inherent in language as a fact about predicates, is seized on by the young. It is at once possible for them to lump all pleasures together, treating them as a single class, and then insist on the differences between them. This allows for the generation of paradoxes to the effect that they are all the same but mutual opposites, or, if done on similarity, for the sophistry of 13d. All these involve taking pluralities as units, because our language inevitably treats them so.

The main advantages of this interpretation are as follows: (i) It saves us from supposing that Socrates has gone off at a tangent. He is still concerned with the same general problem. (ii) It would be more reasonable on Plato's part to expect the reader to see what this passage is about if we suppose it to be picking up earlier remarks and then not elaborating points because they have been indicated earlier. In that case he only has to expect his reader to read the dialogue in the order written and suppose it to be a reasonably competent argument. (iii) It gives a sense which enables one to take the suggestion of the text that the identification of one and many actually occurs, though the fact is abused by the young. On the previous interpretation it is only the young with their false view of predication who would think it occurred. (iv) If it actually occurs and is familiar, it is plausible to take it as a good starting-point. It will be a case of one and many that will not have to be rejected. (v) It allows Protarchus' remarks at 16a8–b2 to refer naturally to release from the sophistical paradoxes—though if so, the passage that follows has to be relevant to that request.

The main difficulties are:

(i) That 15d5 seems to say that every utterance involves this identification. It was an advantage of the last interpretation that immediately you proceed beyond naming and actually say something (*logos*) you are caught up in identifying one and many. Every *logos* is guilty. On the present interpretation it will be true of many statements, but what of 'Hume is Cleanthes'?

To this two replies might be made: (a) The objection is taking too seriously the expression 'in everything that is ever said'. By parity of argument one would have to interpret 16d1–6 equally strictly. But on any reading I have seen suggested the consequence would be that we could never find out how many were between the one and the indeterminate, since we are told that *every* unit we must divide, and we shall *always* be able to. Problems would also arise at 23c4–5 from similar strictness (cf. also 17d6–7 which presumably does not include the problems dismissed at 14d–e). One could not lay much weight on the 'every' unless it was clearly having to carry weight in the argument. If I have a pupil in despair because of a mistake I might comfort him by saying 'even the best philosophers are always making mistakes in everything they write'. Strictly, perhaps, it is not quite true of the best philosophers, but I should expect all but the worst to know what I meant. (b) A stronger defence would be to point out first, that there is no difficulty about statements attributing properties. For either the latter are like 'pleasure' or 'colour', or they are more specific, like 'scarlet'. But just as 'coloured' is only true of X if some shade belongs to X, so a shade belongs to X only if 'coloured' is true of it, and for the young sophist's purposes it makes no odds, the one and many have come together. The young sophist can force his victim to admit that if X is white it is coloured, but if coloured the same as Y, which is also coloured. But Y is coloured in virtue of being black and black is the opposite of white. In this way again a *logos*, not by assertion but by implication, identifies one and many. The kind of statement cited, an identity statement with names at either side of the identity, might look harder. But only because we suffer from prejudices about the difference between predicating and identifying. Arguably for Plato (cf. *Sophist* 252c2) the use of 'is' would be enough. For while in some sense there is one thing, identity, asserted in 'Hume is Cleanthes' and 'Berkeley is Philonous' they are different identities, or 'different parts of identity'. But now the door is wide open to a paradox-hunter to ask how two things (Hume, Berkeley) can be identical but different. In that it must attribute a specific form of a general 'character' or a general 'character' with varied forms every statement is implicitly treating a variety as unvaried.

(ii) It might seem that the style of interpretation advocated preserves relevance at the cost of keeping the argument at a standstill. The refrain seems to be: so he is saying the same thing yet again.

To answer this we have to look back over the discussion up to this point. The difficulty about multiformity in unity is introduced at 12c. The persistent refusal of Protarchus to accept it is meant to underline both the importance of the point, and the difficulty people have in accepting it. But while it is clear from the analogues of colour and figure, and the more generalized *reductio* at 13d, that the point has wider application than pleasure, the argument is at first all directed to that particular case, and when Protarchus is happy to accept the conclusion at 14a it is not because he has grasped either the point or its importance, a success he rarely seems to achieve, but for the debating reason that it is allowed to apply equally to knowledge, so it is not after all going to damage *his* position only.

Only at 14c are we told explicitly that this is an important point, an example of a wider class of difficulties raising important logical (or ontological) issues with wide bearing in philosophy. The type of problem is the same. The development is to put it in a wider context. The tactic is the old one of tackling an issue which arouses heat by fixing it in a wider class and making the points about other less provoking members of the class, where the argument will not be blurred by constant intrusion of *parti pris*.

On the other hand, while indication of the general problem might make the emotional involvement on pleasure seem parochial, the very breadth of the problem makes it daunting, so that by 15d we stand in need of a starting-point. Also, the characterization of the general problem, which is presumably supposed to be recognizable by the reader, is so put as to suggest that it is an open question whether the proposed units are genuine ones, and whether they could possibly admit of plurality in the required way. Also the way of describing the problem as arising from the scatter of the units among things in process would bring to mind central Platonic issues. This would serve well to underline the centrality of the problem, but would also emphasize its vastness.

At 15d, we are invited to make a start on the problem (the same problem) by recognizing a mingling of the one and many of the sort in question as a fact about language, and an inescapable fact. If this is admitted, one advantage is that it becomes clearly everyone's problem, and also not confined to pleasure. Further, the reminder of the futility of the logic-chopping play makes it clear that it is one we all need to solve. The man who rejects the possibility of one/many mingling at this level rejects language and so discussion. So this move might be hoped to put us in a co-operative rather than combative frame of mind and prepare us to look at how it in fact works in language. Of course such a discussion might lead to all sorts of more thorny questions of a metaphysical sort, but it might be hoped that some easing of the relevant one/many dispute might be achieved at this level, and it is, after all, at this level that we met it (cf. 12c6-8). Any other more rarefied ramifications need not concern us. On the other hand such ramifications are part of the same problem. Reflection on facts about language and argument in Plato's view brings to light certain presuppositions of these phenomena which led at one period, and perhaps all periods, of his life, to the postulation of what is usually called the Theory of Forms. The solution of problems that arise about the unity of Forms will be part of the solution of problems that have their starting-point in how we speak. But we may hope for sufficient agreement at an earlier stage of the problem.

Consequently, while the problem has remained the same, the approach to it has changed in a way that might be called progress. This seems to count in favour of the interpretation so far. The next question is whether the passage that follows can be seen as in any way helping with the difficulty it is supposed to meet. The same general interpretation can hold if we accept Badham's emendation which would make 15d4–5 read 'We say that the same thing becoming, as a result of argument/statements, one and many . . .' So this interpretation renders a change unnecessary, though I sympathize with Badham's feeling about the construction of the sentence (see note on 15d4).

THE HEAVENLY TRADITION, 16–19

This section has been the subject of many different interpretations. I can only hope to sketch the main types. As the method described is said (16c2–3) to have brought clarity to every *techne* (skill) it will be as well to start with a few points about this word. No English word quite catches '*techne*', at least at Plato uses it. The connotations of 'skill' are too much of clever performance, so that if one speaks of medicine as a skill one seems to be thinking of the practice of it—the skills of surgery or diagnosis. This leaves out the theoretical element so dear to Plato. On the other hand another popular translation, 'art', is far worse. If rumour got around that medicine was an art, general confidence in doctors would diminish. Not so, if it is a *techne*. In the *Gorgias* (462–5) Plato distinguishes *techne* from *empeiria*. Examples of the latter are skills such as cooking which aim at pleasing people. They fail to be *technai* because no general account can be (or at least is) given of what pleases people, and so there are no general canons for ensuring success. Medicine, by contrast, is supposed to operate with a universally applicable model of health. Calling medicine a *techne* is not calling special attention to its application—the whole theoretical aspect is underlined and its objective, non-relative character asserted. One might, then, try 'branch of knowledge' for '*techne*'. The objections are three. First, it is doubtful whether history or philately would count as *technai*. They are too much concerned with listing or interpreting facts, too little with production. Characteristically the possession of a *techne* gives one the ability to produce good states of affairs in the area covered by the *techne*. Secondly, while, significantly, *technai* are common illustrations of Plato's when he is discussing *episteme* (knowledge?), he tends to reserve the latter term for preferred disciplines such as mathematics and dialectic (though cf. 55 seq. of this dialogue). So even within the restrictions of the first objection it would be false to Plato's use to equate '*techne*' with 'branch of knowledge'. Thirdly, (cf. 55 seq.) *'techne'* can be quite naturally used of instances of skill where the performer has no knowledge of the principles involved, but does in a practical way know the right way of doing things. A person may be able to play the lyre—and there is a right way of doing this—without himself knowing anything of the theory of music. But 'branch of knowledge' is too academic in its connotations to cover such examples of know-how. *'Techne'*, then, tends to be reserved by Plato to cases where there are objective criteria for distinguishing between right and wrong ways of doing things, and there is, as in the examples of medicine or music, a theoretical account to be given of these criteria. For a given capacity to be described as possession of *techne*, however, it is not necessary for it to be a capacity to give the theory. The term can be used of a low level of skill in areas where objectivity and theory are in fact available, though a person who also possesses the theory has attained a higher degree of *techne*. Typical examples of *technai* are cobbling, generalship, carpentry, building, music, medicine, and knowing one's letters. According to 55e (and cf. *Republic* 522c, *Laws* 818) it is the extent of the use of mathematical techniques that makes a *techne* a worthwhile *techne*. One might expect progress in the *technai*, then, to be furthered by the furtherance of their mathematization. However that may be, the Heavenly Tradition is heralded as giving an account of how advance is achieved in the *technai* and it is obviously important to bear in mind what sorts of discipline are included under this heading, and how Plato typically thought of them.

The Heavenly Tradition passage itself falls into three main sections. There is the famous paragraph 16c–17a, where we are told that everything is made up of one and many, *peras* (determinant) and *apeirian* (indeterminacy) (for the translation of these terms see note on 16c10), and how we should try to discover some number between the one and the indeterminate. This is followed by some illustrations of what is meant (17b–18d). These are music and knowing one's letters. Then there is some reflection on the need to apply the points made to the examples of pleasure and knowledge— but that task is ducked when Socrates remembers hearing that neither is the good.

The whole passage has proved extremely recalcitrant to interpretation, and it might help to begin by listing some points that any interpretation should try to accommodate. I say 'try' advisedly. So far as I am aware there is no interpretation that avoids all difficulties. It becomes, therefore, a matter of trading difficulties. So objections have a way of being less than conclusive. Even if an interpretation involves Plato in an inconsistency it is not, after all, unknown for philosophers to be inconsistent or confused, and it is sometimes plausible to suppose that in specific ways they would be. In the end, therefore, the question is one of weighing the difficulties in various interpretations and assessing the likelihood of Plato being enmeshed in this problem or that. Granted this, some of the main points to be accommodated are the following:

1. The method is claimed to be of help with the important one/ many problems of 15a–b, and so with the problems about pleasure and knowledge of 12–14. (Cf. 17d6–7, 18d–19b).

2. The method is supposed to relieve us of the sophistic turmoil described in 15d–e.

3. The method brings clarity to the *technai* and so is held to help with those disciplines covered by that word (16c1–3).

4. It is a doctrine about either the things from time to time said to be, or about the things said always to be (16c9–10).

5. The method is to posit and search for a unit in each case (16d2).

6. The original unit is indeterminate, but one has also to know its number (16d5–7).

7. The plurality (*plethos*) can be described as indeterminate, but not until its number is known (16d7–e1).

8. Once the number is known each unit can be dismissed into the indeterminate (16e1–2).

9. Either knowing the number includes knowing the qualities of the things numbered, or this is additional knowledge required for expertise (17b6–9, d1, 19b3).

10. The indeterminate makes one inexpert (17e3–6).

11. The illustrations of 17b–18d are introduced as illuminating the doctrine of 16c–17a.

12. The illustrations all concern one 'thing': '*phone*' (vocal sound).

13. The doctrine expounded here is taken up and developed at 23 seq.

The first three points should be fairly clear. With 4 there is a problem of the reference of 'the things . . . to be'. With points 5–8 and 10 the problem is giving a satisfactory account, on any given interpretation, of the expressions cited. With 9 the problem is what exactly is involved in finding 'the number' between the unit and the indeterminate, and this runs into point 11 in that one of the problems there is how to fit the role of number in the illustrations to any account of 16c–17a. Point 12 will, I hope, become clear in the sequel. Point 13 should, again, be clear, even if not obviously true.

Roughly, interpretations fall into two classes. First, there are those who take 'the things from time to time said to be' to refer to everything in the universe, possibly taking 'from time to time said' to restrict the reference to those things vulgarly said to exist. Secondly, there are those who take it that universals are under discussion, a point that is ensured by the translation, 'the things said always to be', as this would presumably have to refer to Forms (see note on 16c9–10).

Interpretation 1 (cf. Jowett). If we take the reference of 'the things . . . to be' as widely as possible, then such a view will have to give an account of how Forms and souls and numbers are constituted of the determinant and indeterminate, as well as physical objects. In that case an account similar to Interpretation 2 could be offered with regard to Forms, and then the objections to that would hold. Further, 'indeterminate' will mean something different when used in the description of Forms from what it means in the description of objects, in which case, in addition to any problems concerning objects, there will be the difficulty of supposing (fairly obvious) ambiguity in a key term. A good deal will depend on the plausibility of interpreting the passage as at all concerned with the constitution of physical objects, so for the present I shall confine myself to that.

On such a view, then, the Heavenly Tradition would declare that every object is made up of one and many and has the determinant and indeterminacy as part of its make-up. It is made up of one and many in that, say, a given object belongs to one genus, but also to many sub-genera or species. Thus a Persian cat belongs to the genus animal, but is also a mammal, a member of the genus feline, and so on until we reach the *infima species* Persian cat. In this way, we can make sense of positing and searching for a unit (point 5): we posit and look for the *summum genus* under which our object falls. The next procedure of looking for two, or, if so be, three, is that of properly dividing the genus so as to be sure we have a proper sub-genus or species under which to put our specimen, and so on. There is a constant process of adding differentiae until we reach the *infima species*, and so each specimen is both one (by genus) and many (by differentiae). What, then, of the determinant and indeterminate? These can be thought of as an anticipation of Aristotle's views on Form and Matter. The indeterminate is the undetermined potentiality for manifesting certain properties. But objects are thought of as belonging to a given species, e.g. Persian cat, and 'Persian cat' is the name of a particular form of constitution. It is a particular balance of hardness and softness, heat and coolness, and so on that differentiates it within the range determined for the genus above, Cat. The relative proportions of these can be given mathematical expression and that mathematical expression defines the species. It is only at the level of *infimae species* that we reach precise numerical specifications. When this set of proportions is imposed on that wishwash of potentiality for varying temperatures and solidity that is matter, the result is a Persian cat. So any particular cat is made up of the indeterminate (matter) and the determinant (form). The definition of the *infima species* will give the proportions that have to be imposed and the matter on which they have to be imposed, and every individual falls under some *infima species* and thereby under some *summum genus*. Thus we get distinct points made by the references to one/many and determinant/indeterminacy. The first refers to the genus/species tree, the second to the fact that each individual is the result of an attempted imposition of some infima species form on some matter. Anything higher than an *infima species* gives ranges only of proportions and so not a form that can be imposed on the matter.

There are no doubt obscurities in such a thesis, but we have to remember that Plato lived before Aristotle, and there are signs in the *Timaeus* (possibly a good deal earlier, possibly about the same date) that Plato did toy with the possibility of conceiving of Place as an unformed wish-wash, waiting for structuring by a mathematically inclined Demiurge (cf. *Timaeus* 48 seq.).

If we now look back to our thirteen points (p. 155), the present interpretation would seem to fare moderately on 1 in that at least particular objects seem to be mentioned in 15a–b, and pose some problem, and their constitution, with special reference to Forms, is taken up here. On point 3, presumably understanding, say, the constitution of the human body would be a gain to medicine. How music fares is less clear. As to 4, a good sense seems to be given to 'the things . . . to be'. On 5, an account can be given of positing and searching for one *idea* (form) in the hunt for the *summum genus*. As to 13, there is an interpretation of 23 seq. which makes that passage precisely about the constitution of objects, so the present interpretation would preserve unity of doctrine between the two passages if that interpretation of 23 seq. is tenable. With 10, matter is the unknowable potentiality for knowable properties, and so the point where we have to resort to the description 'matter' is the point where our ignorance begins.

On 1, however, there is as much difficulty as ease. As I have already remarked, the important one/many problem should be one of how a single form has many forms while retaining its unity. On the present interpretation these problems might receive some solution by considering the one/many, genus/species relation. In the passage as a whole, however, it is the notions of number and indeterminate that play the major role. On the present interpretation that should mean that it is the constitution of individual objects that receives the main consideration, and so the problem solved would be that of how one form can be divided among many particulars. The answer presumably is that we take the model of a blueprint instantiated over and over again in different bits of matter. The point is, however, that whether or not this is a good solution it has no bearing on the one/many problem with which we started and to which we return at 18-19, supposedly having been enlightened in the interval.

On 2 it is obscure whether the sophistical play is such that this doctrine could help, but perhaps the first, one/many, part of it might be taken as a demonstration of how in fact the uniting of many species in a genus is harmless. Once again, the notions of number and the indeterminate seem to have no bearing.

On 6 there is an awkwardness. 'The original unit' (16d5) would most naturally be taken to refer to the one form (the *summum genus*), we found a line or two earlier. In that case it is left quite unexplained what it is to discover it to be indeterminate (have matter in it), let alone how we do it. Alternatively, 'the original unit' refers to the particular object, our Persian cat, say, with which we started, but this rather unexpected reference would be a little confusing since hitherto the only units explicitly mentioned as such have been forms.

On 7 we get a further awkwardness, in that now (16d7-e1) the possibility is envisaged of describing the *plurality* as indeterminate. The plurality must be the number of sub-forms discovered. If we take the first option on 6 this means that the passage is concentrating on universals and it becomes hard to discover where the account of the constitution of particular objects is to be found. If we take the second we get a confusing switch. We have just seen that the object is not only one and many and has indeterminate potentiality, we also know its number. We are now told not to attribute indeterminate potentiality to the many until we know its/their number. Since the many in question are genera and species it would be hard for a reader to know what he is being warned against doing. 'The indeterminate' can hardly here refer to a material principle.

All this is aggravated by 8. For now we are told (16e1-2) to let each unit of them all go into the indeterminate. The units, again, must be the genera and species—but what are we to do with them? Perhaps we are being encouraged to consider our Persian cat as a whole again, its genus and species characteristics embodied in the indeterminate, matter. Now that we understand our cat we need struggle no longer to keep its species characteristics abstracted. But in that case the reference of 'the indeterminate' has switched again from the previous sentence, whatever it was there, to what it was in the one before. Alternatively, it has not switched, and we are left with the problem of what the reference of 'the indeterminate' is and so of what we are being invited to do with each unit. If we accept the switching of reference, then we have to attribute to Plato two indeterminates, a material and an immaterial one. For this possibility see Proclus (*In Primum Euclidis Elementorum Librum Commentarii* Prologus I G1, B2 aeq.). The problem is not whether Plato could possibly have held such a view, but how anyone could be expected to pick it up from this passage except as a matter of desperate speculation.

Perhaps the most serious objection is on 11. For in the illustrations the notions of number and the indeterminate are very much to the fore. On the present interpretation this should mean that the illustrations deal with the constitution of individual objects. In fact nothing could be further from the truth. When Theuth notices (18b6 seq.) that *phone* is indeterminate it is not of a particular word or grunt that he has noted this fact, but of *phone* as a general phenomenon surrounding him on all sides in his daily life (and cf. 17b3–4). It is this same 'single thing' that a musician works on, discerning in '*it*' the high and the low and the scales. All this is absurd if taken to be about a particular noise. The absurdity is heightened when we reflect that 'the indeterminate' is used to refer to the fact that 'it' is indeterminately many (16b4), and Theuth observes the presence of vowels (not one, but several), and then consonants, in the indeterminate he first observed. If we take the illustrations as saying that the general phenomenon of vocal sound is indeterminately plural, i.e. there are noticeably many (sorts of) sounds, and Theuth discerned some order in the variety, then it makes good enough sense. But in that case the passage contains little or nothing on the constitution of objects. It might be possible to suggest that the unit with which we start is the (supposedly) single phenomenon, vocal sound, or pleasure. In that case the easiest way to interpret talk of its being indeterminate is as saying that it has an indeterminate variety of sub-forms. If we now cling to the position that the doctrine covers the constitution of individual objects also we are left with having to say that '*apeiron*' is used in two quite different ways. When used of pleasure it indicates the indeterminate variety of sub-forms plus instances. When used of any individual pleasure it indicates the indeterminate potentiality for taking that character which is here determined in that way. So we have to assume ambiguity in addition to the problem of finding any explicit discussion of the constitution of objects.

To sum up, this interpretation can cope quite well with points 3, 4, 5, 10 and 13 (see p. 155). It can do something with 1, though difficulties remain. On the rest it runs into trouble. The remaining difficulties on 1 and those on 2 and 11 seem a particularly heavy price to pay unless one has to, as they combine to make the passage a series of incompetent irrelevances which would involve either a reassessment of Plato's standing or a view about the onset of dotage. *Interpretation 2*. These problems make it attractive to turn to the second type of interpretation which has been the more usual (cf. Ross, Taylor, Hackforth, Gauss, Crombie, Wedberg, Gulley, Robin, Striker). According to this the passage is definitely concerned with universals (for the significance of the translation of 'the things . . . to be' see the note on 16c9). It is such things as pleasure, knowledge, good, man, that come from one and many and have *peras* and *apeirian* as parts of their natural constitution, and not individual objects at all. What we are being encouraged to do is recognize the fact of genus/species relationships whereby many varied species are unified into a single genus. Instead of hopping back and forth from a genus term to the indefinite number of particulars we should carefully map out the various kinds, the sub-species of every genus. In this way our knowledge is extended and we can pass beyond the sterile word-play of polemicists. The process, of course, has its limits. There comes a point when we reach an *infima species*. Beyond that are the indeterminate particulars. But between the single genus at the top and the indeterminate particulars at the bottom lies a determinate number of species and sub-species. It is a grasp of these that marks the difference between the dialectician and the sophist. Without it we might think that since Persian cats and okapis are both mammals they are alike. With it we can spell out the difference and similarities without perturbation.

Now '*apeiron*' does not, on this view, *mean* 'particulars'. It means 'indefinite' or 'undifferentiated' on one version, or 'unlimited' (in number) on another. On the first of these, pleasure may be said to be undifferentiated so long as we do not know its kinds. To work down to the *infimae species* is to find its (pleasure's) number. But we reach a point where no further specific differentiation is possible, viz. there are only particulars, whether these are thought of as always particular three-dimensional objects, or also as including particular colours, shapes etc. (cf. Striker, pp. 34–5). The word '*apeiron*' denotes particulars in virtue of the fact that they mark the end of specific differentiation, although they, like the species, fall under the genus (for Plato makes no sharp distinction between the relation of species to genus and that of member to species or genus).

On the second version the point is presumably that any genus has a finite number of species, but a (potentially) unlimited number of members. So genera and species are distinguished from their members by the possibility of determining their number once and for all. '*Apeiron*' denotes particulars in virtue of the fact that there is no limit to their number (cf. Aristotle *Metaphysics* B, 999a27 and *Posterior Analytics* 86a3–6 for similar uses of '*apeiron*').

Basically, then, the method is that illustrated, on one interpretation, in the *Sophist*, *Politicus*, and *Phaedrus*, with the emphasis
on division. The term '*apeiron*', which does not feature there, is
important here not because it adds anything to the account of the
method, but because it helps to pinpoint the sort of fallacy under
discussion. Plato thinks that by recognizing that there are kinds of
pleasure and knowledge and distinguishing them in a proper scientific manner we shall progress peaceably beyond the sterility of
Protarchus.

This type of view has been the favourite with commentators
despite individual differences. Further, it seems to do better than the
first interpretation on the thirteen points (p. 155). On 1, this view
makes the Heavenly Tradition directly concerned with division into
kinds, and that is just what Socrates wants to induce Protarchus to
accept at 12–13, as Protarchus sees by 18–19. So it is concerned
with the right kind of one/many problem.

On 2, it depends what the sophistic turmoil is, but if, as I have
suggested, Protarchus' early manoeuvres are of the sort in question,
then it might be hoped that if one patiently counted out the kinds
of pleasure one would be less tempted by what would increasingly
seem shallow word-play in contempt of the facts.

On 3 it might well have been thought that careful and thorough
classification would extend knowledge and so help any *techne*.

On 4 a reasonable interpretation is given of 16c9–10. On Striker's
translation, of course, the reference to universals is made obligatory.
On the other it has to be determined by the context of the discussion
(see note on 16c9–10).

On 6, the original unit, say pleasure, does not just have an
indefinite number of pleasures falling under (or within) it. A number
of intermediate determinations is possible. Once that is done one can
characterize each unit (sub-form) as indeterminate in virtue of the
particulars that fall under it (point 7) and then let each drop back
into the indeterminate plurality of pleasure (point 8). That is to say,
pleasure is indeterminate in virtue of the many things that fall under
it, both species and individuals. But part of the plurality is determinate. Once one has mapped out the determinate territory one can
safely return to the one-genus/indeterminate-number-of-members terminology, letting the intervening species disappear into the indeterminate number, because now one has been immunized against
Protarchus' mistake and can recover the intervening territory at need.

At 10, the particulars remain indeterminate, that is to say, they
mark the limit to classification and so scientific knowledge. All the
latter is exhausted at the level of *infimae species*. At the point where
no further specific differentiation is possible no further expertise is

possible, and so the *apeiron* makes one inexpert (17e3–6).

The view copes well, then, with points 1, 2, 3, 4, 6, 7, 8, and 13, though on 3 it is not so clear, if we remember what Plato usually includes under the heading '*techne*'. It would look better if Plato had more Aristotelian interests and models. It fits with pleasure and knowledge, man and ox, but not so well with beautiful and good (15a). Nor is it absolutely clear how successful it is on 1. For the one/many problem is not simply: how can there be many forms of one thing? That is felt as a problem because of an assumption that many things can be called by the same name only in virtue of some similarity, so that talk of variety of forms of *F*, especially 'opposing' forms of *F* seems to amount to talk of dissimilarities in similarity *F*. As remarked elsewhere, (see note on 12c6) the language of 12–13 reads like a conscious rejection of views held in the *Meno* and *Hippias Major*. But if one produced a definition of a genus, that would surely completely satisfy the early dialogue demand for a similarity? If all the Heavenly Tradition does is recommend classification by genus and species it looks as though it would amount to abandoning the earlier point to Protarchus, for the definition of pleasure would yield a point of similarity among pleasures qua pleasures.

More serious objections come on the other points. Thus, it is quite obscure (point 5) what positing and searching for the unit could amount to (16d2), for supposedly we start with it. This point is noted by Hackforth in considering Theuth. For Theuth is supposed to be an example of someone who starts not from a unit but from particulars, and works to a unit. But as Hackforth remarks, in taking all *these* particulars as the ones to study he has already taken them as falling under the single characterization '*phone*'. So he starts with his unit. The idea of hunting for it and finding it is quite bogus. The best one could suggest is that seeking for it is seeking to show that one's supposed unit properly is one and is not, say, like barbarian (cf. *Politicus* 262d)—but there is no sign of this in the text.

More serious is point 11. As Hackforth noted, the illustrations do not illustrate genus/species division. He writes (p. 24): 'In the example of musical sound the procedure is different. The terms 'high', 'low' and 'level' are not the names of species of sound, which can be further divided into sub-species: nor is sound here thought of as a genus . . . It will be realized that this second example . . . does not illustrate dialectic, and is of no direct relevance to that classification of pleasures and kinds of knowledge from which the present digression takes its departure.' The 'third' illustration also fails, on Hackforth's view. None of this disturbs his confidence, for he takes 17b1–10 as a first illustration, making it one by telling us what

Plato would have said if he had expanded it. As Plato does not expand it we have two elaborated illustrations, neither of which illustrates what Plato wants to illustrate, the first because it has nothing to do with genus and species, the second because it is supposed to illustrate working up to the genus from particulars through species, whereas in fact Theuth must be operating with a conception of the genus from the start. Hackforth feels that the illustrations serve notice that the terms *'peras'* and *'apeiron'* have more than just logical significance, and so prepare us for the later passage at 23 seq. This seems to be another way of saying that Plato wants to play fast and loose with some supposedly technical terms and is softening us up. But as the illustrations are supposed to enable us to understand what is said at 16c–e, the result must be confusion. It might be worth trying the hypothesis that it is Hackforth rather than Plato who is mistaken.

Nor can I see that Striker (pp. 26–30) is in much better case. She does, indeed, recognize Hackforth's difficulty, and clearly makes the point that the illustrations ought to be examples, not analogues, of what is described in 16c5 seq. In her view Plato is combating an objection to his theory of Forms, that it would be impossible consistently to allow plurality of the sort envisaged by the argument with Protarchus, and so the Forms, as Plato holds to them, cannot exist. The strategy is to take a unit which Plato considers to be a Form, but which, importantly, would by most people, even without acceptance of the theory of Forms, be admitted to be something which existed, and which can be shown to embody the kind of plurality to which the objector objects. Since he has to admit the existence of units with the objectionable kind of plurality he has to abandon that particular objection to the theory of Forms, and Plato has succeeded in showing that there are units (15b1–2) divided up in the paradoxical manner of 15b–c. There is confusion because on the face of it *'phone'* must mean either 'speech' or 'sound'. If we take 'speech' then the vowels and consonants are clearly not species of speech, but of letters. If we take 'sound', then it is clearly not what Theuth was investigating: the phenomenon he attends to is obviously the narrower one of speech. This difficulty is met if we recognize a general fact about Plato, that he does not distinguish between the use of a term, say 'Change' or 'the Beautiful', to refer to the defining characteristic of a class and the use of the same term to denote the class. There are various things we might refer to by the expression 'kinds of speech': dialects, different languages, different manners of speech, but never vowels or consonants. But Plato is using 'speech' to refer to the defining characteristic of the class he wishes to discuss (the class of speech-sounds) as well as to the class, and here vowels and consonants look better candidates for the status of species. If we remember this terminological weakness of Plato's the letters example becomes appropriate after all—though the sense in which Theuth does not start with a unit remains obscure. The musical example does, however, remain recalcitrant, and we are told that that is added to show the wider applications of the point.

There are six main difficulties with this. The first is that while letters come first, no elaboration is given of that example until we have had the less appropriate illustration of music. Only then, when we have presumably been unillumined about genus and species, do we get the illumination of the letters example. So we have to accuse Plato of bad exposition. Secondly, if music is not an example of genus/species division, then it cannot be an example of the possible wider application of the point if the point is about division into genus and species. It could only be an example of the application of a wider point, of which genus/species division was just one possible example. In that case we have a choice: either 16c–17a describes genus/species division, and the musical example is inappropriate, or else 16c–17a describes something much broader, in which case there is no need to hunt for the example of genus/species division either there or in the illustrations. Even if we take the first it has presumably to be admitted that *Plato thought* the musical example appropriate and so must have been so confused on the matter of genus and species as to raise the question of whether one is at all justified in attributing to him so precise an interest. Thirdly there is point 9, the question of number. On a genus/species account, the finding of a number is finding the number of species, but very clearly in the musical example, at least, finding the number is finding mathematical expression for acceptable relationships between notes and relationships between acceptable notes. Finding the qualities of the notes is presumably finding which will combine with which, and that is finding out what combinations are admitted in the various modes, or, in modern musical theory, keys. Even with letters, the process is not to list kinds of sound, or not only, but, more important, to establish certain ones as elements whose powers of combination with other elements can be expounded so as to make the formation of words intelligible and show it to be systematic. To this whole picture of what is established between the unit and the indeterminate the study of animals, ending with such *infimae species* as Persian cat or common shrew, hardly supplies even an analogue. Fourthly (point 5), Theuth does in fact seem to come up with a unit, in that he calls all the letters elements, but the unit is not the genus *phone*. One might translate *'stoicheion'* as 'letter', in which case perhaps Theuth does reach a genus, if vowels and consonants are species of letter.

More probably it should be translated 'element', in which case, while consonants may be a sub-class of the class of elements of speech-sound, they are not species of the genus 'element', for this word covers notes for music, units for arithmetic, atoms, perhaps, for physics, and so on. Yet the establishing of elements does seem closely bound up with discovering a unit—but of this more later. Fifthly, it is difficult to find an interpretation of 23 seq. such that the role of 'peras' and 'apeiron' there (see General Commentary: The Determinant and Indeterminate) is at all like that in the present passage on this interpretation, so that recalling this passage at 23b–c can only cause confusion. Finally, it is worth noting that both illustrations concern phone (point 12), which is apparently both a unit and an indefinite plurality (17b–c), and (see note on 17c1–2) Plato seems to realize that each techne concerns the same thing. In that case he must think that each techne deals with different species of the same genus, but neither with all, and this would involve even greater confusion on genus and species, to say nothing of the difficulty of interpreting 16d8 where the techne-helping procedure encourages us not to stop until we have the whole number. This must now mean not stopping until we have every techne relevant to a phenomenon.

Thus while this interpretation does well on points 1, 2, 3, 4, 6, 7, 8, and 13 it meets substantial difficulties on points 5, 9, 10, 11 and 12. Further, the examples of beautiful and good at 15a–b do not fit the genus/species picture so well as one would like, so that it is less than perfection on point 1. So while this view does seem to fit the text less awkwardly than the previous one, it is still sufficiently awkward to make one wonder whether more sense could not be made of what we have with less, or less obvious, confusion attributed to Plato. In particular, as it seems that there are difficulties in attributing to Plato any clear grasp of genus/species division even on Striker's ingenious interpretation, it might be worthwhile trying a different version of the relation of one to many.

Interpretation 3. I propose to approach this by considering two points not yet alluded to, one of which at least is not, it must be admitted, more than highly probable. The first is that the terminology of *peras* and *apeiron* is characteristically Pythagorean. Both appear on the traditional table of opposites and were important opposed first principles in Pythagorean theory. It is hard to resist the conclusion that the Prometheus referred to at 16c6 is Pythagoras, as a tradition holding everything to be made up of one and many and to have *peras* and *apeiron* inherent in it (two important and familiar Pythagorean pairs of opposites) would almost certainly be taken to be Pythagorean. This is strengthened by the stress laid on number, which again would have obvious Pythagorean echoes. This stress recurs, in explicit association with *peras*, in the passage at 23 seq. (see especially 25a–b) and there *apeiron* receives the traditional Pythagorean characterization as that without beginning middle or end (31a9–10).

Now the Pythagoreans (i.e. those called Pythagoreans by Plato, whatever their relation to Pythagoras) approached cosmology from a mathematical angle and made considerable contributions to mathematics. A mathematician might dismiss their cosmology, but he would have to take account of their mathematical researches, and any Pythagorean Prometheus could be expected to hand down some mathematical gift to later generations. This is even more to be expected if the gift is to help with every *techne* and is approved by Plato since, as we have seen, Plato considers mathematics to be the bone structure of any *techne*.

The second point is that it is highly probable that in the *Philebus* we have Plato's reaction to the repercussions of Eudoxus. Eudoxus was a very distinguished mathematician who as a young man studied under Plato and some time in the early 360s transferred his own school to Athens. Diogenes Laertius gives the life of Eudoxus at the end of his series of distinguished Pythagoreans (*Vitae Philosophorum* Book VIII), and he is generally reputed to have worked with the famous Pythagorean Archytas. But he did not confine himself to mathematics. According to Aristotle (*Nicomachean Ethics* 1172b9 seq.) he taught that pleasure is the good on the ground that everything, possessed of reason or not, can be seen to pursue it, and what everything pursues must be the good. *Philebus* 11b, 60a, 67b clearly suggest a thesis based similarly on what everything pursues. Further, Aristotle attributes to Eudoxus an argument that pleasure, added to anything, makes it preferable, and comments that at best this shows it to be *a* good, not the good, since any good is preferable in conjunction with another good than on its own. He then goes on: 'In fact Plato also uses this sort of argument to show that pleasure is not the good.' This is clearly a reference to 20 seq. of the *Philebus*, and while the inference is not obligatory, it seems likely that Aristotle is thinking of a known dispute where Plato turns Eudoxus' argument against him. For the argument for the combined life is that if you add intelligence to a life of pleasure the result is preferable. Eudoxus' argument is allowed in pleasure's favour so far as human life is concerned, but as the same argument can be used in favour of intelligence, the result is, as Aristotle says, that neither is *the* good. So Eudoxus' principle is used to yield a preferred test for the good life by reference to perfection, adequacy, and chooseability. This last, again, looks like an echo of another principle attributed to

Eudoxus by Aristotle, that that is good which everything pursues. It looks as though Plato is trying to convince us (see General Commentary: Victory to the Mixed Life, pp. 181 seq. and note on 12c6) first that there is more to what some beings pursue than just pleasure, and secondly, perhaps, that this more is what anything would want if it were capable of it. This again seems to be an attempt to use Eudoxus' principle against him and in a way that enables Plato to reject the appeal to the pursuits of the 'lower' animals. The whole reads as tailored to Eudoxus' position, and one gets the impression that Aristotle is recording Plato's reaction to Eudoxus. This becomes more likely when we remember that Eudoxus was an old pupil of Plato's and taught in the same city. Again according to Aristotle, his views were believed because of his general sobriety. In other words, the thesis was commonly interpreted as in favour of sybaritic pleasures and Eudoxus was believed because his sobriety showed him to be free of the charge of *parti pris*. So not only is Eudoxus a distinguished opponent whose views would be considered in the Academy, but his thesis gets interpreted in a vulgarly hedonistic way which would make it important in public moral debate (for further points see the Epilogue to General Commentary). It is therefore highly probable that the *Philebus* is a response to Eudoxus and the repercussions of Eudoxus.

Now Pythagoras and Eudoxus are not two unrelated phenomena. As noted, Eudoxus had Pythagorean connections. Further, one problem that the Pythagoreans unearthed and that much exercised mathematicians in the first half of the fourth century B.C. was the problem of irrationals, and this was a problem which much exercised Eudoxus and in dealing with which he won much of his well-deserved fame. The Greeks tended to think of mathematics primarily in terms of geometry. Many problems that we think of as arithmetical can be posed and solved in geometrical terms and this is how the Greeks tended to do it. Thus the problem of solving the equation $x^2 = 9$ has an equivalent geometrical problem of what length sides a square has whose area is nine square units. But for the Pythagoreans and early Plato 'numbers' meant 'rational numbers', that is numbers expressible as ratios between integers, and so the length given in the answer, to be numerically expressible, must be expressible in rational numbers. Suppose, then, we have a rectangle of 9 square units. The proportion 1:9 determines a given proportion of figure, viz.

$$1 \quad \begin{array}{c} B \rule[0.5ex]{4em}{0.1pt} C \\[-0.3em] A \quad 9 \quad D \end{array}$$

The problem set is: what length of side must a square have to produce a figure of identical area. Clearly a square on the shorter side is too small, one on the longer side too large. If we represent the two lengths on a single line, thus

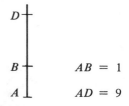

where AB is one unit, AD 9 units long, then clearly the required length must terminate at some point between B and D. In this case the problem is soluble in the system of rational numbers and the length of the required line is three units, or, arithmetically: if $x^2 = 9$, then $x = 3$. But if '8' is substituted for '9' in the above problem the equation is not soluble in rational numbers. So it ought not to be possible to construct a square of equal area to an oblong of sides 1:8. Yet on crude intuition it seems we must be able to. After all, on the following diagram

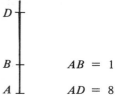

the problem is the same as previously. A square on AB is too small, one on AD too large, but if one either keeps extending AB or shortening AD each successive square must approach in area the area of the original oblong, until, surely, we shall arrive at the required point. But while we know that the length, let us call it AX, must be such that $AD > AX > AB$, any length expressible in rational numbers turns out to be either too large or too small. Methods were devised for refining on the limits (*perata*) within which the point fell, but refinement from above or below could go on indefinitely (*eis apeiron*) or *ad infinitum* without anything more than increasing approximation being achieved. The degree of excess or defect is progressively reduced, but some degree always remains.

The results of this can be variously put. Thus, in terms of rational numbers it is not possible to give the relationship between the required length and any other length: there is no length that it is either double or half. Again the discovery that $x^2 = 8$ cannot be solved in rational numbers is equivalent to the discovery that there is no common measure such that AB, AC, and AX can all be described as of so many units of that measure—the lengths are not commensurable (*symmetra*). Again, it does not seem possible, either, to say that

168

AX is equal to anything, for it is natural, especially if one starts from rational numbers, to think of equals as those things that have the same number of measures, whereas *AX* turns out to have no number of the relevant measures. So equality and the irrational are at loggerheads. Thus we get equality, double, commensurability (*symmetria*), measure, proportion ('*logos*' means 'proportion' as well as 'reason') on one side, and resistance to these things, *asymmetria*, the *aloga* (one word for irrationals) on the other. The first set are bound up with the possibility of mathematics and rational progress, the latter with its limits. Further, the discovery of irrationals was the discovery that a continuum can be divided *ad infinitum* (*eis apeiron*), that is that there is no length in terms of which to measure all divisions of a continuum, and so '*apeiron*' becomes associated with irrationals and the continuum.

This set of contrasts: *peras*, number, equality, double, proportion, measure, etc. on one side, and *apeiron*, lack of proportion or measure, etc. on the other, runs through the *Philebus* treatment of *peras* and *apeiron* and makes it highly likely that Plato has in mind these mathematical problems which exercised the Pythagoreans and also the man who was probably responsible for provoking the *Philebus*, Eudoxus.

The question, then, is: how could Eudoxus' interest in irrationals have any connection with his hedonistic tenets, or how could Plato think it had? To approach this we might first turn to the Heavenly Tradition and ask how remembering disputes about irrationals might help understand the gift from the gods that is supposed to help with every *techne*. The first illustration that receives any detailed treatment, the musical one, is of a *techne* that was a major Pythagorean interest. (There is some evidence that the Pythagorean Archytas thought grammar came under music (cf. Quintilian *Instit. Orat.* I. x. 17), and Eudoxus worked with Archytas. So it is likely that both *technai* selected are particularly appropriate.) What the Pythagoreans discovered was that if one takes a lyre string and stops it at the half way point by a bridge, either half length of the string will give a note an octave higher. So the interval between a given note and one an octave higher can be represented in terms of the ratio between the lengths of the string for each note i.e. 2:1. Now all the notes on the scale can be similarly represented in terms of various ratios, and in geometrical terms the representation takes the form of proportions between sub-lengths of a line. A scale, then, could be represented as a line with a series of points marked on it, the various lengths being expressible in rational numbers and the intervals as ratios between them. Once represented this way, however, certain things stand out as obvious. First, most points on the line are not marked. This represents the fact that for a given note there are endless possible further sound-pitches which bear no musical relationship to that note, that is do not fall at a point whose relationship can be expressed by one of the ratios permitted by the representation of the scale. They are therefore not concordant and, as falling above or below every permissible point, are either too high or too low. Secondly, complete systematization of sounds in this way is impossible. For any given one, further refinements also expressible in terms of rational numbers are possible. Thus classical Western musical theory does not allow of quarter-tones, but they could be accommodated in the geometrical representation without abandoning rational numbers. The continuum, however, is infinitely divisible, and that is another way of saying that there are points that will fall outside every such refinement.

If, with Plato, we think of the Pythagoreans as advancing the *techne* of music, and consider that advancing a *techne* is increasing the role of mathematics in it, then, using Pythagorean terminology, we might describe the process as follows. At first vocal sound strikes one as a single thing, but also indeterminate, allowing of infinite possibilities of sub-division. A person who has only got this far is no musician. A musician will first note that sound can be high or low. This can be represented by a line

High |

Low |

Next he will note that there are relationships between concordant notes expressible as ratios between lengths on such a line. He has now passed beyond realizing that he has sound and that it constitutes a continuum. He has a major division in his continuum, and then further mathematically related sub-divisions. It is the discovery of this that makes the expert. The *apeiron* as such does not yield expertise, but only the 'number' does that. Yet the line remains and is irretrievably *apeiron*, admitting of infinite division, and so remaining in the last resort indeterminate. The point where the line remains undetermined is the point where musical theory stops, where expertise is not possible. Expertise is limited to the determinate points.

None of this, of course, is an interest in the ordinary concept of '*phone*'. Musicians are treating the phenomenon of *phone*, vocal sound, as the subject of the single skill of music. (Music and song are at this period inseparable.) This is that phenomenon considered as varying in pitch (also, of course, tempo—see 26a—but that aspect is not explored here). It constitutes a single object of skill, but also admits of infinite division. Expertise consists in discovering the mathematically expressible relationships between concordant notes. The discovery is that actual noises are either related as required by musical theory, or one or more can be criticized as falling on the indeterminate part of the line. The phenomenon of vocal sound shows both the indeterminate variety that makes the linear representation appropriate, and also capacity for proportionately related sounds so as to make musical theory applicable. So the phenomenon shows *apeirian*, and yet there is 'number' to be found so that proper relationships can be described and discerned, and musical expertise is possible. This expertise involves a geometrical representation of the continuum, the *apeiron*, and we can see expertise as a matter of discovering relationships between a finite number of elements which are represented as selected points from among an infinite set of possible ones. This Pythagorean picture of a *techne* and its relation to a Pythagorean problem about the *apeiron* and irrationals would be familiar to Eudoxus.

If we turn to Theuth we find that he takes the phenomenon of vocal sound, and notes that it is not just indeterminate but can be distinguished in terms of what can be spoken alone, what cannot be spoken alone, and that half-way house, the semi-vowels. This again seems to invite linear representation, and what Theuth does is to see that there are main points on the continuum, and that permissible combinations can be expressed as relations between these points. There are many sounds which, from the point of view of knowing one's letters, are simply not represented, but fall somewhere on the *apeiron*. The discovery of the alphabet-system is the discovery that the vocal-sound phenomenon allows of systematization into elements such that permissible sound combinations are represented by combinations of elements, while many kinds of sound receive no representation.

There is a problem in the letter example about how far the geometrical model can be taken. I shall return to this later, merely remarking for the moment that Plato does not give up the number terminology which has received its first elucidation in the music example. Leaving that aside, the Theuth example does seem to give some idea of what hunting for a unit might be. For Theuth finally gives the letters the name 'element'. But elements are the basic units for explaining a subject-matter. In other words he realized (18c7 seq.) that the letters could not be learned independently. As a set they constitute the elements, and knowledge of elements is knowledge of their mutual interconnections in explaining permissible sound-combinations. The letter C can be recognized, but knowing it is knowing that it is a consonant, not a vowel, and the kind of consonant it is, and so on. But none of this can be known without knowing about the other letters and their powers. Theuth considered this mutual need for intelligibility a single bond that made the elements one i.e. a unified set (18c–d). In music the same would hold of the elements there, the notes, and similarly, presumably for other *technai*. So in each case the discovery of elements that have this particular bond with regard to their knowability is the discovery that they constitute a unit, and at the same time that there is a single *techne*. So Theuth might well start with a concept of *phone*, but he only discovers that, in the respect in which he is considering it, it is not only *apeiron* but a unit, by discovering a way of systematizing it in that respect, and that is a matter of discovering elements united by an intelligibility bond, and so showing that there is a relevant *techne*. In the case of music, because a man starts with the fact that music is a *techne*, he starts with it given that there is a unit in *phone*, though how it is one has still to be discovered. But if we think of someone starting simply with *phone*, then he has first either to look for a *techne* concerned with *phone*, or try to devise one. In either case he supposes there is and looks for a unit in the thing said to be—in this case *phone*. So we consider the phenomenon *phone*, which we consider to be something, we take the doctrine that it is one, many, and has *peras* and *apeirian*. So: we posit that *phone* is a unit. This is not supposing it to be a genus, or a phenomenon describable by the term '*phone*', but supposing that it can be unified by a *techne* and we have to search for a way. There may well be more than one, and Plato gives two. The search may be concluded by finding a *techne* already developed, e.g. music, in which case we can start from the musical way of unifying sound. Or we may be like Theuth and suspect there is a way of doing it, in which case we suppose there is a unit and devise a way of unifying sound. It is sound that we assume to be a unit. On either way of unifying it it remains an indeterminate, but by showing that either notes or letters constitute a unit we show *phone* to be a unit as well, a single object of a *techne*. But, of course, what are elements, and so among the many things numbered by one *techne*, do not enter the other at all. Consonants have no part in music nor B flat in grammar.

If we now consider those of our thirteen points (p. 155) that concern simply the passage of the Heavenly Tradition, how does this line of interpretation fare? With regard to point 3, if we remember typical Platonic examples of *techne* and Plato's prejudice in favour of those using mathematics, the Pythagorean example of music and its proposed treatment fits very well. On 4, the things said to be are neither observable particulars, nor Forms, but phenomena such as vocal sound, pleasure, considered as manifold phenomena in our experience, susceptible of general study. This reference has to be secured by context (see note on 16c9). On point 5, we have just seen that searching for a unit is very much connected with *techne*. The advice is, in effect, always to look for a *techne*, whether this is one already to hand or one that, like Theuth, we must establish. It has nothing to do with either defining *'phone'* or finding genera and species. The same phenomenon, *phone* yields at least two units as there are at least two *technai* concerned with it. Thus point 12 is accommodated. When we know the elements of music, the notes, we have a *techne* of sound in respect of relative pitch, and the *techne* shows sound to form a unit in respect of relative pitch. But sound in that respect is also *apeiron*. For *techne* one has to grasp the proportions of the points on the continuum which constitute it as a unit as well as *apeiron* (point 6). When we have reached that point we can safely characterize the plurality of sounds as indeterminate/a continuum, but only when we have its complete number, i.e., in the case of music, all the points representing notes and the ratios between them (point 7). Then each unit (each point) can be allowed to relapse into the continuum. That is to say, we can now safely declare them to be on the continuum and to belong to it. Safely, in that in doing so we are not *just* declaring *phone* to be *apeiron*, we have the divisions of the line which are its number. But they are divisions of a line. So an interpretation can be given to 16e1–2 (point 8). On the Pythagorean theory of music, the ratios discovered are those that hold between concordant sounds. If we take a simplified illustration from very elementary musical theory, there is a particular progression of notes in terms of tones and semitones defining a major scale, so that if we wish to determine the notes in C Major we can read off the notes that fit together in that key. We thus discover the qualities of certain notes, that they do or do not fit into C Major, and so will be concordant in a piece of that key. So knowing the number is related to knowing the qualities of the elements (point 9). We have already seen that the indeterminate as such is that of which no final *logos* can be given. Expertise and the *apeiron* do not mix (point 10).

The question remains whether point 11 can be met, that the illustrations should illustrate the doctrine of 16c–17a. In part this has been answered in giving interpretations for points 5–9. It is worth recalling, however, a point made at the end of the discussion of the second type of interpretation, that even if we try a genus/ species version of 16c–17a we have to declare Plato confused on the subject. In fact the Pythagorean-sounding introduction of the Heavenly Tradition makes it unlikely that a Greek would or would be expected to pick up the use of '*peras*' and '*apeiron*' required for that interpretation. But apart from that, Plato makes Protarchus at 17a6–7 claim only partial understanding and ask for further illumination. Now we may admit that some commentators are more intelligent than Protarchus, but the point is that Plato presumably puts this into Protarchus' mouth so as to give himself the opportunity to clarify what is not so clear as to need nothing more. Indeed, when one reads 16c–17a, while one can read genus/species into it, that is what has to be done. As it stands there is just a general picture of proceeding from one through a number, with a Pythagorean notion of *apeiron* intruding. If that were all, the genus/species interpretation would be an intelligent speculation as to what is being said, but no more. If the illustrations are to help, then, as we have seen, trouble starts for that interpretation. The present interpretation has started from the illustrations. If we take the music example, then it all fits well enough to 16c–17a. We start with the music *techne* which assures us of a unit in *phone*. We divide it into high and low and continue until we have the complete set of ratios and then we characterise it as *apeiron* and so on. 16c–17a gives a general sketch description which fits the illustration perfectly well so long as we are free of the genus/species straitjacket. The problem comes with Theuth, but it is a problem common to all interpretations, that Theuth reverses the process described at 16c–17a. The proposed solution is therefore also available to all: that 16c–17a gives a sketch which concentrates on the order of exposition. If Theuth is successful he will expound his discovery starting: 'Sound can be studied via a set of sounds that can be distinguished into vowels, semi-vowels and consonants; the vowels are, a, e, i, o, u', and so on. The difference is in the order of discovery—though even Theuth posits a unit and searches for it.

The interpretation, then, fits well all the points internal to the Heavenly Tradition, that is points 3, 4, 5, 6, 7, 8, 9, 10, 11, and 12. As to the relation to 23 seq. (point 13), that will have to wait discussion of that section, but for what it is worth, one expects '*peras*' and '*apeiron*' to have Pythagorean roles from 16c, and they are receiving Pythagorean descriptions in 23 seq. That leaves points 1 and 2, and it is here that the most obvious objections arise.

To take point 2 first: if I am right, the sophistical turmoils referred to at 15d–e trade on the supposition that if the same predicate can be applied to two subjects, those subjects are alike, while relying on the facts of language which enable one to say that black, white, etc. are all colours and so the same while opposed, and so many. The latter fact seems paradoxical because of the assumption. But once this is recognized, the Heavenly Tradition is obviously apt and pointedly ends with the Theuth example where it is underlined that if we examine *technai* we shall see that the justification for taking *phone* as a unit is that for putting elements into a single class: not that they are alike but that they have a Theuthian bond. A reader put into a Pythagorean mood at 16c will expect that this makes possible the putting of opposites into a single category, as *techne* involves the blending of opposites. It is therefore characteristic of intellectually respectable disciplines not to rely on similarity as the basis of treating their subject-matter as one thing, and indeed the elements cannot be known/defined in isolation but only as parts of a system, which presumably underlines the absence of similarity. So the assumption underlying the sophistic turmoil and also Protarchus' original resistance to Socrates is undermined by examining the basis for putting things in a single class that actually operates in areas of intellectual repute. It is all particularly apt as a *techne* characteristically unifies *opposites* (cf. 12–13 where opposition is causing the problem). So point 2 is accommodated.

This leaves point 1. Here there might be two objections. First, how does this view accommodate the examples of man, ox? Secondly, how does it apply to pleasure and knowledge? As to the first, one might start with a defensive point. Good and Beautiful (fine) might be accommodated into the general picture in that it is possible to consider every *techne* as concerned with what is good or fine in its area. True, the illustrations do not deal with these items, but that is a brute fact about all the units mentioned at 15a–b. It might still be that the best hope with any such unit is to observe the *technai.* Remarks to the effect that every one and many must be dealt with this way may be Platonic extravagance if this way always involves a number between one and *apeiron* (but see below, pp. 202 seq.). Good, like harmony, measure, and so on, may not be indeterminate, though understanding of them all is gained by considering the *technai* into which they enter, and to which *apeiron* will also be related. At least these fit no worse than with a genus/species account. As to man, ox, the discovery of a *techne* will be the discovery that there are respects in which these items vary indeterminately, ways capable of linear representation, and a *techne,* e.g. medicine, is devised with regard to them when a means is discovered of 'unifying' respects of variation so as to produce certain points of temperature, weight, and so on which should not be exceeded. The elements of medicine would be temperature and weight points, say, for various parts of the body or stages of its development. It is no objection that this involves more than one *apeiron.* As remarked above (and cf.

17d) a musician will also have expertise on tempo, and this was well recognized in Greek musical theory. So either a note is, as an element, to be thought of not just as a point of pitch but also a time-value, or there is more than one set of elements. Plato only says enough in the musical illustration to get the general point across. He is not writing a musical treatise but supposing his readers to be sufficiently familiar with the theory. There is no obvious block to supposing he thought the same applied to medicine. The difference between this interpretation and the previous one on Man and Ox is that there there would be one way of dealing with them. On the present interpretation, there could be various skills to do with men (e.g. medicine, statesmanship in Plato's view), and they would not be helped particularly by genus/species division but would be concerned to work out the relevant proper forms of combination of elements of the skill.

So on this point this interpretation fares no worse than others, though the fit is less than perfect. The major objection comes from the other, which also is one main source of support for the genus/species interpretation. For it is natural to feel that what Socrates wants Protarchus to see is that there are *kinds* of pleasure and knowledge. This would be appropriate. On the present interpretation, however, we have to suppose Plato interested in *technai* of pleasure and knowledge, which is implausible. Yet only in this way can Eudoxus' interest in irrationals be related to his doctrine on pleasure.

To begin with, in answer to this, it is worth remarking that the kind of variety in which Socrates is most interested at 12–13 is opposition, and the examples he gives with regard to pleasure are not obviously species. Secondly, Protarchus is defending a thesis that pleasure is the good. It is defended in a way that suggests that pleasure can be used to determine how to organize one's life and in whose production one could be skilled. Once doubt is thrown on the similarity thesis it becomes a good question how you have *one thing* to be skilled about. The Heavenly Tradition makes it clear that this sort of dissimilarity and multiplicity is no bar to a skill, but anyone holding that pleasure is the good would have to expound the pleasure-skill. Knowing about pleasure is going to be the important thing after all. This serves to prepare us for the view that the good life needs not only pleasure but knowledge. Also, however, there is, by the *phone* example, opened up the possibility of various skills concerning pleasure. We might be able to 'unify' pleasure in terms of intensity (44 seq.) and duration, or in terms of unadulterated pleasure (53), or certain points on the unadulterated-cum-duration continua might be determined by considerations to do with knowledge. However it is to be done we should no longer be held up by

Protarchus' objections, and perhaps this is just what Socrates thinks Protarchus should be telling us, just as a musician is expected to produce an account of the rules for combining notes, so Protarchus should tell us how pleasures are to be combined and so how we are to consider it a single thing. Similarly, of course, with Intelligence. There are, according to 55c seq., varying degrees in the capacity of an *episteme* (knowledge) or *techne* to yield accurate results and also degrees of usefulness. There will also be questions of duration of exercise of various capacities and so on. Once it is recognized that 'Intelligence' covers a variety of capacities and activities Socrates, too, will have to produce the relevant *techne*.

It should be remembered, in all this, that Socrates never does what is in this section declared necessary, because at 20 seq. he secures agreement that neither pleasure nor intelligence is the good. In this respect all interpretations are in the same boat, and it would in each case be possible and true to say that we just do not know how Plato thought the Heavenly Tradition applied to the initial problem. The above has, in fact, been a defensive argument against an objection that on the proposed interpretation it could not conceivably be relevant. In fact it could, and so this part of point 1 constitutes no objection.

It remains that this interpretation is less than perfect on this point and has to be tested on point 13. On point 2 it does at least as well as its nearest rival, and otherwise accommodates more difficulties than the others. If Plato has Eudoxus in view it has an added advantage. For Plato would then seem to have noted that Eudoxus' thesis involves a simple-minded view of pleasure; and that once this is recognized a Eudoxan can be invited to reflect on how *technai* are developed. This can readily be done by Pythagorean examples which use a geometrical representation, i.e. use the notion of a continuum, which would be apt for Eudoxus as this recalls the area of his investigations. Further, implicit in the Heavenly Tradition is the importance of intellectual activity in devising a skill, and the importance skill would have for a hedonist once he had abandoned a simplistic view of pleasure. This prepares the way for 20 seq., and also, indeed, for the role of Intelligence in 23 seq.

One last point before I return to the example of letters. In some respects this view can sound close to the first interpretation in that it can seem that particular healthy bodies, say, must be made up of *peras* and *apeiron*. But the present interpretation makes the passage primarily about *technai*. It is only derivatively about their products. In so far as it is about them '*apeiron*' does not indicate an element in their constitution. In the first instance '*apeiron*' indicates a continuum used in a *techne* on which, in the account of the *techne*, points are plotted. In so far as the *techne* is being used to produce or criticize e.g. a tune, *it* (the tune) will, in virtue of its measurements (pitch, tempo) be able to be plotted onto the continuum. If some of its constituents have to be plotted on the undetermined part, they will go down as *apeira*, and the whole tune will also either go down as *apeiron* in that it does not correspond to what is allowed, or will count as *apeiron* to the extent that this is true. Nothing allows us to judge which. In the present passage nothing is in fact said about individual noises being *apeira*. What is *apeiron* is some 'unit' like pleasure or *phone*. But it is a result of the interpretation that individual products will be assessable in the terms of the *techne* in a way that would make the above natural. Nor would it involve ambiguity in '*apeiron*' only in 'is an *apeiron*'. For the present, however, it is enough to note that nothing is said about the constitution of individual objects.

As was noted earlier, the letter example seems to be an odd man out on this interpretation, and this deserves a few words. To begin with, whatever the difficulty in it, it does seem that Plato held that advance in a *techne* went hand in hand with the greater use of precise mathematical techniques in it, and this view is not peculiar to the *Philebus* (see pp. 154 seq. above). Secondly, the use of the notion of number is uncompromising in this section of the text, as it is in 23 seq. in relation to *peras*. It is hard to resist the conclusion that to the extent that he thought the *techne* of letters to be a *techne* he thought that the subject-matter allowed of mathematization. He could still hold that at the stage it had so far reached this was not very evident. The passage 55–9 shows him prepared to call something a *techne* even if the method used does not in any serious sense involve mathematics, so long as more sophisticated methods are or (in faith) will be found. Even in these cases some embryonic form of measuring doubtless takes place. A builder who builds by eye, by eye matches his walls and assesses his angles, which is perhaps the beginning of measurement. The various letters do at least mark certain standard sounds which are at a point to which acceptable sounds have to approximate. There are intervening sounds between the stages of *p*, *b*, *v*, which do/should not occur in words, and it is not impossible that Plato thought the signs were that there were various forms of indeterminacy, as with music, that would allow the development of a theory of letters of a full-fledged mathematical sort.

It is also possible that Plato was succumbing to the temptation to use mathematical terminology where it was not strictly applicable. Thus in the *Gorgias* (508a) and *Laws* (757) he talks, as does Aristotle (*Nicomachean Ethics* 1106a26 seq.), as though the notion of geometrical equality was the appropriate one in discussing virtues as well as *techne*. Two quantities are said to be geometrically equal if the proportions between each and the second of its pair are equal. Thus 3 in relation to 6 is equal to 4 in relation to 8. Granted this notion a distribution can be said to be equal in two different ways: first, if equal quantities of what has to be distributed are given to each person and secondly if the proportion between what is given and what is due is equal in each case. As it stands, this is an extended use of the notion of geometrical equality, though if what is due can be quantified it becomes literal. Thus if we are considering the payment of debts in a bankcruptcy case, it can be literal. In the case of justice it is not clear, but if clear quantities could be given to such things as a soul's needs or a body's needs, and a means of determining them could be supplied, then rulers and doctors could be thought of as concerned to distribute their wares with an eye to virtue and health, and equal (and, because of the purposes, good) distributions would be assessed geometrically. It is not easy to judge to what extent Plato put trust in this hope, to what extent he is trading on extensions and would not expect numbers, in any serious sense, to be useful.

To end, it might be appropriate to refer to certain external evidence. So far I have confined myself to the *Philebus*, either to the text or to hypotheses about the dialogue's purpose. It is worth noting two general pieces of evidence which do not directly bear on the *Philebus*. The first is remarks of Aristotle's on the contrast between Plato and Pythagoreans, the second is from Aristoxenus' treatise on musical theory. In interpreting the *Philebus* I have supposed that Plato is adopting a Pythagorean view of *technai*, but that he does not consider *peras* and *apeiron* as entering into objects and being somehow parts of their constitution. They are to be seen rather in relation to a geometrical representation in terms of which phenomena can be understood, but which are separate from the phenomena. This at least fits Aristotle's comments when he contrasts Plato with Pythagoreans (*Metaphysics* A, 987a–b). It is open to dispute whether the Pythagoreans in question are, or are predominantly, pre-Platonic Pythagoreans, but the important point is that Aristotle emphasizes that while the Pythagoreans in some way thought of *peras* and *apeiron* as entering into things, so that they were prepared to call number the essence of everything, Plato posited number distinct from objects. These remarks have attracted attention because they suggest that Plato posited an intermediate order of reality between Forms and physical objects. Yet the significance of the move is surely the refusal to consider mathematical items (units, lines etc.) as in any way constituents of objects. This refusal would make it possible, not to say necessary, to take a different view of the relation of geometrical discoveries to the physical world. If Aristotle is right, then the interpretation proposed for the *Philebus* shows Plato separating numbers from things as one would expect.

I have also assumed that Plato is wanting to make certain geometrical problems relevant to the study of music, letters, medicine, and so on. It is worth remembering, therefore, that geometry was not considered as just the study of spatial properties in the common sense of 'spatial'. We have already seen that Socrates in the *Gorgias* and the Athenian Stranger in the *Laws* (see above, p. 178) see geometry as applicable in non-spatial contexts. It is interesting also to note Aristotle's comments in *Metaphysics* K, 1061a28 seq., where he says that mathematicians consider heaviness and lightness, hardness and its opposite, warmth and coldness and generally perceptible opposites, but prescinding from their perceptible properties consider them only in so far as they display quantity and continuum in various dimensions, and all this comes under geometry. There would be nothing startling to Eudoxus in the suggestion that his geometrical investigations bore on the development of *technai*. That was well recognized.

Finally, Aristoxenus. Aristoxenus was a musical theorist who studied under the Pythagorean Xenophilus before transferring to Aristotle. He was writing, therefore, not long after Plato and with knowledge of the Pythagorean tradition. He considered himself a great improvement on his predecessors, who only treated of enharmonic and not diatonic or chromatic scales. This, he says (*Elementa Harmonica* A 2), is clear from their diagrams. In other words, the sort of representation of the scale that one might expect was in fact familiar. Further, (A13.31 seq.) he at one point turns to a problem of whether the contrast of high and low proceeds indefinitely (whether it is *apeiros*) in each direction. He proceeds to argue that so far as the voice and ear are concerned there is a. an upper and lower limit and b. a limit to the intermediate possible differentiations. If we consider the contrast of high and low in itself, however, it will proceed *eis apeiron*. The discussion does not have much point unless Aristoxenus is combating some known approach. In that case he has come across someone talking of the high and low and claiming it to be *apeiron* i.e. infinitely divisible, indeterminate, and he is countering that this is not true of the high and low considered as perceptible or producible. At least this argues the existence of a use of '*peras*' and '*apeiron*' in relation to music in the way I have suggested and at a date quite close to Plato. The probability is that Aristoxenus has in mind either the *Philebus* or the musical theorists alluded to in the

Philebus or both. So not only is it antecedently probable that musical theorists represented their view diagrammatically, with relationships between notes given as relationships between measures on a continuum, but there is evidence that not only was this done, but the language of *'peras'* and *'apeiron'* was used in discussing music in the way that I have suggested as best fitting the Heavenly Tradition. For another possible echo of the *Philebus* discussion cf. *Elementa Harmonica* Γ 67. 11 seq. For a general discussion at latest soon after Plato of problems concerning *apeiron* see Aristotle *Physics* Γ 4–8.

VICTORY TO THE MIXED LIFE, 20–23

Socrates affirms the relevance of the Heavenly Tradition to the question at issue. The task, however, is clearly daunting as it would necessitate establishing branches of knowledge concerning pleasure and knowledge, (and perhaps about good, too?) and comparing them. The whole previous section has made it less attractive to hold the pleasure thesis on at least one interpretation; for if pleasure is to be an operable criterion it must be the subject of some *techne* and so one would expect intelligence to be important; so Socrates' memory of a compromise view has been prepared for. Strictly, even such argument as is offered could only prove that the mixed life is better than the present candidates, not that it is the good. On the other hand, in so far as it is admitted that a life lacking either pleasure or intelligence cannot be the good life it is admitted that the good life is at least a mixture of these. But the door is open for Plato to add other ingredients.

Three important questions arise about this section:
(i) what is the criterion used for deciding that neither protagonist can be the good?
(ii) what do the arguments for a mixed life commit one to?
(iii) what is to govern the awarding of second or lower prizes?

(i) Socrates obtains the admission that the good life must be complete, adequate, and such that any subject that knows of it will want it and pursue it. Though apparently three criteria these do not get applied separately in what follows. Socrates builds up a description of the life of pleasure only until Protarchus agrees that no one could choose it—they would want intelligence as well, thus showing the life to be incomplete and inadequate as it stands. But incompleteness and inadequacy are shown in that something is left to be desired. The relevant desire, however, is not every being's desire. The desire of beings that cannot know what intelligence is is discounted. Although some things in the passage suggest that Plato thought it would be better for an oyster if it could think, the argument is predominantly about the good for man. The criterion, then, is whether an intelligent being, and specifically man, would or does choose the life in question. In fact, it seems to be 'would'. The tactic is to face Protarchus with the description and ask him whether he thinks it chooseable by us. As Socrates has characterized the life as a jelly-fish existence, not a human one, Protarchus' answer is not surprising. Suppose, though, that faced with the choice, someone chooses the other way? Socrates might claim it as an aberration. Certainly his argument does not seem to be that everyone does choose as he says. It hardly could be, as the set-up is artificial, and the majority never faces such a choice. The point, then, is that any one who *reflected would* choose this way. The alternative choice would show lack of reflection. But how are we supposed to know this? It is well enough for Protarchus to admit it about himself—though even here questions might be raised—but not to make any more general claim. It is tempting to suggest that Plato would say that anyone who would make such a choice would thereby show himself either irrational, or not really to have reflected. But this is not just going round in a circle, it is pirouetting. The test of whether X is a good life was whether a rational being who knew what X is would want or choose it. Now the test of whether a being is rational or knows what X is becomes whether it wants or chooses X. The way that a hedonist might take, of claiming that a rational being would be dissatisfied, is not open to Plato, and does not look very long-lived in itself. Presumably if the profered life is wholly pleasant and wholly without intellection it will be by any pleasure test wholly satisfactory to its possessor, though also its possessor will cease to be intelligent. It is no help to say that while intelligent it would not choose it, as that would only show that not all choices were directed to what would in fact be satisfying.

Socrates' point gets its pull, of course, as an appeal to the individual honestly to declare his preferences. Doubtless most of us would show some opposition to a proposal to reduce us to the condition of contented jelly-fishes, at least at the level of declared preference. It may be that Socrates should be read as conducting an *ad hominem* examination of Protarchus, which Plato hopes will elicit the same admission from any honest reader. The argument then reveals to Protarchus (and perhaps to the reader) that *he* does not take seriously the life of pleasure as a goal to aim at. This fits well with a common Socratic approach to moral discussion, that as the issue is how best to live, the important thing for each individual is to be clear where he stands. But *knowing* where one stands seems to involve being clear that what one pursues is really good. For this to amount to more than being sure that one is serious about it one would need some way of distinguishing between good and bad answers on the good form of life. No such way seems to be offered in the *Philebus*. The organizing intelligence spoken of later does have to determine how to mix pleasure and intelligence, but the criterion takes it as given that those ingredients constitute the good life or are least necessary elements in it. The only justification for saying that is the present passage. It is instructive to compare this with, for instance, the imagery applied to the Good in *Republic* VI–VII, and with the setting of the question in *Republic* II and the form of answer in *Republic* IX, as also with the procedure of the *Gorgias*. The *Philebus* does not seem to supply any general means of deciding whether or not a given life is good. It may be that the point that the proposed life would not be a human life could be developed, but in fact it is not. So we lack any clear criterion for deciding what is good. On the other hand, if Eudoxus is a hoped-for reader, the appeal to what is pursuable might have *ad hominem* force, in that his thesis was based on what is clearly taken as an object of pursuit. The present passage invites him to admit that he, at least, wants more than pleasure.

(ii) The second query is: what does the admission that neither contestant is the good commit us to? So far as allowing in pleasure goes, the admission is that no human being, at least, would want a life that was pleasureless; but whether this means without at least enjoying his intellectual activities or without at least some non-intellectual pleasures is not spelled out. The admission that intelligence is needed, on the other hand, is extracted on straight hedonistic grounds, or can be interpreted so. Protarchus is not asked to contemplate with horror a life where he cannot do mathematics, but one where he cannot remember or recognize or predict his enjoyments. The first two could be seen as adding to one's pleasures, the last as giving as assured means of obtaining them. So Protarchus could be admitting intelligent activities simply in so far as they either constituted or were a good means to pleasures. The form of the admission does not commit him to asserting the value of any intellectual activities independently of their pleasantness or power to lead to pleasure. It does *seem* to commit him to the position that the simple fact that a life is all pleasant and in no way distressing is insufficient to make it good (but see below). For realizing that one is enjoying oneself is preferred to just enjoying oneself. But it has not been shown to be impossible to make sense of saying that a pleasure realized is greater than one of which we are not aware; and the power to organize oneself so as to have nothing but pleasures might obviously be claimed to be desirable on the grounds that it would be the most effective way of ensuring the goal. Intelligence would be desirable for us, but irrelevant to deciding the goodness of the whole life. When we are considering what equipment we should like, intelligence is included, but the only feature required of the constituent occurrences is that they be pleasant.

Even if we admit that no account of degrees of pleasantness can be given to justify the preference for realizing that one is enjoying oneself, it might still be claimed that to realize one is enjoying oneself is itself a pleasure, and Protarchus could claim first, that his admission still allows that only a life consisting of pleasures is in fact good, and secondly, that what determined the success of intelligence in organizing a life was that the life should contain only, or so far as possible only, pleasant episodes.

The role ascribed to intelligence in the above is largely that of producer, partly that of enjoyer. The first role is that suggested at 28c6–9 at the end of the second *peras/apeiron* passage. But by 56 and following various *branches* of knowledge are being treated as candidates for inclusion. It is true that at 63 a pleasure-justification is given for including these branches of knowledge, but they are in turn used as a test of what pleasures to include. Further, the criterion for admission does not seem justified by the present passage, although it is the only basis for it. For at 61d–e it is announced that we should only mix the purified (see note on 61e6–9) cases of knowledge and pleasure in the first instance, mixing less clear examples only as permitted ·by these. This only seems justifiable if Protarchus' admission in the present passage is interpreted as allowing that there must be knowledge of a sort that does not admit of any ignorance. For the later point about purified or true knowledge seems to be ‚that some branches of knowledge are so only with qualifications, as they allow a margin of error/ignorance (see notes on 51a5, 58a2); the argument is then presumably that all Protarchus has admitted is that knowledge has a place in the good life; he has not admitted ignorance; so most empirical techniques are not thereby allowed in. This seems an unjustifiable interpretation of the form given to Protarchus' admission in the present passage, where memory of the past and prediction (qualified cases) were let in, but no preference shown for knowledge in this ‘pure’ sense. It may be that Plato felt that we all do, or should, admire intellectual accomplishments irrespective of any connection with pleasure, and that the high point of intellectual achievement is in areas where there is no uncertainty, but no such admission has in fact been extracted from Protarchus here, nor does it follow from what is admitted, nor is it anywhere proved. See below, pp. 196–7 for a passage with further bearing on this, and note on 58d4–5.

(iii) The first prize has gone to the mixed life. The second prize spoken of at 22c8 is not a prize for the second best *life*. The contest is for an award to an element of the good life. The criterion is one of relative responsibility for it. What does this mean?

It is fair enough that at this stage the answer to this question should be uncertain, but we are not helped by being offered, in addition to responsibility, or as a gloss on it, the criterion of 'being more related to' (*suggenesteron*) or 'more like' (*homoioteron*). The term translated 'responsible for . . .', '*aitios*', is picked up at 26e, where it is glossed as 'what produces'. The word is often translated 'cause', but has a more general sense than that word is usually given in contemporary English philosophical discussion. 'Explanation' is a fair translation, but slightly more puzzling than the vague 'responsible for . . .' in the present passage. Either way, it needs further specification before it is clear what we are looking for. This it seems to receive at 26e, and then at 30c seq. intelligence is roundly said to belong to the class of producers, those responsible for products. With pleasure classed as an *apeiron* that seems to settle the issue. But it seems that is not enough, and we have to wait until 65 seq. for our final answer. Why?

As it stands, the victory for intelligence at 30c–e could be hollow. For it is not yet clear that there are any other ingredients than pleasure for intelligence to organize. Its value could be simply to discover the 'number' of pleasure. In the rest of the argument two further things are done. First, it is made clear that *peras* makes a good mixture good, in the sense that that, not facts about pleasantness, is what distinguishes a good mixture from a bad; secondly, it emerges that branches of knowledge are among the ingredients, with a value independent of their power to produce pleasure. It looks as though *peras* makes a combination the right combination, and that branches of knowledge are always concerned with right combinations. Consequently knowledge 'is more closely related' to the good. This serves to give them a higher place. For further discussion of this ordering see below, pp. 224 seq. In the present section intelligence is only shown to be responsible for the good life in the sense of being its producer. *Peras* is responsible (cf. 64d) in another sense, and intelligence is just more close related to that.

THE DETERMINANT AND INDETERMINATE, 23–28

The aim now is to decide whether intelligence or pleasure is more responsible for the good life. Socrates declares that we shall need to add some new tools to our old ones. The old ones are *apeiron* and *peras*, then there is the union of these and the producer of the union. '*Apeiron*' is explained as the name for such things as the hotter, the colder, the excessive, in opposition to equality and such like which come under '*peras*'. The union of these is a mixed thing and intelligence is the cause of the mixture, and so responsible for it. Thus intelligence wins the laurels and pleasure comes as part of the product, though, as remarked in the previous section of the commentary, described just like that the victory could turn out hollow.

Like 16–19 this passage has proved difficult to interpret, and once again there are certain points that interpretations should try to accommodate:

1. This passage is supposed to take certain tools from the earlier one. The natural way of taking this is as saying that the tools used in the earlier passage in the Pythagoreanizing doctrine will be useful again. But to be the same tools they must not just be the same words, but the same technical terms. If the contrast of *peras* and *apeiron* there was between form and matter, so should it be here, if between countable kinds and indefinitely varied particulars, so should it be here. Anything weaker would make the reference confusing and so should only be accepted as a second-best.

2. At 24a–d *apeiron* is described as being destroyed by *peras*, but 25d seq. describes a category of things produced by blending these two, so that somehow *apeiron* must have a place in the mixture.

3. *Apeira* are first defined as what allows of more and less, *peras* as what is or produces specific quantities (24a–d), but later *peras* is or produces only good quantities.

4. While the good life, possibly in general, is allowed to be a mixed thing (*meikton*) (27d), predominantly the suggestion is that fine days, healthy bodies, the cycle of the seasons are examples of *meikta*, that is, observable phenomena (cf. 26a–b, 30b–c).

5. *Apeiron* is spoken of early on as though *apeira* are things like hotter, colder, in other words as though Plato is interested either in elements of things, or in predicates; but also (cf. 52c) particular items can be put in that category.

Once again there are two main lines of interpretation, though with many internal variations, and once again what follows will be a sketch of these types.

Interpretation 1 (cf. Bury, Appendix D, Jowett, Ross, Taylor, Gauss, Hackforth, and, with qualifications, Robin). This follows the lines of the first interpretation of 16–19, the Heavenly Tradition (so possibly meeting point 1). *Peras* and *apeiron* are cousins of Aristotle's form and matter. Plato has seen that objects can be described as of such and such a temperature, weight, and so on, and takes it that corresponding to different elements in the description will be different elements in reality. So there must be capacities for greater or less heat, weight, and so on, a material receptacle with these potentialities, waiting for the imposition of a form to produce some object with these qualities. But Plato also makes his material principle a principle of change. It is not only a potentiality for heat but a tendency to change heat, so that the imposition of *peras* not only actualizes a potentiality for a given temperature, but restrains a tendency to change to another temperature. The universe is to be seen as a battlefield where disorderly material elements, potentially manifesting any of various degrees of certain properties, are also tending to change degrees of those properties. On the other hand the divine intelligence is trying to produce certain good combinations of elements and so to restrain the tendency of matter to change. This explains the general picture of hostility between *peras* and *apeiron* and of the turbulence of the latter (24a–d). It is of the nature of the *apeiron*, material, element to be on the move, and this is destroyed by the imposition of form. But it is also of its nature to be a potentiality for e.g. degrees of heat or cold, and this becomes actualized when form is imposed and so the material element survives in the mixture. There is no need to attribute to Plato any conception of pure potentiality. The hot element is already as it were fire constantly changing temperature, and only potentially some definite temperature. Fire has to survive in any product of divine operations, but with its natural uncurbed movement destroyed (point 2).

For this it has to be accepted that '*peras*' is not equivalent simply to 'number', but only includes those proportions whose imposition produces something corresponding to a Form. This has sometimes been felt too restrictive. Thus Hackforth is quite clear that 'the instances given are states or conditions of bodies or souls, or of the physical universe and though these do not cover the whole ground indicated by πάντα τὰ νῦν ὄντα ἐν τῷ πάντι (everything at present in the universe) there can, in my opinion, be no doubt that the classification intended is a classification of phenomena or γιγνόμενα (things that come into being) alone.' He wishes to make two points: first, that the intention is simply to give an analysis of the constitution of the observable world, not of Forms. Secondly, he wants it to be an analysis of the constitution of every observable object, so that he thinks that we are meant to see that there are mixtures of the determinant and indeterminate that are not right, to cover all the bad combinations. With this Ross and Taylor are in basic agreement.

This would certainly enable one to take '*peras*' as simply covering quantities and relationships between quantities, but this in itself seems questionable (point 3). *Peras* seems to be of its nature opposed to disorder, when that is an evaluative notion (cf. 25d11–26c2, 27d7–10). In conditions of storm, frost, arrogance, and so on, *peras* is lacking. This is also suggested at 64d–e. There it is claimed that what is responsible for any mixture is measure and commensurability. The mixture under discussion is the good life, a mixed thing in the terminology of 23 seq. So far this might seem to support Hackforth as there is a strong statement that there just is no mixture without measure, i.e. not even bad ones. But in fact this point is immediately taken to show that the power of making something good has gone into hiding in the cover of what makes something fine (64e5 seq.). For measure and proportion emerge always as what constitute fineness and excellence. This entails that a poor mixture is not in the required sense a mixture at all, and so not all states of objects are mixtures.

Secondly, if Plato's thesis is so general, and despite appearances he meant physical objects in all states to be mixtures, then he missed a golden opportunity of making this clear. At 29a seq. he compares the constitution of our bodies to that of the universe at large, and mentions the traditional four elements. There is no mention of any connection between, say, fire and the hotter or any *apeiron* mentioned earlier, nor any indication that some familiar previous point is being elaborated. Worse, none of the language used to describe the results of blending *peras* and *apeiron* is used for describing the constitution of the body or the universe. All previous talk of the things that 'come into being' is in the language of mixture (*meixis* and corresponding verbs) or blending (*koinonia*). Neither set of terms features in 29a seq. Instead we have words that are the origin of 'synthesis'. The only exception is that a verb is used at 26a4 (*sunhistamai*) whose noun occurs at 29a11, but neither is a dominant term of the exposition. Yet if the constitution of bodies generally were what Plato had in mind in the talk of mixtures of *peras* and *apeiron* it is strange that what should have been the natural terminology is quite absent when he does unequivocally talk of their constitution.

For these reasons it seems better to stick with the view that Plato has good states of bodies, souls, etc. in mind. In that case one has the problem still of point 3 that *apeira* are what allow of more and less, *peras* seems to be purely quantitative, but mixed things are good states. This seems to be conflating the idea of a straight scale with points on it and that of desirable proportions.

This objection might be met by a two-pronged defence, first on *apeiron* and then on *peras*. The proposed position is that Plato sees the possibility of varying degrees in certain respects and holds responsible for this observable fact a variable material element. But the talk of varying degrees is misleading. The Greek comparatives commonly carry connotations of excess and defect. Like the English positives 'fat', 'thin', 'bold', 'timid', the Greek comparatives of the words for 'hot', 'cold' can indicate that the heat or cold is overdone, and mean something like 'rather hot', 'too cold'. If this is the way in which Plato thinks of varying degrees, as varying to excess and defect, it would be natural to think of the corresponding elements as turbulent, and also natural to think of bringing a limit to the too hot or too cold as producing the right temperature.

Even so, this would involve some confusion, for one could stop the element, in theory, at any degree without thereby stopping it from being, say, excessively hot. This point can be met by the second prong. The assumption of the objection about *peras* is that when Plato talks of number, equality, he has simple quantities such as number of degrees Fahrenheit in mind. Yet this is highly improbable. As early as the *Gorgias* (508a) Socrates complains that Callicles is ignorant of geometry and geometrical equality. The point is that geometrical equality is what is thought pertinent in knowledge. Thus a well-developed medical theory will have a concept of health that does not require, even of one species, such as human beings, an identical amount of muscle or blood per person, but an identical ratio between the amount of muscle, or blood and, say, the size of skeleton. It may be that muscle makes up the same percentage of the body mass, but that does not mean the same amount of muscle. As we all know, an identical percentage pay rise is not the same as an identical across the board pay rise. When one talks of arithmetical equality this typically has nothing to do with what is appropriate. In the *technai*, where one is concerned with the best arrangement, the appropriate amount of heat, the appropriate amount of muscle, and so on will be the amount whose proportion to size of skeleton or whatever is the same as the proportion $A:B$. In these areas it is geometrical equality that is important (see above, pp. 178–9). I have no wish here to argue the question of how clearly Plato grasped the distinction prior to the *Politicus* (283–5), or whether the fact that the distinction is not made in the *Philebus* shows it to be earlier than the *Politicus*—though it seems to me that by itself it is not enough to show this. The point is that whereas we, if we talked of the more and less and number and equality, might be thinking primarily simply of degrees and precise quantities, the chances are high that Plato would be thinking of possibilities of excess and defect and geometrical equality. So either by the time he wrote the *Philebus* he took the *Politicus* distinction for granted and assumed the important form of measurement was in question; or he had not yet, when he wrote the *Philebus*, made the distinction clearly, in which case it is still probable that he had primarily geometrical equality in mind.

If that is so, then introducing number and equality to the too hot and the too cold is not just introducing precise temperatures, but producing temperatures which are proportionately equal or whatever, that is, those temperatures etc. required to preserve a ratio equal to the ratio *A:B* as specified by some *techne*. That to which the temperature has to bear a given ratio may be another temperature or a degree of something quite different. The important point is that introducing number, equality, etc. to temperature is thought of as introducing a way of relating the amount of temperature to some other quantity, the latter, together with the determining ratio given in the account of health, yielding the appropriate temperature, the one that is proportionately equal. In that case it will be natural to expect that imposing equality, number, etc. on the too hot/too cold has the result of producing the right temperature. All we have to remember is that Plato moves from the possible truth that an account of health must yield a specification of the right proportions striking a balance between certain excesses, to the dubious conclusion that corresponding to the elements in that description (proportion of heat to fat, with possibilities of excess or defect either way) are elements in any healthy body struggling for control.

It seems, then, that this view might escape the charge that it has to make Plato pass quite unintelligibly from talking of points on scales to talking of good arrangements. It would remain that objects in bad states do not have a place in this account of 'everything at present in the universe', and one has to accuse Plato of the move mentioned at the end of the last paragraph.

How, then, does it fare on the five points mentioned on p. 186? On point 2 it manages quite well, allowing that *apeiron* is destroyed in the sense that its typifying changeableness is restrained, but remains in the resultant mixture in that it is the material element whose capacity for precise temperature is required to produce something of such and such a heat. Point 3 I have just dealt with. On point 4, the thesis is precisely that mixed things are good states of observable objects. When it comes to the good life, it is true that there may never have been an example and yet Plato talks as though a philosopher's description of the good life would be a description of a *meikton*. This does not, however, seem either a seriously objectionable or unlikely usage, the point of the philosopher's description being that anything that was a good life would be a *meikton*. On point 5, there would be peculiarity in talking of pleasure as a quasi-physical element, but if we allow that Plato might, as perhaps in the *Republic* at least he at times seems to, think of it as an alluring as well as pleasurable element in experience, then it is natural that he should consider it *apeiron*. But there might be pleasures in correct proportion, which would be *meikta*. As to the particular pleasures put at 52c into the *apeiron* category, that would be fatal to a view like Hackforth's that considers all observable particulars to be *meikta*, but the present view has been devised to protect against that. If we think of pleasure as, in virtue of being *apeiron*, an element tending to different degrees, then it might be easy to think of violent or disruptive pleasures as raw manifestations of this phenomenon. To the extent that one does one's material principle is not potentiality to receive a certain character, but something with that character in flux with the potentiality to have it in a precise degree—but that has already been allowed for in the interpretation. It is more difficult with conditions of extreme heat (26a) which are all too often stably unpleasant, although apparently exhibiting *apeirian*. So on point 5 the performance is mixed: less unfortunate than Hackforth's view, but not perfect.

So the view does well on point 2, moderately on 5, and all right on 3 so long as we are prepared to attribute to Plato the view that the hotter, the cooler, etc. are turbulent elements. This last is hardest to swallow in relation to music (26a). One can think of instruments, such as the bagpipes, where the picture of producing a tune as a struggle to keep in check recalcitrant tendencies to excess fits well, but it will hardly do for most singing, the lyre, the flute, and so on (and cf. 25c for other odd 'elements'). On point 4 it cannot cope with stable bad conditions, although these are familiar enough. On point 1 it is prima facie strongest in that *'peras'* and *'apeiron'* are clearly the same technical terms if one takes the first interpretation of the Heavenly Tradition. It is only sad that it should be the weakest candidate there. So either one accepts Interpretation 1 there, at a high price, or else accepts a different interpretation there and consequently fails on point 1. The end of the Heavenly Tradition (19b) is so close to 23b as to make such a sudden shift in the use of the terminology not easy to accept.

Interpretation 2 (cf. Stenzel, Crombie, Striker, and, with qualifications, Robin). On a first reading, the description of *apeiron* at 24a–d strikes one as highly metaphorical, but as an attempt to isolate not a set of elements but a set of concepts. This is strengthened at 25c where more and fewer and faster and slower and larger and smaller are added as things that receive more and less. It becomes difficult to see how anyone is going to consider these as material elements. As Striker argues (pp. 50–1) Plato has no terminology for making it clear that he is talking of concepts. He uses the rather uncertain word *'genos'* (kind? category?) and calls *apeiron* a *genos*. He also calls hotter and colder *gene* (plural) in which the more and less dwell. Whatever else is true, *'genos'* is not a very appropriate word for talking of the element of fire (the hot). It certainly looks as though Plato is wanting to say something about the concepts 'hot', 'hotter', 'faster', 'fewer', and their like, that it is possible to qualify them by 'more', 'less', 'too', and so on. Strictly, this is only true of the positives: 'hotter' does not in any obvious way, any more than 'colder', receive 'less', but it is not hard to think of them as at least already having 'more' in them. If one now introduces specific quantities the description is changed from the indeterminate, possibly relative, description 'hot', to a particular degree.

Now, if, in talking of '*apeiron*', Plato is primarily making a point about concepts, so presumably must he when talking about *meikta*. The point is that a concept like 'health' is to be analysed into (is a compound form) some concept giving qualities of which there can be degrees and some number giving the degrees of the quality in question. Similarly, if we wish to get a clear grasp of the concept 'a good life' we have to search for its formal, numerical element and its 'material' indeterminate aspect. So health is a *meikton* in that the concept of health requires analysis into a formal component and a material component. The formal component is thought of as a set of ratios, the material one as some notion of possible degrees, and the combination is a set of ratios between degrees of various properties. The analysis, of course, is not of the ordinary man's concept of health. Rather a fully elaborated medical theory will expound a concept of health to be analysed in this way.

At first sight there are two obvious problems to be met. First, just what concepts has Plato in mind as covered by the term '*apeiron*'? Secondly, if this account is right, how about point 5, that particular states and phenomena, not concepts, seem to be accounted *apeira*?

To take the first: as Striker points out (pp. 51 seq.), it will not do to say that if you have an adjective 'A' admitting of a comparative, then you can truly say 'the A admits of more and less' (or, for 'the A' an equivalent abstract noun), for on that count 'health' or 'the healthy' would be *apeira*, since there is a comparative of 'healthy'. But (25e, 26b) health is clearly a *meikton*. Perhaps, then, we should confine ourselves either (i) to those cases such that if it is true that X is A it is possible to describe a Y such that Y would be more/less A than X; or (ii) to those cases where if it is true that X is A, then 'A' carries implicit comparison to some Y less A than X. Both criteria exclude 'healthy', since what 'X is healthy' says is that X conforms to a certain standard. Taken as an unqualified assertion (i.e. X is perfectly healthy), it excludes the possibility of any Y more healthy than X, and there is no implication of comparison with any *Y* less healthy than *X*. It could be, though alas it is not, that every man and animal was perfectly healthy, and 'healthy' would remain applicable. By contrast, if weather is hot, there is still always a description of even hotter weather; and if all weather were uniformly of the same temperature, none would deserve the description 'hot'. So either criterion would exclude 'healthy', and would include 'hot', etc. The first criterion suggests that *apeira* are without limit (cf. 24b, 31a), but does not readily catch 'too much' (24e8), which can apply even if there is no possibility of more or less (there is no comparative of 'too'), and which does not, as 'hot' and 'hotter' do, naturally suggest comparatives of the sort in question. On the other hand criterion (ii) catches 'too much', which always implies relation to something less, and is directly suggested by 24c4. It also explains the tendency for Plato to think in terms of pairs of opposing adjectives, in that the hotter is always relative to something colder, etc. Further it can accommodate 24b, 31a in that 'hot' (relative to something colder) does not determine any boundary (*telos*) but only an indeterminate range of upper temperatures.

Consequently (but for full detail she should be read) Striker prefers criterion (ii). But she recognizes, first that this criterion leaves out many adjectives ('friendly', 'enthusiastic'), which do not imply approximation to a standard, and secondly that there is a residual problem about excess. The first is not a serious objection, in that Plato might be expected not to have covered all possibilities. The second is more troublesome. The problem is that if we take *meikta* as suggested, and health as a *meikton*, then it is natural to think of the *apeira* as the hot, the cold. Then health is a certain combination of the hot, the cold, the dry, etc. In that case the *phenomena* covered by the term '*apeiron*' would be the things that are hot and cold. But that would include *meikta* and in fact in so far as Plato talks of *things* as *apeira* they are states of *excessive* heat, etc. So we might take *apeira* as the too hot, too cold, too dry, etc. That would allow these particulars to be covered by the concepts. But then it is implausible to think of health as a combination of the too hot, too dry, and the rest. So there seems to be a vacillation between thinking of *apeira* as receiving more and less and receiving excess and defect.

Striker, if I understand her, puts this down to a confusion on Plato's part, not recognized until the *Politicus*, between straight talk of relative quantity and talk of excessive quantity, a confusion encouraged by the Greek comparatives, as already pointed out. Granted this, Plato might have had in mind the idea of relative quantities when thinking of *meikta* but passed easily to the notion of excessive quantity when thinking of observable phenomena as falling under '*apeiron*'.

This brings us to the second problem: how '*apeiron*' can be used to describe particulars and, with it, how particular states can be considered as *meikta*. This difficulty is met by pointing out that Plato does not distinguish between class inclusion and class membership, nor between referring to the defining concept of a class and the class it defines. The hot, the cold are forms of *apeiron*, and so, as classes, members of the class of *apeira*, in that they are defining concepts of classes, and defining concepts that 'allow of more and less' (the defining concept of the class of *apeira*). Consequently, the class of hot things is thought of as a member of the class of *apeira*, and thereby as included in the class of *apeira*, so that members of the class of hot things are members of the class of *apeira* and so merit the description '*apeiron*'. So granted his characteristic confusions it is to be expected that he will think particulars can be described as *apeira*, and granted the confusion of more/less and too much/too little it is to be expected that things like excessively hot weather, falling into the class of hot/hotter things, will be seen as members of the genus *apeiron* and so as *apeira*. There will similarly be no problem about '*meikton*' applying to particular states.

So individual states of things are described as *apeira* in virtue of deserving some description 'too *A*', and could be so described in virtue of being *A* relative to something less *A*. But Plato conflates these, trading on the 'relatively *A*' strand for talking of *apeiron* as an element in *meikta*, and on the 'excessively *A*' strand for talking of observable instances as *apeira*. While the passage is confused, it is confused in ways to be expected of Plato, and in ways that allow one to say that he is not talking here of the constitution of observable objects but is struggling to a view whose clear exposition would require concepts he does not possess.

If we return to our five points (p. 186), this view explains point 2 by holding that *apeiron* is preserved in the mixture in that a concept in the *apeiron* category appears in the analysis of the *meikton* concept, but is destroyed in that the concept alone is indeterminate, and its indeterminacy is removed by giving of precise degrees. Not only that, but the result (warm to degree 32) does not imply reference to something less warm. Point 3 is met by declaring Plato not yet clear on a point to be clarified in the *Politicus*. Points 4 and 5 have been dealt with in the recent discussion.

Thus point 2 is well catered for, and points 3–5 accommodated granted certain confusions. On the latter it is perhaps worth noting that if the use of '*genos*' (kind) here is supposed to be in tune with the supposed genus/species proposals of the Heavenly Tradition, we have to suppose Plato in an early, naive stage on genus and species.

For one purpose of that form of classification is to produce an exhaustive set of exclusive classifications, such that X cannot be a member of two different species or co-ordinate genera. If Hot and Dry are *gene*, however, since X may be hot and dry, this requirement is broken, *unless* we limit the range of what can be hot so that physical objects do not count, but in that case there are difficulties with the text, where particular states of weather capable of being both hot and dry seem to be *apeira*, and similarly pleasures capable of being too intense, too attractive, etc. In that case one has to accept lack of clarity on Plato's part about genus and species. If that is so it reflects back on the interpretation of the Heavenly Tradition, and reinforces earlier misgivings about trying to enforce any precise genus/species account of division on that passage.

The view does worst on point 1. As this is the major objection here it might be worth elaborating. Crombie rightly points out that there is no need to suggest any ambiguity in the terms *'peras'*, *'apeiron'*. They mean 'limit' or 'determinant' and 'unlimited' or 'indeterminate' respectively. Thus in the early passage observable particulars are referred to by *'apeiron'* in virtue of being indeterminate either in number or as regards further specific difference; in the present passage the Hotter is called indeterminate in virtue of the indeterminate reference of 'hot'. In either case the reference is secured by the same sense of the word *'apeiron'*. So this view can be protected against the charge of requiring *'apeiron'* or any other technical word to be ambiguous.

To see why this is not enough, suppose we take an analogy. Professor Erudite is discussing education in classes of mixed ability. He thinks it a good idea to mix abilities granted the numbers are not too high and the individuals mix temperamentally. So he declares it important in considering any class to distinguish, for separate consideration, the number of the class, and the individuals in it. There is a separate study to be given to the question of number and to the question of individuals. This distinction is used to show that some apparent counter-evidence to his thesis is not really so and confusedly runs together examples where failure was due to numbers and ones where failure was due to individuals. Later in his book, but not much later, he moves to talking of teaching mathematics to such groups, and wishes to make the point that we need to distinguish the numbers we are asking them to deal with and the individuals we are asking to deal with them. It is no use giving large numbers to slow individuals: numbers must be matched to individuals. Now the words 'number' and 'individual' are not ambiguous here, but suppose Professor Erudite started his later discussion by saying: 'It will help here to remember our earlier tools, the distinction between number and individuals.' In that case he would start us off in quite the wrong direction. For we should, of course, expect 'number' not simply to mean the same, but to be the same tool of analysis, and so we should expect once more to be using the distinction between the number of a group and its individual members. But that is not at all what we are going to get.

Similarly, if 23 seq. is going to put the contrast of *peras* and *apeiron* to quite different use from what it had in the Heavenly Tradition, Plato is being deliberately confusing, unless he has failed to see the difference. Nor could the shift be rendered harmless by pointing to the distance between the passages which might make it likely we had forgotten the earlier passage. Quite the contrary. The distance is so short that our heads should still be swimming from the Heavenly Tradition.

Granted this, the present interpretation requires a fair shift, even from Interpretation 2 of the Heavenly Tradition. For there finding the number was finding the number of genera and species—a matter of counting—while '*apeiron*' referred to observable particulars, and this was the burden of the distinction of *peras* (*poson, arithmos, metron*) and *apeiron*. But now the *peras* (*poson, arithmos, metron*) is a set of proportions of certain degrees of properties and '*apeiron*' refers to certain comparative concepts and to individuals only in so far as they fall under these concepts. It seems a very obvious change and we have to attribute to Plato a fair (or unfair) degree of either stupidity or carelessness if we are to hold that he made it.

Interpretation 3. In what follows I want first to recall the objection to Interpretation 1, that Plato does not seem to be considering the constitution of physical phenomena. On the other hand, the defence of Plato proposed in relation to that interpretation on the subject of equality seems to me to be on the right lines. Whatever is true on the relative dating of the *Politicus*, it seems most likely that Plato would be thinking in terms of geometrical equality. As the main objection to Interpretation 2 has been on its failure to relate this passage adequately to the Heavenly Tradition, and as that is also a problem for Interpretation 1, I shall start by seeing whether, allowing that it is neither the constitution of objects nor arithmetical equality that is in question, there is an interpretation in line with Interpretation 3 of the Heavenly Tradition applicable to this passage.

To recapitulate briefly (see above, pp. 165 seq.): the suggestion there was that '*peras*' and '*apeiron*' should be taken as having a Pythagorean/mathematical background, '*apeiron*' being a term for the mathematical continuum, conceived of as infinitely divisible, without measure etc. Any *techne* starts from the observation that some general *phenomenon* shows variation of degrees in certain respects, the variation being representable geometrically by a continuum. The *techne* is finally established only when certain elements are arrived at, represented by points on the relevant continua, such that they and certain relationships between them describe arrangements permitted by the *techne*. The purpose of the exposition of the Heavenly Tradition is to make a point about the problem of one and many. Plato does not describe any *techne* in any great detail, but hopes to give enough to make the point. For this the important thing is to make it clear what is needed for a discipline to count as a *techne*. There is thus little mention of the products of a *techne*. There is talk of working out the scales, but not of the music composed. Even the composer only gets a side-glance in that having the number between the unit and the *apeiron* is said to be what makes an expert.

This is all very proper, since what would be in question would be whether there is a *techne* covering pleasure and so what would have to be discoverable if there is to be one. By 23 the direction has changed. We now know that what we hope to produce is a mixed life, and that the mixture is good, so we get a general discussion of the production of such mixtures. One would expect that the production of such mixtures might be a matter of skill. It is no surprise, therefore, to discover that 'the things that come to be' covers only good conditions and is said to be a product of intelligence. According to 17b−c it is knowing the number (e.g. scales), not just the *apeiron*, that makes one clever (*sophos*); according to 30b−c the cause that arranged the universe should, like that responsible for our own skills, be called *sophia*. The difference is that it is now the products of *techne* and producers that are being considered rather than what has to be true for something to be a *techne*, or for a *techne* to be acquired. But clearly the knowledge a musician acquires is the knowledge he applies. The theory he learns yields knowledge of scales (points on continua); his actual composition involves the selection of notes as required by the rules governing scales, tempo, etc. The theory says that only pieces of music whose sounds correspond to points on the scale correctly combined are permissible; the practice must involve producing combinations obeying these rules. So the Heavenly Tradition tells us what a person has to know to be *sophos*, the later passage what the typical products of *sophia* are. One would expect the latter for conform to what the *sophos* learns. At a general level, therefore, it would seem that one might expect the earlier account of *techne* to be relevant, but with emphasis on two further factors: the product and the nature of the producer. These are needed for the new argumentative objective, but the previous tools are extremely apt because not only are they to be reused, but implicit in their earlier introduction was reference to the additional tools, intelligence and *meikta*.

At a sketch level, then, one might hope to see continuity, with a shift of emphasis to products of *techne*. Now if one is going to be able to apply one's *techne* it must be possible to measure phenomena in the required respects. Thus, it must be possible to measure both pitch and tempo, heat and dryness, and so on. Otherwise theory is all up in the air. So with respect to pitch and tempo a particular musical effort will either measure up to what is required by the theory—its notes as measured will be properly related—or in some respect or respects it will not. If it does, then it will correspond to an arrangement of measures permitted by the skill, and so be a *meikton*, something not just of some pitch, but of a correct pitch, and so on. But to be a product of *techne* it must succeed at all points. If it, for instance, is not of proper tempo, its measures fail to fall at points determined by the skill. As its tempo falls at some point(s) not permitted by the skill, it corresponds to points on the continuum that are not marked. It therefore goes down as *apeiron*.

On this account '*apeiron*' does not stand for elements, nor for a class of concepts exactly, though this is nearer the truth. The word '*apeiron*' will already suggest that the continuum is what Plato has in mind, and the continuum is thought of as that which is divisible *ad infinitum*, and therefore not such that there is a common measure of all its sub-divisions. It therefore is such that whatever set of measures is applied it keeps on falling above and below that set of measures—that is to say parts remain undetermined by the measure. So we might see the situation as follows. 'The hotter' (or perhaps 'the hotter and colder') stands for a continuum of degrees of heat that is indeterminate, uncut-up into measures. We just have

We might hope to mark off certain distances as measures of heat thus:

But this can go on for ever. If it could be brought to an end there would be no points that were simply hotter or less hot but of no measurable heat, and the indeterminate would be destroyed. As it is the continuum remains indeterminate and so does away with precise quantification or the question 'how much?' When we select points of measurement we cut the continuum at a point, and a point is not a sub-stretch of continuum with more and less still in it. So we stop the process of more and less there. But however many such points are selected there are stretches of continuum always in excess or falling short for any given set of measures. The language of 24a–25a is not intended to indicate a set of predicates that Plato has in mind, but rather to remind one of the features of the continuum and suggest that certain terms suggest continua. The result is that others, such as 'healthy' do not, for the sort of reason Striker suggests. But Plato is not either confusing or interested in distinguishing between concepts conforming to criterion (i) and those conforming to criterion (ii) above (see pp. 192 seq.). References to having no end, proceeding on and on, excess, and so forth come not because of the type of word in question directly, but because the words in question suggest continua, which all have these features. Thus every continuum contains the 'too much' in that it always has parts that fall in excess of any nearest measure. The way in which the continuum came to be thought of in the study of irrationals makes all these descriptions appropriate. What Plato is doing is trying to persuade us to consider the hotter, the higher, and so on as continua. In that case the same talk of endlessness and excess will apply to them even though the word 'hotter' does not necessarily imply excess.

Only one *techne* is in common to the Heavenly Tradition and the later passage, music, but as the Heavenly Tradition only mentions two anyway this is a fair proportion. The later passage suggests a broader field. With regard to music, according to the Heavenly Tradition we have to move from the high and low to discover the complete number, i.e. the scales, etc. According to 23 seq., the imposition of number, etc. on the high and low is required to produce music. That is to say, the sounds produced have to be made to conform to the measures of pitch and tempo required by the theory. It is the same continua, the same number, but now production is in question.

But Plato is not, when he talks of number and equality, thinking arithmetically, as though any selection of measures would produce results. There is, after all, an indefinite number of ways of cutting up the continuum of pitch, or heat, or whatever. The view is that certain *technai* can be shown to select points that are determined by reference to required ratios between these quantities and others (see above, pp. 167 seq.). The hope is that this can be extended to all *technai.*

In short, the terms '*peras*' and '*apeiron*' as used in this passage will be used in expounding the same view of *techne*, and will be used unambiguously. The association *peras*-number-measure has the same process in view, and '*apeiron*' is in both cases used of the continuum. It is true that on this view, as on Striker's, there is an ambiguity in 'is'. Thus sound is *apeiron*, the hot is *apeiron* and certain pleasures are *apeira*. The account to be given of '*apeiron*' is in each case the same, but the 'is' has to be glossed differently. Roughly sound is *apeiron* in that it admits of representation by a continuum or continua, the hot is *apeiron* in being a form of continuum, certain pleasures are *apeira* in that they fall simply on the continuum (but of this more later). But I think that if the passages are read with the proposed interpretation in mind these different glosses on 'is' are not hard to pick up—one would naturally interpret the 'is' in these ways—and no damaging confusion is involved. Indeed (see below) even these glosses may be too starkly different.

Thus on point 1 (p. 186) this interpretation looks hopeful. On point 2 the characterization of the opposition between *peras* and *apeiron* is intended to recall features of the problem of irrationals, and recalls the point at 17e that the *apeiron* is incompatible with *logos.* The imposition of measurement, to the extent that it occurs, destroys indeterminacy, and so to that extent stops the continuum being indeterminate. But the measurement is always on some continuum which remains in the last resort immune to complete measurement. And so the combinations produced by a *techne* are *meikta*, they are proportions of measures on a particular continuum. Point 3 has already been dealt with. On point 4, it is questionable whether Plato would have thought it important to distinguish here. He does not have in mind an important contrast between Forms and particulars. He is thinking of a person producing the objects of his skill. Such a person must know the proportions to which such an object must conform and so be able to give a description of any such object. So general descriptions of the good life will be descriptions of (possible) *meikta*, and actual *meikta* will have to conform. But either is an equally good illustration of the point. It is not the concept of health that is a *meikton*, but the concept of health is the concept of a *meikton*. In fact one would expect actual states of things or described possible ones to be the examples. And this is what one gets. The important thing is that in order to count as *meikta* their measurements have to correspond to selected, not just any, points on the continuum.

This suggests the answer to point 5. As remarked above, '*apeiron*' does not stand for a class of concepts, but certain words suggest *apeira*. It might be better to think of the Hot and the Cold as the general phenomenon of indefinite variations of heat falling on a continuum. The Hot is not the element, Fire, nor the concept of heat, nor the Form of heat, but heat as a general phenomenon in our experience. This is the way *phone* is thought of in the Heavenly Tradition, and the division of *that* phenomenon into the High and Low involves considering it in its aspect as a general phenomenon of varying pitches. The terms the Hotter, the Less, and so on stand for the phenomena of heat and so on that can be represented by continua. Thus they are *apeira* in much the same sense of 'is' as *phone* is an *apeiron*. The skilled musician works within the general phenomenon of variable pitch and tempo and produces actual combinations that accord with the theory of music. But there will be many combinations of sounds whose pitch or tempo does not accord, and which, therefore, in the required sense lack measure: they fall above or below the measures required by music. In the terminology of the *Philebus*, therefore, they are not mixtures (cf. 64d–e). They are not of any quantity determined by *peras*, and so are not according to musical skill determinate. So they are indeterminate, because their pitch or tempo falls on the undetermined area of the continuum.

Thus excessive heat might count as an *apeiron*, and out of it, by bringing the right quantity of heat out of the excess, the god produces good weather (26a–b). Excessive heat might, as remarked earlier, be a relatively stable condition, hard to shift and so stably *apeiron*. In Plato's view certain pleasures are such that there is no stability of measure (cf. 52c and 46d–e). It might be that their intensity passed through permitted points, but the pleasures are such that they cannot be measured, but have to be plotted on a stretch of continuum which is either entirely or largely outside the proper measure. This reflects Plato's bias in favour of thinking of good states as relatively stable, as conditions of balance. In theory a condition of varying intensity of pleasure might be frequently passing through a permissible amount, so that quite often the pleasure experienced is a *meikton*. But Plato thinks of that which is varying as the pleasure, and because intrinsically given to variation incapable of precise measurement, and so only to be put down as on the indeterminate. But it is not necessary for something to be unstable in order to be *apeiron*.

In all this '*genos*' has to be taken as a not particularly precise term, such as 'category'. When we are told that everything in the universe can be divided into four, and these are four *gene*, the point is that in interpreting the observable universe at least four categories are needed, *peras*, *apeiron*, the results of imposing the first on the second, and intelligence. These are not classes of which things are members, still less genera, but they are four different tools. This looseness of '*genos*', '*eidos*' seems in keeping with the rest of the *Philebus*.

So on point 1 this interpretation does well, as neither of the others does. For this style of interpretation is less open to objection on the Heavenly Tradition than Interpretation 1, and preserves unity of doctrine as nothing else but Interpretation 1 applied to both passages could hope to. On point 2 it is neither better nor worse than the others. It copes with point 3 without the need to attribute damaging confusion to Plato, and manages points 4 and 5 with less complexity and less attribution of confusion than either of the other views.

There is one remaining objection. In the discussion of *apeiron* in particular, there is a good deal of talk of its being one and many, and of the need to round up the scattered *apeira* into a unit (23e, 24e–25a, 25d). The second passage has a clear reference back to 15b. Now it was those problems with which the Heavenly Tradition was supposed to help, and it was introduced as a long-time favourite method with Socrates. There are two points to be made. First, the word for 'rounding up', *synagein*, is the verb used in the *Phaedrus* discussion of the method of collection and division. Here, as there, it is part of dealing with a one/many problem, but neither there, nor in the passage about the many *apeira* being one, is anything done that remotely resembles what, on the present interpretation, the Heavenly Tradition recommends. Yet surely this must be what is meant by Socrates' favourite method, and we ought to make the Heavenly Tradition conform. Secondly, the Heavenly Tradition (17d) is supposed to be the way of dealing with every one and many, yet if the present interpretation of *peras* and *apeiron* is right, how could it be applied to the one *apeiron*/many *apeira* problem? Yet unless these questions can be answered the claim that the interpretation successfully relates the two passages has at least to be qualified.

The assumption behind this objection is that the Heavenly Tradition is in Plato's view the only method of dealing with the relevant one/many problems and is therefore identical with the method of collection and division, whatever that turns out to be. Yet there is nothing to prove this assumption. The claim that this is the way to deal with every one and many (17d) is a claim from within the tradition, not by Socrates. It could only be attributed to Socrates if he claimed this as the only method. But he only claims that he knows no *better* way out of the sophistical turmoil than this method, and though he says he has long been enamoured of it he does not say that this attachment comes from its power to solve all one/many problems. In fact it is billed as a help to *technai* and as we have seen Plato's own view on *technai* is that their value is proportionate to their mathematization. So if my interpretation is right we have a description of an approach to *technai* which Plato shows signs of liking at least as early as the *Republic* (and cf. *Gorgias* 501). It happens that if we examine this approach we find that there are things that are both one and many in the supposedly paradoxical way, and the appeal to *technai* is appropriate in face of the clever-clever young sophists. But it is not necessarily Plato's approved method for dealing with all one/many problems. Indeed, while it is his approved approach to *technai*, 55 seq. (especially 58) suggests that there are disciplines superior to the *technai*, and there other methods might be required. In 23 seq. the discussion of one/many is not from within a *techne*, but in a discussion about the terms to be used in describing *technai* and their products. It is perhaps significant that the back reference at 24e–25a is to 15b, before the Heavenly Tradition, to the general description of one/many problems. But by the Heavenly Tradition we have already ducked the general problem and have agreed to approach it by way of a familiar fact of language. The Heavenly Tradition helps us meet confusion raised by those who trade on this fact, and in a way that will be appropriate to pleasure, but there is no guarantee that it will cope with everything envisaged at 15b.

This, of course, might seem to allow us to reintroduce the possibility that pleasure itself, like *apeiron*, needs other than Heavenly Tradition methods to show how it is one and many. But Socrates himself agrees (18d–19a) that the Heavenly Tradition method is appropriate for the problem about pleasure that they started with, and this confirms the view that he considers it a subject for *techne* and assumes a hedonist will have to answer the challenge of achieving one.

It is part of this interpretation that the Heavenly Tradition is a borrowing from Pythagoreanism, chosen because it is an aspect of Pythagoreanism associated with the study of irrationals, in which Eudoxus was particularly interested. It is also a part of Pythagoreanism which fits well Plato's own view on *technai*. It should be clear from this that on the present interpretation it is vain to hunt these sections of the *Philebus* for development or abandonment of the theory of Forms. Granted Socrates' statement of long attachment, one might find an elaboration of Plato's view of the role of mathematics in *technai*, but that is all. This is not to deny (but not to assert either) that he still thought there was a Form of the hot and so on. But while 15a–b almost certainly alludes to Forms, and Plato very likely still held, as in *Republic* X, that things studied by *technai* were somehow related to Forms, the *Philebus* is silent on the subject. None of the categories in 23 seq. is to be taken as the class of Forms, nor is any to be taken as being a Form. The discussion is about *techne* and its products, conducted in Pythagorean vein, but doubtless with Plato's approval.

While I think, then, that we get some indication of how Plato viewed *technai* in the *Philebus*, it is worth noting the limitations of his analysis. As already remarked in discussing the word *techne* (see above, pp. 153–4) the analysis can only claim to apply to a limited range of intellectual competences. But it does seem that Plato had a prejudice in favour of what came within that range. Yet even if we accept that limitation there are unsatisfactory points. It has already been noted that the mathematical emphasis is either no more than an act of faith, or amounts to a metaphorical use of mathematical terms. Further, it seems that Plato is assuming that whenever you can speak of right combinations or arrangements it will be possible to represent the subject-matter in the appropriate geometrical way. Yet sometimes it is not just a problem of taking notions of measuring etc. with any seriousness, it is also difficult to see what the proposed continuum for plotting excess and defect might be. Suppose we take something which Plato himself in the *Sophist* speaks of by implication in terms of skill, the correct arrangement of words so as to yield meaningful sentences (*Sophist* 261–3). It is fair enough to say that we call 'Fido if horse but' an improper combination and 'Fido bites the horse' a proper one, but it is hard to think what the continuum is such that the first is excessive or defective. 'Grammatical' will not indicate one since it, like 'healthy', indicates a norm from which the ungrammatical deviates, not something certain degrees of which are grammatical others ungrammatical. In this case the notions of too much and too little have become unilluminating and simply serve to describe anything that is not right.

There is also a limitation of Plato's model for *technai* that may at least in part come from the fact that not only does he want them mathematicized but also the mathematics in question is confined to rational numbers. For he seems to want to give an account of, say, health, in terms of proportions between various factors, between, say, degrees of heat, solidity, size, and so on, but the proportions are fixed. Now putting it in terms of proportions certainly has advantages over straight quantities in that it allows people with different absolute quantities nevertheless to count as healthy. But the picture seems to be of humans of all ages having to approximate to the same proportions to count as healthy. Why could one not have a formula which made the proportions a function of age, as e.g. that in respect of two factors Health $= 2aG : \frac{100-a}{a} F$, where a stands in for age and F and G for properties representable by continua? We should then get varying proportions according to age: 4:49 at age 2, 20:9 at age 10, and the formula for health is for a constantly changing condition. That is, to remain healthy would be to be in a constant process of changing proportions between elements. Yet while this formula yields a rationally expressible ratio for every rational value of a, it is fairly clear that growing older is a continuous process. Consequently a person will pass through ages not commensurate with years, days, etc., so that a could not be given a rational value in the relevant measure. Similarly the value of $2aG$ will not always be rationally expressible. Formulae for continuous change of this sort suppose more than rational numbers. So long as one is confined to the latter it will be natural to think of health in terms of fixed proportions, the continuum as, as it were, that along which change takes place. Growth undoubtedly occurs. Animals change along a variety of continua. Consequently even the healthiest will commonly only be approximating to the proportions of a healthy condition. Change is associated with the *apeiron* and is not susceptible of precise mathematical expression, but it can be to some extent understood as approximation to expressible proportions. This is, I think, a strong influence on Plato's way of thinking of number, precision, stability as coming on one side, lack of number, instability on the other. It does, however, severely restrict the possibilities in *technai* that he will envisage.

Accepting these limitations, it seems that for the passage at 23 seq., Plato wishes to take up again the analysis of *techne* in the Heavenly Tradition. The emphasis is on what a *techne* produces because the good life is a putative product. As the products have to meet the requirements of the *techne* they have to display the required *peras* on the relevant *apeira*. The range of *apeira* in particular is widened because Plato wishes to display the universe at large as an arrangement (*kosmos*) (30a—c) and various features in it, such as health, seasons, etc., as sub-arrangements (26b—c). Further, he is now concerned not simply to indicate what marks a *sophos* or intelligent person, but to make out that certain sorts of product require intelligence. As the good life is such a product it will require intelligence for its production. So in this section there is, because of the question at issue, an interest in the role of intelligence. The issue also explains the broadening out to the cosmos at large, as this helps build up the role of intelligence by giving it a part in the divine strategy (see below, pp. 207 seq.). While the new tools were implicit in the Heavenly Tradition, they were no more than that. Together with the old ones they are now put to work to answer the new question. Neither this passage, nor the Heavenly Tradition, is a digression. Each is a relevant part of the argument in hand.

THE MICROCOSM/MACROCOSM ARGUMENT, 28–30

The argument develops as follows: first (28d–e) there is the general admission that the universe as a whole is governed by intelligence. Then (29a–d) there is an argument that the elements of which our bodies are constituted are a weak reflection of those in the universe at large. It is inferred (29c), fallaciously, that as the universe is constituted of the same elements as our bodies it must be a body too, which is responsible for the development of our bodies. But we have souls, so the universe must have a soul (30). For granted the general dependence of ourselves on the universe, and the physical analogy, it seems arbitrary to allow the role of the soul in our case and deny it in the other.

The invalidity of most of the steps is too obvious to dwell on. It is probably kindest to suppose that Plato thought of it as what is sometimes called an inclining argument. There are, however, problems as to quite what is being said, and also as to what the passage from 29a onwards adds, for the purposes of the argument, to what is granted at 28d–e.

To take the first first. This is in fact a succession of problems. To begin with, what is meant by saying at 29c5 that the fire in us is cherished and increased by the heavenly fire? It cannot be the bare point that the body takes in any increase of a given element from the environment. That is too weak for the notion of cherishing, and leaves puzzling the talk of greater power and beauty at 29c1–3. A possibility is that when Plato talks of the greater power of fire in the universe he is not thinking of its greater incendiary force, as a modern reader might infer. Rather he has in mind that if one studies the body one gets some idea of the functions and operations of the different elements in the system. This is very impressive and wonderful but only a small part of the total operations of these elements as observed in the universe as a whole, where their inter-action is more splendidly revealed. There we can see the interplay of earth, air, fire, and water in the seasons, the sun, the balance of nature, and so on. In this perspective it is easy to see individual organisms not as independent theatres for the elements' interaction, but as minute parts of a larger, finer operation. This invites the idea that the cherishing of heat in individual organisms is part of a more complex operation whereby the natural balance of the universe is achieved. This makes the moves at 30a–b less abrupt. For in effect the picture is already of the universe as a complex interacting system tending, like bodies, to a balance of elements. This suggests that our lives are aspects of the life of the universe, of its organic operation.

This may be the picture intended, and certainly the passage flows more easily if so. It leaves problems about the soul. In previous dialogues the prime operation of the soul has been rational thinking and ordering (cf. e.g. *Phaedo passim*, *Republic* I, 353d, *Phaedrus* 246b). Other operations, such as spiritedness and desire for physical satisfactions, which sometimes enter as part of the nature of the soul, are influences on decision and action of which the agent is aware. In the present passage Plato needs a tie between souls and universe closer than that of designer to product designed or even of pilot to ship piloted in the way Descartes envisages the use of that image. He wishes (30a–b) not only to speak of a directing intelligence but of a living body. Living—*empsuchos*—means 'possessing a *psuche*' (soul?). The language of 30a–b suggests that Plato is thinking of digestion and various living functions of the body as functions of *psuche* as well as more ratiocinatory performances. The question therefore arises how this fits with earlier views of the soul (cf. *Phaedo passim*, *Republic* IV and X, *Phaedrus* 245 seq.; cf. also *Laws* 898).

A further problem arises about individuation of souls. It may be well enough to speak of fire both in the universe at large and in its parts, but 'bits' of fire tend to be distinguished by their place of operation or identified initially by place at a certain time and then individuated by tracing history backwards or forwards to that place. This latter operation, however, becomes very complex as bits get absorbed in larger masses, complex to the point of impossibility. Souls, however, seem to be individuated by memories, character traits, intellectual interests and capabilities, capacity for entering into certain personal relationships. It is hard to see what the distinction is between their absorption into the larger mass and their destruction. This is crude, but the point is that Plato's way of talking of souls 'coming from' the world soul raises problems of the interrelations of concepts such as those of life, mind, soul, person. But in some way he seems to be inviting us to view the universe on analogy with the body, and the operations of various intelligences on analogy with the divergent but ultimately coherent operations of parts of the organism.

If this is so, the question then arises: what advance have we made by 30e over the position at 28e? The answer is twofold. First, we have, supposedly, some support over and above the authority of 'those with any claim to intelligence' for the view admitted at 28e. Secondly, there is a rhetorical point in favour of intelligence. For it is now seen not just as the organizer of individual lives, but each person's intelligence is in some sense part of the directing life-principle of the universe. This puts all our minds in good company, and gives them a role that might be hoped to make the pursuit of an individual's pleasure look meagre.

The passage in general is of interest not only as a relative of the theistic argument from design, but as an example of Plato's normal tendency to tie intelligent activity to the production of arrangements that can be assessed as better or worse done (cf. e.g. *Gorgias* 503-4, *Phaedo* 97-9, *Republic* VI, X). It is this point, not a simple fact about regularity, that leads to the postulation of intelligence, and such orderings are the characteristic outcome of intelligent operation.

THE EXAMINATION OF PLEASURE, 31 ad fin.

There are three general problems about this passage, (i) concerning the form it takes, (ii) concerning its relation to the dialectical method just discussed, (iii) concerning the use of the word for 'true'.

(i) The whole of the passage 31-55 is taken up with 'mixed'/ 'false' pleasures—except for 51a-52c, where we get a brief mention of some unadulterated pleasures. The rest is taken up with physical pleasures, pleasures of anticipation, and the mixed pleasures of the mind alone. Why this imbalance? The reason is probably that the argument shifts so as to be directed more immediately at Philebus. It has been noted (note on 27e1-2) that it is from Philebus that the admission is extracted that pleasure is *apeiron*, and extracted in a form which seems to show a misunderstanding of what Socrates is saying. In the present passage that admission is several times recalled (just before it, at 31a, at 32d, 41d, 52c-e). The context of the earlier of these passages is that of mixed pleasures—and for the first time Plato talks of pleasure and distress forming a continuum—in the last it is the mixed pleasures that are specifically characterized as *apeira* in contrast with others. Now Philebus is billed as someone whose interests are in what are usually called physical pleasures, and when we are discussing this *apeiron* it is Philebus' candidates that are always in mind. Various themes hostile to these pleasures run through the passage. In addition to these, we get a treatment of pleasures of anticipation, but the discussion starts from and remains within the limits of anticipation of pleasures or states seen in contrast with a present state of felt distress. The typical 'false' pleasure is the sort that Socrates might expect someone of Philebus' way of life to experience frequently. When we come to mixed pleasures of the mind alone at 47c, we move from thirst-quenching and scratching to more refined pleasures of the theatre and the emotions. It is not likely that Philebus, any more than Callicles in the *Gorgias*, is concerned to advocate simply the pursuit of physical pleasures. A life of pleasure will involve more cultured indulgences. The analysis of comedy was doubtless undertaken partly because in itself intriguing, but also because comedy might seem pure pleasure, and the analysis of it as mixed helps underline how much of life is in the same case (cf. 50b). Consequently, the whole passage up to 50d analyses the mass of pleasures espoused by the average hedonist. The 'pure' pleasures at 51−2 stand out as not the sort such a man would spend much time on. The aim is clearly to contrast one set of pleasures with another, a contrast preserved at 63d−e, 65c−d, 66c−d, when all the 'mixed' pleasures are rejected except such as are necessary for life.

In short, the main burden of the passage seems to be to exclude certain pleasures as having any part in the good life (so showing not all pleasures to be desirable, cf. 32d), and the pleasures concerned are ones one would expect Philebus to advocate. This is why at 44b the dour scientists are described as Philebus' real enemies. Their analysis may not be right as a general analysis of pleasure, but it tells against one main class of pleasures that Philebus favours.

But this raises a question as to why the direction of the argument has changed. Up to 31a there has been no consideration of a thesis in favour of certain pleasures, but only of a more general hedonism. The reason is not, I think, far to seek. Plato sees Philebus (cf. 66e) as representing a very common view of life, strengthened, no doubt, by the authority of Eudoxus, which observes the general tendency of animals and men to pursue pleasure, and infers that pleasure is the good, while interpreting 'pleasure' as referring to certain classes of pleasure, and, without great thought, tending to reject out of hand the claims of other factors to be desirable. There is no place for an analysis of particular types of pleasure so long as the view is deployed with the singular 'pleasure', referring differences to difference of source. If the singular presentation can be broken down, then one can consider particular candidates. But Plato makes the critique of that presentation in a form that leads naturally, via rejection of the view that pleasure alone is sufficient to make a life good, to a consideration of the ideal as a particular organization of life. This enables him to distinguish two 'explanations' of the goodness of the good life: productive intelligence, and the order whose presence makes the life good. Pleasure is clearly in neither category. This constitutes a criticism of other than Phileban hedonism. If cogent it tells against more refined Eudoxan views and in general against attempts to give pleasure the role of arbiter between candidates for inclusion in the good life. But it leaves open the possibility that all pleasures are desirable (cf. 32c−d), and also therefore that all Philebus' pleasures are. They might even be the main thing desirable. Since we can now allow pleasures to differ, the way is open to tackle the specifically Phileban candidates, and this Socrates proceeds

to do. So the criticism of Philebus has three stages:
(i) Pleasure should not be spoken of in the singular, and so hedonism is either holding that *all* pleasures are good, or some particular ones; (ii) the fact that a life contains pleasures is not what makes it good; (iii) the particular pleasures favoured by Philebus are not only not the good but ought to be excluded.

In considering the anti-Phileban direction of this section it is worth noting the use made of the notion of an intermediate state and of two appeals to known views on pleasure. At 32e seq. Socrates draws the conclusion from the analysis of physical pleasure and pain that when the body is neither being disturbed from nor restored to its natural balance there will be neither pleasure nor distress, and points out that the ideal intellectual life might be in this state. All that strictly follows of this state is that it is free of physical pleasure or distress. So we get a contrast between a life with (spent in) (cf. 35e) physical pleasures, and a life without. The theme of a neutral state is picked up again at 42d seq. (and cf. 43c8−11). The picture is now refined: pleasure is not simply the restoration to natural balance but the perception of that restoration. Once again we get three lives spoken of (43c13). The argument requires no talk of lives, and mention seems to be inserted in order to harp on the point that the pleasures under discussion are in fact being put forward (by Philebus) as an object of pursuit in life. These same pleasures come under the analysis of releases from pain (44c) and show their true colours in the intense forms discussed at 44−6, following the views of certain physicists. As remarked above, the reserve expressed about this view is as a general analysis of pleasure. There is no reason to suppose the analysis is rejected as covering this sort of pleasure. The language at 52c, 63d−e, and 65c−d suggests that the general picture of the true character of these pleasures is accepted, and the talk of release from pain can be accommodated in the analysis of 31c seq. At the end of the account of these thinkers' views we are reminded again that the pleasures in question are possible candidates for the status of main goal in life (cf. 47b).

At 53c4 seq. another appeal is made to a well-known view that pleasure is a process towards an end state, but not itself an end state. As with the thesis that pleasure is a flight from pain, this view is not accepted but we are told that gratitude is owed to its proponents. As in that case there is little cause for gratitude if it is just another bad analysis of pleasure. The reason for gratitude is that it is considered to be true of a large number of those pleasures that characteristically feature prominently in the sort of hedonism for which Philebus stands. Consequently someone who says pleasure is good is holding that one should make it one's goal in life to indulge in activities

directed to a goal but only in so far as they do not achieve that goal
(cf. 54d5 seq.); and while this may not be true of pleasure in general,
it will hold for Plato's own analysis of physical pleasures—a large
part of those Philebus wants us to spend our life pursuing. Thus the
general context of what we are to make our goal in life is kept before
us throughout the analyses of sorts of pleasure, and always in a way
that invites us to see the oddity of devoting our lives to a particular
sort of pleasure. No attention is given to a view that selects other
more refined pleasures for pursuit. It is always those of the 'life of
pleasure' that come in for attack. So what we get is not a thorough
study of pleasure, but a thorough study of Phileban pleasure, with a
brief glance at some unadulterated ones.

(ii) It is commonly held that from 31b onwards we ought to find a
working-out of the programme of 23 seq. In fact, there is a notable
absence of all talk of number or equality. Yet there is surely a listing
of kinds of the sort we were led to believe at 20c4—6 that we should
be let off. What, then are we entitled to expect, and do we get?

Not a great deal of weight can be put on 20c4—6, which could
easily be explained away by reference to its tentativeness and the
general vagaries of conversation. Still, it is perhaps worth noting that
we do not get what is envisaged in that earlier context. While there is
a certain listing of pleasures we get no examination of the pleasures
of health and virtue (cf. 63e) or of the exercise of knowledge
(66c4—6) (the discussion at 52a is of the acquisition of knowledge).
Further, we get no account of why 'pleasure' might be taken to
denote a single class. There are statements (e.g. 31d8—10) that
might be construed as doing this for certain classes of pleasure, but
such statements seem only provisional, and never to cover pleasure in
general. So in fact we do not seem to have anything that would meet
the requirements of the Heavenly Tradition—statements such as
34c10—d1 concern how pleasure comes about, and that only for
certain sorts of pleasure.

Nor do we seem to have an application of the theorizing of
23 seq., unless Plato thinks that greater and less truth is in fact an
apeiron on which he begins to impose some measure. But *apeiron* is
never used of this scale, and is only used in this passage of pleasure,
and specifically of certain sorts. With regard to those sorts there is
no discussion of in what measure to have them. As already noted
there is in this section a shift to the examination of Phileban
pleasures. While we are told that we shall inquire whether all
pleasures are desirable or only some (32d), there is no indication
that we should expect a detailed exposition of the good life *meikton*.
The reason for supposing we might is that it would surely make the
dialogue more of a unit. But this, I think, misconstrues the plan of

the dialogue. The purpose of 23 seq. was to determine the respective roles of intelligence and pleasure, and the notion of a mixture is important here. For the mixtures in question have intelligence as cause, and the *apeiron*, to which pleasure is relegated, has a lowly status. For settling the question of relative status there is no need for a detailed account of the good life. It is enough that it is a mixture of the required sort. As remarked earlier, however, at this stage it remains a possibility that all pleasures are good and that Phileban ones are what intelligence has to produce. So Plato turns to the question whether all pleasures are desirable, since until this is settled Philebus' position remains more nearly intact than Plato would like. The aim is not to give a detailed account of the good life but to lay down principles for deciding which pleasures/forms of knowledge to include. The result is a more Socratic, less Phileban set of ingredients. As a result Plato can have a final prize-giving with a distinction between those pleasures that will be allowed and those that Philebus advocates (66c). If this point about the structure of the dialogue is right one would not expect an application of either the Heavenly Tradition or 23 seq. to the examination of pleasure. Consequently no view of *peras/apeiron* has to measure up to the test of applicability to this section (cf. Introduction pp. 13 seq.).

(iii) The final general point is the unnerving use of the word translated 'true' some of the time, and 'genuine' some of the time. It seems impossible to acquit Plato of the charge of rank equivocation. Briefly, the difficulty is that sometimes (e.g. 37 seq.) 'true' and 'false' seem to operate as with belief, so that falsity of pleasure carries no suggestion that the pleasure is not genuine. At other times (e.g. 52d seq.) calling pleasures false (not true) is tantamount to questioning whether they are really pleasures. By 52d seq., where lack of admixture of pain is taken as arguing for greater 'truth' of pleasure, it seems fairly clear that X is a true pleasure to the extent that it is true of it without qualification that it is a pleasure. When knowledge is discussed, on the other hand, the criterion of 'true' knowledge is capacity to yield precise truths. If we can set aside 37 seq. some coherence can be brought to the use of 'true', perhaps. The basic interest would be in isolating examples of things called pleasure or knowledge to which the descriptions could be applied without demur, i.e. of which they were strictly true. Demur is justified either by clear absence of pleasure/knowledge, or by the present of their opposites: distress/ignorance. Thus, all 'mixed' pleasures, as well as neutral states, are 'false'. Even the false pleasures discussed at 37 seq. are, for reasons that are not at all clear, supposed also to be mixed. The fact remains that these examples are supposed also to be false in a sense that has nothing to do with the strict falsity of calling them pleasures. The argument about true (= genuine or unqualified) becomes important at 61d seq. as governing the mixture. None of the moves there would serve to rule out false pleasures of the sort discussed at 37 seq., unless it could be shown that these must always be mixed ones. It seems that the important sense for the main argument is that of 'genuine' or 'unqualified', but it is hard to resist the suspicion that the equivocation is played upon via the feeling that all falsity must be repugnant to the intellect. (Cf. the use of 'truth' at 64b2–3, and e9–10, 65d2–3 and *Laws* 726 seq. esp. 73 oc.) I have aimed to insert the word *'alethes'* in brackets when that family of words is being translated, and *'to on'* ('being') or *'ontōs'* ('really') where those are translated 'true' or 'genuinely'.

A word is in order on the sense in which we are given an analysis of pleasure at all. What we seem to get, early on, is a general description of conditions under which certain pleasures occur. Plato talks as though the pleasure of quenching one's thirst *is* the perception of a restoration of natural harmony. It has been claimed (cf. Gosling, *Phronesis* VI (1961)) that Plato thought of pleasure as the satisfaction of desire, and in *Republic* IX, 585d–e, at least, he certainly seems to toy with that idea. It will not do for the *Philebus*, however, where it looks as though neither pleasures of anticipation, nor of malice, will fit this account, nor should those of virtue or the exercise of knowledge (cf. *Symposium* 204a: the wise do not desire wisdom, though presumably they enjoy its exercise). We have in fact quite different sorts of pleasure requiring different accounts. The sort of account envisaged is not conceptual analysis but a theory of the conditions for the occurrence of pleasure, and statements of what pleasure is have to be construed in that way. In consistency with the earlier sections, however, Plato would not be expected to be attracted by the prospect of an over-all account of the sort envisaged in *Republic* IX and by Aristotle in the *Nicomachean Ethics*. 'Pleasure is the replenishment of a lack (or satisfaction of a desire)' is the sort of answer demanded in the early dialogues, and gives a point of similarity between all pleasures. But that search is rejected in 12c seq. Just as there is no account of what a letter is that one can learn without learning one's letters, and armed with it identify the various letters independently, so there is no account of what pleasure is that one can learn without learning about all the pleasures and their mutual connections. They can be put in one class, but not in virtue of a similarity formula. A science of pleasure is needed to justify their being put into a single class, and that is not being supplied in the *Philebus*. In short, Plato does not, in the *Philebus*, give us an account of pleasure, if at that time he had one.

•

FALSE PLEASURES, 32–43

This section divides into three parts. The first and longest ends at 41a4 and argues that pleasures of anticipation can be false in the same sense as the false beliefs on which they are based. The second is from 41a5 to 42c4 where it is argued that certain future pleasures seem larger than life from the circumstances of present distress and so affect our judgement, because much of the pleasure foreseen is apparent only. The rest considers examples of states which are as such neither forms of pleasure nor distress, but are commonly called pleasures. In both these last sections the future pleasures that affect our judgement and the states that are neither of pleasure or distress have been thought, wrongly, to be false pleasures (see below). This would be straightforward equivocation like that on 'true' (see above, pp. 212 seq.). The general purpose is, however, clear enough. Plato thinks the situations of anticipation envisaged are common and typically Phileban. Error of judgement is consequently a common Phileban situation. Further, as the errors are in judgements about pleasure, they are not ones that even a Phileban is likely to consider admissible.

The first section. Here it is important to note that Plato wants to argue that pleasure can be false in the same sense that judgement can, and to refute the view that he puts clearly into the mouth of Protarchus (37e12–38a2) that only the judgement can be false, not the pleasure. This is the form of the conclusion at 40c4–6, and the point of making Protarchus find the thesis prima facie unacceptable (36c–d), and then give the common-sense analysis at 37e12, is to make it clear that the common-sense view is not what Plato wishes to hold. What is introduced between 37e12 and the conclusion is something else besides judgements or statements, viz. pictures that can be straightforwardly true or false (39c4–5) and the following sentences establish that we can suffer this (i.e. picturing) with regard to the future, that is, we are pleased and distressed in anticipation, and these pleasures are hopes. In short, Plato is rejecting the view of these pleasures that there is a judgement about the future which may be true or false, which gives rise to pleasure which is neither. And this is done by identifying the anticipatory pleasure with picturing the future pleasure, another name for which is hope.

The thesis is supposed to hold for fear, anger, and the rest as well (cf. 40e2–4 and 36c10–11). Indeed it is at first sight more acceptable to think of fears, and even more of expectations, as true or false, so that the tactic is like that later with spite, of taking the hard case. The use of the word for hope at 36a in relation to pleasant anticipation of pleasure and its recurrence at 39e (and cf. 47c7) to sum up the picturing of future pleasures is not accidental. Talking of false hopes is also more acceptable than talking of false pleasures, but if the anticipatory pleasure and the hope are one and the same thing, then they will be equally capable of truth or falsity. In this connection, however, 40a6–7 should be noted. While 40a9–12 identifies hopes with the writings *and* pictures, this sentence seems to confine the hopes to the writings. This is *just* possible, but would necessitate taking the sentence as saying, 'There are statements in each of us, which we call hopes', and then taking Socrates' next statement as 'And moreover there are painted images'–the latter not being called hopes. But the introductory phrase means something like 'and especially (the painted images)'. In other words the paintings are more especially what we have in mind in talking of hopes.

That is, in sketch, what Plato seems to be saying, but the account has been disputed and it will be as well to note some of the crucial points in the interpretation. As I take it, Plato is inclined to approach the topic of pleasure via the plural 'pleasures', this being the plural of which 'the pleasure of quenching one's thirst', 'the pleasure of winning a game of tennis', etc. are singulars. He is then inclined to ask what makes them all pleasures, and this is a problem because the pleasure of quenching one's thirst seems to consist in quenching one's thirst, which is very different from playing tennis (for more elaboration see notes on 12c6 and 13a7). By the time of the *Philebus* (see above, p. 213 and note on 12c6) he had abandoned earlier flirtation with a general characterization, but it is still true that there are more specific types of characterization such as, e.g., 'picturing a future pleasure', 'perceiving the return of one's constitution to its natural state', and so on which give what constitutes the pleasures of the various types.

J. Dybikowski (p. 151) (cf. also T. Penner, p. 177n.) claims that while Plato's general theory may be along these lines, in the passage at 37a–e he clearly distinguishes the pleasure of anticipation from its object, and so facts about the general theory cannot be used to interpret this particular passage. The difficulty here is that talk of 'object' is Dybikowski's and it is not clear how it is being used. For on the account of Plato's general theory sketched above Plato could be described as not distinguishing between pleasure and its object in that he treats the pleasure as the activity or experience enjoyed, as that in which we take pleasure. (The 'object' is given by what is governed by the verb 'enjoy'.) It is not clear that this is abandoned at 37a–e. That which the pleasure is there said to be about is some absent, and, in anticipatory cases, future state of affairs, and it becomes false just and only when the *logos* becomes false, i.e. when that state of affairs does not obtain. But this is not the object of the present anticipatory pleasure, where the object is given by the object of the verb 'enjoy'. For what he enjoys is anticipating. The future state of affairs is the object of the anticipation. What he enjoys is picturing himself enjoying the future circumstances, and Plato might still think the pleasure consisted in that. It could be, of course, that Plato fails to distinguish 'enjoy' from 'be pleased about'; that we need the second for the present passage; and that he for once rightly distinguishes taking pleasure in X from X. But in fact, although I have used the 'pleased that . . .' translation, this is *faute de mieux*. Plato has something more limited in mind, viz. gloating. I can be pleased at the prospect of a fortune without even thinking about the fortune, and my pleasure take the form of a more relaxed and cheerful generosity to my friends. But Plato is thinking of a person who is now enjoying seeing himself in his mind's eye enjoying his fortune. (Cf. 32c1–2, 36a, 39b–c, 40a: the examples are only of enjoyment in advance of future pleasures, by picturing them, cf. *Republic* 584c9–11.) There is, then, something that he is enjoying, the picture, but the picture is related to the 'facts', or is 'about' them, and it is they that, for Plato, the pleasure is 'about'. If they are the object, then 'object' is now being used in a different sense.

There is, then, no call to take this passage as indicating that Plato is not as usual thinking that the pleasure is the activity or experience enjoyed, and if that is his general tendency there is something to be said for not attributing to him a marked but unmarked change. In that case it will be most natural to suppose that when Protarchus at first rejects the idea that pleasures can be false and is asked by Socrates whether he then thinks that no one ever, in waking life or asleep, thinks he is enjoying something when he is not, Socrates is expecting him to think that of course a person sometimes thinks he is enjoying things when he is not. He will expect this because people obviously dream they are indulging in pleasures when the activity in question is not taking place. So this question serves the purpose of introducing some hesitation in Protarchus' outright rejection (cf. note on 36e5).

In 37 Socrates tries an analogy between pleasure and belief, but Protarchus will not accept it. In 38–9 Socrates introduces a myth about the mind. We have a Scribe who writes in beliefs/statements, and a Painter who paints pictures of what the statements assert. These operations are distinct. A man at times gazes on these pictures (39c1), the pictures can be true or false according to whether or not the *logoi* are (39c4–5), and just like anticipatory pleasures they can be about the future. In fact such pleasures are hopes (39e4–5) and hopes are *logoi* (40a6–7), but more especially pictures (40a9–12). In other words: pleasures of anticipation are hopes, which are pictures, which can be false. At this point Protarchus is lost. For while the pleasures are not beliefs, but accompany beliefs (for they are pictures based on them), still they can quite strictly be called false, since pictures can (39c).

Dybikowski (p. 152) objects that this involves equating picturing with pictures, and both he (p. 164) and Penner (pp. 176–7n.) suppose that it involves a strange translation of 'pictured pleasures' to mean 'pictures of pleasures'—the one takes the expression to mean the pleasures of which the pictures are pictures, the other the pleasures portrayed in the picture, which are false if the picture is false (though why is not explained).

As to the first point, as Penner brings out, Plato shows some vacillation in the use of '*doxa*' as between the operation of judging and the proposition judged to be true, especially in the Scribe/Painter passage. There is no reason to suppose him aware of an important contrast in the Painter simile. In fact, once one recognizes that Plato's example is not of being pleased, but of gloating, then it is clear that the important point is the viewing of the picture (cf. 39c1, 40a9–12: it is this, not constructing the picture, that is picturing). Now if we are thinking of three-dimensional pictures there is an obvious independence between pictures and viewings. Further, if we speak of someone having a strange picture of Athenian democracy, we can describe the picture without supposing him to be 'viewing' it. But if we are thinking of the picture of a future fortune as what the gloater gloats over, then it is a moot point what there is in any distinction between the picture and the viewing. The 'image' lasts just so long as the viewing and conversely. Further, quite apart from Plato's equations mentioned above, it seems all too common that those who use the picture/image terminology for talking about the imagination conflate the image with its viewing. As an analogous conflation is made with judgement, this seems even more likely in this case.

As to '*phantasmata ezōgraphemena*' (40a9) (painted images) and '*hedonai ezōgraphemenai*' (40b6–7) (painted pleasures), it is a familiar usage that the participle should not imply that the originals of the painting are referred to. Cf. *Phaedo* 73e where 'the painted Simmias' ('the painted horse' etc.) is clearly not referring to the Simmias who is painted or the Simmias in the painting but to the *eikon*, the painting or image of Simmias, or the picture-Simmias. Here too, 'the painted pleasures' can naturally mean 'the paintings of pleasures' and 'the painted images' 'the paintings of the images'.

In short, it seems that Plato does not distinguish picturing a fortune from the picture of a fortune in the context of gloating, and that he does identify the picture/picturing with the pleasure. As the picture/picturing is agreed to be true or false, so are (these) pleasures. Consequently Protarchus is brought to agree to something he had originally rejected, and Socrates is holding something stronger than a view that pleasures accompanying/dependent on false belief might as well be called false by extension too. For if this were all he wanted to say it is not clear why Protarchus would want to object so vigorously, except on the grounds that it is a way of talking that might mislead people.

As I have pointed out, 'anticipatory pleasure' has to be interpreted narrowly as covering gloating anticipations only, where the point is not that the subject is gloating over anyone, but simply over the prospective pleasure. There certainly seem to be occasions that fit this general description. It remains that it is only a sub-set of what would usually be considered as pleasures in anticipation. A child, excited at the prospect of going to a fair, a woman pleased at the prospect of retirement are not necessarily, or even typically, picturing the prospect to themselves. Plato has not, in fact, given a general account of anticipatory pleasures. What, then, of the set he has selected? There is, of course, a problem of what is meant by saying that the pleasure is the picturing of a future pleasure (see note on 12c6). Apart from that at least three points are worth making: first, that picturing a believed-in future pleasure is not sufficient for anticipatory pleasure. A person of ascetic aspirations may successfully picture himself enjoying giving in to some future temptation he believes is coming his way and be depressed or disgusted at the prospect. Secondly, there is no need for the sort of pleased picturing that Plato has in mind to be confined to the subject's supposed future pleasures: he might delightedly picture some believed-in future pleasure of some other person. Plato is, in fact, further confining himself to enjoying in anticipation a future pleasure of one's own. Thirdly, although the conflation of picture and picturing is one that Plato almost certainly committed, it is a conflation nevertheless. The pleasure is most plausibly identified with the picturing, but all that can strictly be said to be false is the picture. No doubt if we are concentrating on the gloating episode, picture and picturing are coterminous in the sense that a picturing and the occurrence of a picture live or die together. But it must always be possible to distinguish the questions whether A was picturing something and what his picture was like and was of. When we have the answer to the second question, we get a description of a portrayal as a portrayal of certain supposed facts. This will be assessable for accuracy against the facts, and this will be discussable without reference to particular occasions on which the picture is entertained. It is the picture considered this way, not the picturing, that might be called false. The case is parallel to belief, where it is not the believing that is false—the belief in that sense—but what is believed.

The second section. This passage makes out that when a person is in distress, but hopeful, the judgement tends to be distorted by the mixed distress/pleasure situation. But while that is briefly right, the exposition is less than lucid. We start with the point that the typical anticipation situation embodies a combination of physical distress and mental pleasure. One can see how this disturbing situation might make it difficult to form judgements about the future, but that is not Plato's point. He thinks it sends them askew. We then get a reminder that pleasure and pain are capable of degrees of excess and defect and that we need a means of measuring relative size. But in visual perception distance can lead to false judgements. So too in pleasure.

The point, expanded, presumably is that pleasure and pain can vary in degrees, so that false judgement about degrees is possible— there is not a known degree that all pleasures or any pleasures have. But just as judgements of size can be bedevilled by distance, so can judgements of future pleasure. At this point, two obscurities arise. First, what distance tends to do is make more distant things look smaller; but with pleasure the situation is more complicated. If I am at present fairly contented, the distant prospect of some great pleasure tends to be unexciting, and so, Platonically, my picture of it is not true, even if my judgement is; though also, but not so obviously commonly, my judgement also may be false. But if I am in a state of considerable distress, then I tend to view exaggeratedly even slight possible releases. But what governs the exaggeration here is a combination of the degree of distress and the degree of likelihood of release, more obviously than distance. If I am engaged in a boring course that I can at any time abandon, though I am determined to stick it out, the pleasure of release will not get so exaggerated as if I cannot give it up but must stick it out. If, therefore, one has in mind familiar facts about distorted anticipation in situations of present distress, the analogy with sight is not immediately illuminating. For in so far as it does any more than simply reassert that we make mistakes it casts a shadow by suggesting that the mistakes are typically to underestimate the size of distant pleasures and so not easily fitting familiar cases (cf. *Protagoras* 356).

The second obscurity is that at 42b Socrates contrasts this example with the previous one in that there judgement infected pleasure with its falsity whereas here the pleasure infects the judgement. As the pleasure that infects the judgement is the (falsely) apparent future pleasure, and this is made much of in the passage, it is easy to suppose that it is this that is being said to be false (cf. Gosling, 1 *Phronesis* IV (1959)). But in fact 42c1–3 makes it clear that Plato has the right conclusion in mind. This particular form of false anticipation is doubtless typical of the mixed pleasures to be discussed later, which is why at 41b1–2 they are said to be important for the final judgement. Consequently some time is spent on the tendency to illusion. But it is the present anticipation as directed to the merely apparent pleasure that is false.

The third section. This might make one doubt whether a common view on the third sort of false pleasure is right (cf. Hackforth, Runciman, Gosling, op. cit.), that it is false in virtue of not being a pleasure at all. If this is right, then Plato is guilty of rank equivocation. He does not in fact, however, say that they are false in virtue of not really being pleasures. He does say that certain conditions are not pleasures although some people think they are, but it is quite possible that what he had in mind was that people who are in a disrupted state look forward with pleasure to states that are ones of neither pleasure nor pain. In fact he does not elaborate on this class in terms of anticipation but uses the discussion as a lead in to the physicists' views at 44b. If, however, he still has the anticipatory pleasures in mind, then the distinction between the three types will be that in the first a false judgement as to what will occur takes place, though if it did occur it would be pleasant, in the second there is a false judgement of the amount of pleasure, though that some pleasure will occur is right, in the third there is a gross mistake about the nature of pleasure altogether. In all cases there is a false anticipatory pleasure based on the judgements; the difference is in the sorts of mistake, and their gravity as mistakes about pleasantness.

PLEASURE AS BECOMING, 53–54

This section, together with 55b, does not continue the argument of the preceding passage. It is rather an abrupt introduction of a current view on pleasure which is hostile to hedonism. One gets the impression that Plato had this piece to hand, was unwilling to abandon it, could not blend it in smoothly, so in desperation inserted it badly at this point. The inference from baldness to incoherence, however, may be as unwise here as elsewhere. The discussion of pleasure from 31 onwards displays a certain pattern. We begin with an account of physical pleasures which sees them as processes of re-establishment of physical harmony. Then there is a discussion of anticipatory pleasures—the anticipations concentrated on being of physical pleasures. Then we have the physicists' analysis of physical pleasures as releases from pain, and the examination of those organic processes that produce violent pleasures. Then there is a discussion of mixed pleasures of the soul alone, and of pure pleasures, and finally we come back again to physical pleasures. The return to physical pleasures is like a refrain. But it is a developing refrain. The refrain is a constant reminder of the pleasures that play a central role in the hedonism of Philebus (and countless others cf. 66e seq., and for an example see Callicles in the *Gorgias* 491-4). The development produces a gradually more precise account of these pleasures. At first they are described simply as returns to a normal state, then as perceived returns to a normal state, though on the assumption that both lack and replenishment are perceived. The perception requirement makes possible the admission of pure physical pleasures which are still thought of (51b) as replenishments of lacks, but the lacks are unperceived. These contrast with the normal subjects of Phileban advocacy, which are typically mixed, but they are still processes. The criticism canvassed in the present passage also embraces pure physical pleasures. For if all these are processes (and this point is never rejected, but only suspect as a general account of pleasure) then there results the oddity that not only Philebus with his typically mixed pleasures, but anyone who advocates physical pleasures of any sort as a main object in life is inviting us to make our main pursuit situations which are themselves the pursuit of something else. This is like encouraging people to go in for the process of learning while declaring the truth to be unimportant. As with the physicists earlier, so now Plato accepts these thinkers as allies, without accepting their view. Once again, the hesitation is probably with the view as a general account of pleasures, but they are allies because right about physical pleasures and about the oddity of spending one's life in their pursuit. For related criticisms cf. *Gorgias* 493-4, *Republic* IX, 585-7. For a criticism of any attempt to say pleasure is a process of becoming cf. Aristotle *Nicomachean Ethics*, 1152b12 seq., 1173a29 seq.

It might be objected that this point holds equally against pleasures of learning, and this is I think true. It is noticeable that the only pure pleasures of the mind alone that are treated are those of learning, and while Plato does not in so many words commit himself to saying that they are processes of coming to know, the language invites one to think of the pleasures of acquisition. But the fact is not an objection. The point of deciding on the truth of a pleasure is to decide on its acceptability in the good life. The oddity highlighted in the present passage is not one involved in their inclusion, but in making them a main objective. There is no reason to suppose Plato would not have thought it odd to make a main objective of the pleasures of acquisition of knowledge. It is certainly noticeable that mention of other pure pleasures of the soul is kept until later (63e).

FORMS OF KNOWLEDGE, 55–59

In this section it becomes clear that Socrates' candidate is not only the organizing intelligence of life, but also the practice of various particular skills. This was hinted in the talk of forms of knowledge at e.g. 13e seq., but hitherto intelligence as needed to produce a good mixture has stolen the limelight. As in the *Republic*, considerable weight is put on the extent to which mathematics enters into an inquiry, and this is used to grade pursuits by reference to their capacity to produce precise and accurate results, though allied here to a more tolerant view of the use of the word '*episteme*'. The grading is not used to exclude aspirants for the title, but to explain the principle of inclusion. As in other dialogues the inability of practical branches of knowledge to produce firm results is related to the changeable nature of their subject-matter. It is not altogether clear just what the principle of grading is. It seems that there are two, one according to the method employed, the other according to the subject-matter studied. The first is to the fore in distinguishing flute-playing from building, and both from arithmetic. Here it seems that a branch of knowledge is to be preferred to the extent that it is more purely mathematical, and the reason seems to be the increasing precision as we move up this scale. Someone may be quite good at constructing houses by eye. As a result of long experience he has a feel for the right angles and elevations. But his instructions will be of the form 'a little more to the left', 'not quite so high as that', and so on. In other words, they will be imprecise. A builder who uses measuring instruments will be able to give measurements of angles for the pitch of the roof, or for the height of the ceiling. But he still works within a permissible margin of error as he has to use measuring instruments and judge the measurement. A geometer, by contrast, is dealing in exact lengths and angles and their relationships,—exact because the measurements are given and it is relations between these, not objects measured, that he studies. At 59a, however, a slightly different point seems to be made, in terms of eternal truths as against others. On this view, builders would only be able to give information that held for the most part either because of the variability of materials, or because statements about actual houses were always about objects that, however slowly, were nevertheless changing (see note on 59b4–5). In these last respects the builder who builds by eye is no worse off than one who goes in for measuring. So we have a means of discriminating between practical skills, and another for grading theoretical ones above practical ones.

There is now a problem. Plato wants to put dialectic above all others (57e6–7). But it does not seem to employ more arithmetic, or to produce, as it were, truths even more eternal. The word translated 'precise' now has to catch the idea of a sharper delineation of the truth, and the comparative and superlative of 'true' indicate greater completeness. (For a longer, but still obscure treatment cf. *Republic* VI, 505–VII, 534.) It seems a mistake to look for a single scale here. It seems that the claim that one has a full grasp of the truth on something needs various conditions satisfied for its substantiation. The something must be such that some universal descriptions hold of it (where 'is in a process of change' is incomplete or for some other reason does not count), there must be no areas of obscurity, there must be no margin of error, and there are possibly some other conditions. It looks as though Plato treats these as related in that, say, only if there is no margin of error are we dealing with subjects that allow of universal truths, and so only if that condition is satisfied is there hope of satisfying the condition of removing all obscurities.

It is noticeable that very little is said about dialectic except to laud it. Ryle (*Plato's Progress*, p. 252) claims that this shows its receding importance. In part the settlement of this issue depends on what one takes 'dialectic' to refer to. Within the *Philebus* (17a) it seems to refer at least to a proper procedure for dealing with one/many problems, and in particular therefore with pleasure, though the use of the term there is from within the Heavenly Tradition and so not necessarily Plato's. The context suggests that the results would be a proper understanding about pleasures which would enable one to produce proper arrangements of them, and dialectic (58a) knows the nature of all other skills, including any about pleasure. This may be why it is chosen first by the pleasures at 63b7–c3, and declared by Protarchus to render the others safe (62d). It looks as though Plato might seriously have considered such knowledge important, and indeed the earlier description suggests that the passage on Gorgias in 58 is as ironic as one would antecedently have expected. For the point of the pleasures wanting the branch of knowledge that knows them cf. *Laws* 732 seq. The reason why little illuminating is said about dialectic here is probably that what is needed is some indication of how forms of knowledge vary in truth analogously to pleasures. This is most easily illustrated by reference to the examples relied on. The difference between dialectic and mathematics, on the other hand, would require elucidation of the way in which mathematics falls short of the whole truth, which could be expected to be a long business, and not needed for getting the main point over. For more, see notes on 58a2, 58a4, 59b4.

THE PRIZE-GIVING, 59—66

As has been pointed out (cf. above, pp. 208 seq., pp. 181 seq.) the prize-giving has effectively been settled by 31a, at least so far as the question at 22c—e13 is concerned. But, as argued in the notes referred to, that does not justify any special hostility to Phileban pleasures. For the final judgement, however, it is appropriate to recall the earlier passage, while giving an extra twist against popular hedonism. The prize-giving, however, presents problems. The main burden of 23 seq. seemed to be to show that pleasure neither served to mark off a good organization of life from a bad, nor brought a good organization about. The analyses from 31 onwards are of 'pleasures', in the plural, as the early discussion with Protarchus recommends. So far as pleasure goes, the prize-giving seems to be considering pleasures, and telling us what members of that class should be admitted. It is interesting that not only violent, but even necessary (cf. 62e8—9) pleasures are omitted here. The reason presumably is that the prize-giving is not between elements in the good life, but elements that make some contribution to its goodness. The admissions of 20 seq. allow that pleasure is needed to make a life good for man, and as remarked in the note on 53b1, the 'pure' pleasures are also held to be fine in an evaluative sense. The pursuit of knowledge contributes both as a pleasure, and as desirable anyway for living at all. But it is not clear why pleasure's contribution to the goodness of the good life is inferior to the others. Its contribution must be different (a further sense of 'making it good' would be needed), but why inferior? It is not clear how one would *grade* a cook, a recipe, and the ingredients in their contribution to making a good cake.

This question may be helped by considering another one: what the connection is between the first three prize-winners. After all, the first prize has already gone to the mixed life, and this is recalled at 59d—61c. The first prize in the present passage, then, should be first prize in a competition for the second prize in the original competition, but now the grading is in terms of their status in 'making the good life good'. The problem is: how to distinguish and relate the first three on any such scale.

As has been remarked (cf. note on 64b2) the first two seem hardly distinct. Indeed they are distinguished not by description, but only by measuring pleasure against them at 65d and 65e. It then emerges that measure is contrasted with lack of moderation, fineness with shamefulness. So the good life is characterized by measure and giving no ground for shame or criticism. The interchangeability of the descriptions suggests that these are two sides of the same point: that criticism giving ground for shame must always take the form of pointing to lack of measure, and the latter is always sufficient for the former. In that case the ordering seems not very significant, and the distinction made simply because Plato had two polemical points against Phileban pleasures to make (65d, 65e) which made a distinction convenient, and perhaps because they served to help put pleasure further down, and so thoroughly bear out the prophecy of 22e3.

The first two, then, are aspects of the *peras* of 23 seq. and make the mixture good in that sense. But we are supposed to have three 'aspects', 'marks', 'descriptions', or whatever it is with which to track down the good, i.e. the good life; and three that we can treat as one thing responsible for its goodness (65a1—5). Whatever the truth about 'truth' (*aletheia* cf. note on 64b2), it emerges by 66b5—6 that one of these is intelligence. Part of the justification for this might be that if we take seriously the description of productive intelligence at 23 seq., then clearly there cannot be a good mixture without intelligence, or intelligence without good arrangement. As was noted (see above, pp. 206 seq.) Plato 'argues' in that passage, by the microcosm/macrocosm argument, for a closer association between intelligence and the arrangement than simply that of designer and design, so that one could as well talk of the arrangement being good through the presence of intelligence as of *peras*: for present purposes the distinction is theoretical only. Further it seems that Plato in that earlier section is wanting to insinuate two things: first that intellectual activity, and in particular organizing one's life, get their glory from association with the working of the world soul, and secondly, that that sort of operation at its highest has no interest in pleasure. If this is the line of thought it is easy to think that what makes the good life admirable is not, or hardly, that it is pleasant, but that it is divine (for a pupil preserving some such idea cf. Aristotle *Nicomachean Ethics* 1178b20 seq.). While pleasure needs intelligence for its security and for supplying a wider variety, there is nowhere suggested any reason why intelligence should *need* pleasure. That *men* would not choose a life without it is conceded, but a life of intellectual activity unenjoyed, while being inhuman, would be so by being divine (which is a laudatory description), not bestial. If Plato toys with the idea (cf. above, pp. 181 seq.) that a rational life is somehow better than a non-rational one, a man's than an oyster's, then he might well also be hinting that a god's life is better than a man's, so that the undesirability to man of a pleasure-less life is a sign of man's inferior social status: it is thought, not pleasure, that makes man even as admirable as he is.

If this is so, putting the first three 'prize-winners' together as in effect a single cause of goodness, and at the top, may be not only reaffirming the mutual connection between intelligence and order, but reminding one that what makes the good life admirable is that it is sharing in the divine ordering activities. Even the other branches of knowledge (cf. 66b8—c2) tend, like building, to serve mundane needs, and can hardly be thought to occupy much of the time of the divine mind. Still, they deal with *peras* in their way, and maybe (cf. *Republic.* VII) they are stepping-stones to better things. So they are closely related to what makes the good life good. The fact that they are pleasant adds to the desirability of the life for men, as do other pure pleasures. Other pleasures do not add to the worth of a life: they are either just necessary, or undesirable.

EPILOGUE

If we now look back over the *Philebus*, I think it is clear that it should not be looked upon as a series of digressions of ill-assorted dubiously consistent passages connected by similarity of language only. Doubtless like many works it is not wholly consistent nor well-polished at all points. It does, however, seem to have a definite strategy and a structure to suit. If we consider Aristotle's remarks on Eudoxus (see above, pp. 165 seq., 181 seq.) and consider both the position opposed and certain arguments used in the *Philebus* it begins to look as though the *Philebus* is geared to Eudoxan arguments. The introduction of the Pythagorean Heavenly Tradition would be appropriate to the Pythagorean and mathematician Eudoxus, especially when we consider his known mathematical interests. Again it seems from Aristotle that Eudoxus' arguments on pleasure were interpreted as supporting vulgar hedonism, so that it is likely that Plato would give his views consideration not simply because of his distinction and impact in Academic circles, but because of the way his views were generally interpreted.

If we see the work as directed at Eudoxus and those influenced by him but using his authority in support of a sybaritic life, then the portrayal of Philebus and the structure of the dialogue become more intelligible. Philebus is a lover of Aphrodite, who makes pleasure *apeiron* because he wants unlimited pleasure, and his main enemies as Mr. Loveboy are those who think physical pleasures to be a process of escape from pain to a painless state. He is not himself particularly intelligent, but he is relying on Eudoxus, and Eudoxus' main argument gets its force from supposing that all pleasures can be treated as alike, and so the observation that all animals pursue pleasure and the conclusion that pleasure is the good are unproblematic. The first move therefore is to attack that assumption. It now becomes more difficult to see how pleasure can operate as a criterion usable either in public debate or private deliberation for deciding between actions or ways of life. Anyone putting forward pleasure as the goal has to give some account of what justifies his talking of pleasure as a single thing. This is a difficult problem, one perhaps inherent in the Theory of Forms, but it is anyway endemic to language, and we shall be clearer on it if we note how the *technai* operate. It there becomes clear that similarity is not important, but that is not the only function of the Heavenly Tradition. As pleasure has been offered as a criterion but agreed to be multiform, the *techne* examples are apt, as presumably it is up to a Eudoxan now to supply a *techne* of pleasure which would also supply his justification for treating pleasure as one thing. The appeal to Pythagorean mathematical tradition is also, as remarked earlier, appropriate. The suggestion of the illustration, so far as pleasure is concerned, is that it will require a *techne* to deal with it and to work out the desirable proportions of it. This prepares one both for the arguments to pleasure's insufficiency in the next section, and for the subordinate role allotted to pleasure in 23 seq. We then get the argument that neither pleasure nor intelligence is the good, which so far as pleasure is concerned simply shows that further equipment will be needed besides pleasant episodes, but not that any other than pleasant episodes will be required.

The argument now turns to the relative roles of the protagonists in the good life. Recourse is had to the same view of *techne* illustrated in the Heavenly Tradition, but we are now concerned with producing the end-products. If the good life is a mixture then pleasure at least is something of which we shall have to ask what number and proportion of it is to be included, whereas answering that question and putting the answer into effect will be the function of intelligence. Pleasure does not supply a criterion for judging whether all or only some pleasures should be included, and has no productive power with regard to the desirable mixture. Consequently intelligence wins a prize above pleasure, and is in passing shown to be in divine company. Strictly this does not show that intelligence is not primarily interested in producing (the right combination of) pleasure, but the argument concerning the relation of the individual to the World Soul has the role of billing the operation of the intellect as having wider interests, especially as, as is hinted later, the gods will not be interested in pleasure.

Up to this point, the argument has been against the Eudoxan thesis, and it does not show that there are not certain pleasures, perhaps even Philebus', which are all desirable and such that they constitute all desirable activities or at least justify the inclusion of other activities. It does not even show that not all pleasures are desirable. The production would still be the function of intelligence, and the intellect's judgement that such a life was best would still be based on something other than pleasantness, but that would hardly worry Philebus. It is probably significant that the admission that pleasure is *apeiron* is extracted from Philebus on a misunderstanding of the point, one that takes '*apeiron*' as meaning 'some thing that is not limited'. This allows the concentration on certain pleasures in the discussion of the *apeiron* pleasure. The discussion of pleasures is almost entirely of false and mixed ones, which are described as at least potentially or typically disordered, insistent beyond limit. All this is expressly done to see whether all pleasures are desirable or not, and to exclude Phileban candidates *in toto*. Those who thus rely on Eudoxus' authority, therefore, are first deprived of any support from that source and then shown that the nature of what they advocate is at odds with one factor agreed necessary for a good life, and is not, as described, anyway very glamorous. In the final ordering of importance only pleasures that Philebus would hardly be interested in are given a place, with the suggestion that the presence of pleasant activities is not very important. His own candidates do not appear.

The *Philebus* leaves open the possibility, for any argument that is supplied, that all the episodes in a good life are pleasant episodes, and that therefore the goal is in this sense a pleasant life, though made up of rather 'philosophical' pleasures. Against this there is propaganda and suggestion in the discussion of the world soul, the suggestion that the gods are uninterested in pleasure, the reference to an innate interest in the truth. But in the treatment of pleasure the main target is the sybarite and the programme of making his sort of pleasure an objective in life. This accounts for the imbalance of the treatment of pleasure, the use of views on pleasure that are not accepted, the motif of the life that is neither pleasant nor painful.

I am not claiming that all the arguments are good arguments—the commentary and notes should make that clear—nor that all sections are honest or are clearly relevant parts of the argument. There are other ways of pursuing a coherent strategy than developing a close-knit argument and Plato is not above them. The claim is simply that the inconsistencies are less than they can seem, so that Plato could well have thought there were none, and that other awkwardnesses become less awkward or not at all so if seen in the light of the overall strategy.

BIBLIOGRAPHY

ANSCOMBE, G. E., *Monist* 1966.

ARCHER-HIND, R. D., 'Note on Plato *Philebus* 15A, B', *Journal of Philology* XXVII.

BADHAM, C., *The Philebus of Plato* (2nd ed.), 1878.

BURNET, J., *Platonis Opera*, O.U.P., Oxford. 1901.

BURY, R. G., *The Philebus of Plato*, C.U.P., Cambridge, 1897.

CROMBIE, I. M., *An Examination of Plato's Doctrines*, Routledge & Kegan Paul, London, 1963.

DIELS, H., and W. KRANZ, *Die Fragmente der Vorsokratiker*, 7th ed., Berlin, 1954.

DYBIKOWSKI, J., 'False Pleasure and the *Philebus*', *Phronesis* XV, 1970.

GAUSS, H., *Philosophischer Handkommentar zu den Dialogen Platons.* III/2 Herbert Long & Cie, Bern, 1961.

GOSLING, J., 'False Pleasures: *Philebus* 35c–41b', *Phronesis* IV, 1959. 'Father Kenny on False Pleasures', *Phronesis* VI, 1961.

GULLEY, N., *Plato's Theory of Knowledge*, Methuen, London, 1962.

HACKFORTH, R. *Plato's Examination of Pleasure*, C.U.P., Cambridge, 1945, (Bobbs Merrill: The Library of Liberal Arts, Paperback).

JOWETT, B., *The Dialogues of Plato* (4th ed.), Vol. III, O.U.P., Oxford, 1953.

OWEN, G. E., 'The Place of the *Timaeus* in Plato's Dialogues', in *Studies in Plato's Metaphysics*, ed. R. E. Allen, Routledge and Kegan Paul, 1965.
'A Proof in the *Peri Ideon*', in *Studies in Plato's Metaphysics*, ed. R. E. Allen, Routledge and Kegan Paul, 1965.

PENNER, T., 'False Anticipatory Pleasures: *Philebus* 36a3–41a6', *Phronesis* XV, 1970.

POSTE, E., *The Philebus of Plato*, O.U.P., Oxford, 1860.

ROBIN, L., *Platon*, Presses Universitaires de France, Paris, 1968.

ROBINSON, R., *Plato's Earlier Dialectic* (2nd ed.), O.U.P., Oxford, 1953.

ROSS, D., *Plato's Theory of Ideas*, O.U.P., Oxford, 1951.

RUNCIMAN, W. G., *Plato's Later Epistemology*, C.U.P., Cambridge, 1962.

RYLE, G., *Plato's Progress*, C.U.P., Cambridge, 1966.

SCHLEIERMACHER, F., *Platos Werke*, Berlin, 1817–28.

SCHOFIELD, M., 'Who were οἱ δυχερεῖς in Plato, *Philebus* 44a f.?' *Museum Helveticum*, Vol. XXX, 1971.

STALLBAUM, G., *Philebus*, Leipzig, 1820.

STENZEL, J., *Plato's Method of Dialectic* (tr. D. J. Allan), O.U.P., Oxford, 1940.

STRIKER, E., *Peras und Apeiron*. Hypomnemata. Vandenboeck & Ruprecht, Göttingen, 1970.

TAYLOR, A. E., *Plato: Philebus and Epinomis*, Thomas Nelson & Sons, London, 1956.

WEDBERG, A., *Plato's Philosophy of Mathematics*, Almquist & Wiksell, Stockholm, 1955.

ADDENDA

21b3 '. . . you would be glad . . .' Or possibly: 'so living this way constantly throughout your life you would enjoy the greatest pleasures.' The sense I have given better fits the run of the argument. What follows does not show that Protarchus would not enjoy the greatest pleasures, but persuades him that he would not be glad to lead the life described. This tempts one to follow Badham, in his second edition, in bracketing ταῖς μεγίσταις ἡδοναῖς (*tais megistairs ēdonais*: the greatest pleasures) and translate: 'so you would be glad to live constantly in this condition in this condition throughout your life.'

44b10 '. . . that they are pleasures.' (and cf. 45c8). Or: *i* 'who completely deny that pleasures exist,' or: *ii* 'who completely deny any reality to pleasure.' If *i*, we must either suppose the remark to apply to pleasures as conceived of by Philebus, or to pleasures properly conceived. If the first, then it is odd that they proceed to define such pleasures as flights from pain, and make it clear that they exist with baneful results. If the second, then presumably they have a view of pleasure whereby it is never instantiated. Then the point must be that Philebus' candidates also fail to be pleasures. But if flights from pain are all we can get, the person who declares that that is what they are and that real pleasure does not exist, is a toothless opponent. If *ii*, the point might be that pleasures are processes that lack stable being (reality). This might be suggested by 43a1–3, but the point is obscurely made. After all, the claim there is not that there is a condition of stable being, but that there is one of not perceiving bodily changes. In fact these theorists are portrayed as arguing, by means of a view on nature, a. that Phileban pleasures are manic in tendency and b. that they are not really pleasures (46a–47c, 51a) but mixed experiences. To start looking like enemies they would have not merely to deny the title of pleasures to Philebus' candidates, but hold that there is a state free of physical distress or pleasure and that true pleasure is found there. Had Protarchus agreed at 44b to go back on the admission of a neutral state, Philebus' pleasures would have been safe enough as the best we can aspire to. Hackforth will have it otherwise at 44b, but for no reason that I can discover. His suggestion (p. 86) that the view is Plato's own will not survive Republic Book IX, let alone the discussion of pure pleasures to follow.

It remains that 45c8 is awkward to translate this way.

45e3 '... roaring about.' OR: 'makes them the talk of the town' (Hackforth). Certainly περιβόητος (*periboētos*) usually has this passive sense in prose. Liddell and Scott cite the present passage for the active sense, together with Sophocles, *Oedipus Tyrannus* 192, which is probable, but not certain. There is no undisputed active case known to me. On the other hand, the active sense fits well with the trend of the passage (cf. 47c4–10), and the rare but related ἀμφιβόητος (*amphiboētos*) seems to have had both active and passive senses. So it seems possible that the word can be used actively, and as nothing philosophical hangs on it I have preferred the dramatic colour of the active sense.

References to the text are in bold type.

Accuracy **57-61, 65-6,** 128
Akon see Hekon
Aletheia, capacity for truth **68-70,**
134-6, 138, 224-5
see Alethes
Alethes **32-7, 51,** 128, (forms of
knowledge) **60-2, 64-6,**
128-9, 131-2, 184, 222-3,
(genuine) **53-4, 64-6,** 121, 133,
145, (mark of good) **68-70**
equivocation on 212-13
see On, Pleasure: falsity, Truth
'All' Plato's use of 97
Anger **38, 46-7, 50**
Anscombe, G.E. 84, 146-7, 229
Apeiron x-xi, xiii-xix, **5, 7-10, 14-20**
ambiguity of 158-9, 177-8, 195-6,
200
and change 204-5
and comparative concepts 192-4,
198
and the continuum 167-81,
196-205
and matter xvi, 156-9, 186-91, 198
and musical theory 180-1
and particulars xiv, 160-4, 193-4,
200
translation 84-5
Aphrodite ix, **2,** 141
Archer-Hind, R. 146, 229
Archytas 166, 169
Aristotle, *Posterior Analytics* 86a 3-6,
160
Metaphysics A 987a-b, 179;
B 999a27, 160; K 1061a28,
180
Nicomachean Ethics 1096b22, 83;
1097a15-b21, 87; 1103b17-19,
104; 1106a26, 178; 1109b30-
1111b3, 89; 1115a9-b6, 132;
1148b4-14, 132; 1152b12,
125, 221; 1153b1-7, 89, 102;
1154b26, 103; 1172b, ix, 139,
141, 166; 1173a29, 125, 221;
1174a13, 103; 1178b20, 225
Physics Γ 4-8, 83, 181; 194b16-

195b30, 95; 197a36-199b33,
125
Aristoxenus 180-₁
Arithmetic, two kinds **58-9,** 127, 129
Art **51-2,** 121-2

Beauty *see* Fine, 121-2
Badham, C. 82, 97, 101, 138, 146,
153, 229
Becoming, **18-20,** 94-5, 134-5
pleasure as **54-6,** 125, 220-1
see Mixtures
Being *see* Becoming, *On*, Truth
Body, not subject of desire **28-30,**
104-6
Book, simile for mind 35, 110-11,
214-18
Building **58, 65,** 131-2, 222-3
Burnet, J. 82, 229
Bury, R.G. 82, 97, 99, 119, 123, 128,
186, 229

Cause, category of **15, 18-24,** 98-9
causal law **19,** 95
of the Good Life **13-14, 20-4,**
68-70, 95-6, 135, 185, 224-5,
227
see Good
Collection *see* Division
Comedy **49-50**
Commensurability
17-18, 68-9, 93, 168-9
see Irrationals
Concepts, analysis of 75-6, 104-6,
170-3, 213-14
Plato's lack of terminology for
163-5, 191-4
Cosmos (23-30) xv, **14-23,** 91-9,
185-208
Crombie, I.M. 129, 160, 191, 195,
229

Desire **28-31,** 104
bodily 115-16
as criterion of good **11-14, 60,**
87-90, 139-142, 181-4

not a function of the body 104-6
strength related to intensity of
   pleasure 43, 116
Determinant *see Peras*
Dialectic 5, 7, 23-4, 60-1, 65-7,
   128-30, 133, 134, 222-3
Diels, H. (and W. Kranz) 83
Diogenes Laertius 166
Distress, opposed to pleasure 24-5
   see Pleasure
Divine 13, 22-3, 27, 52, 103, 122,
   136, 207-8, 225, 227-8
Division method of 82, 87, 91, 160-4,
   202-3
Doxa, common opinions 130-1
   see Judgement
Dybikowski, J. 215, 217, 229

Envy 46-7, 50
Episteme, translation 128, 153-4, 222
   see Knowledge
Equal *see* Geometry, *Peras*: number
Eudaemon 1, 140
Eudoxus ix, 87, 89, 102, 139-142,
   166-7, 169, 171, 177, 180,
   183, 209, 226-8

Falsity, and worthlessness 38
   see Pleasure, Judgement
Fear 32, 38, 46-7, 50
Fine 18, 23, 53-4, 68-70, 93
   (= beautiful) 51-2
Finite *see Peras*
Forms 83-4, 132, 136-7, 143-53,
   156-9, 186-91, 203-5, 227

Gauss, H. 160, 186, 229
Genesis see Becoming
Genuine *see Alethes*, Truth
Genus (and species) 84-5, 156-8,
   160-4, 173-4, 194-5
Geometry, two kinds 58-9
   opposed to arithmetic 178-80,
   189-90, 199
   and equality 178-9, 189-90
Gluttony 115-16
Good, and being *versus* becoming
   54-6

Cause of 13-4, 67-70, 185, 188-9,
   224-5, 227
and divine intelligence *see* Divine
marks of 64, 132, 135
and perfection 11-3, 62-4, 87
and pursuit *see* Desire
synonymous with 'pleasant' x, 126
   see Good Life, Good Man, Intelligence, Pleasure
Good Life, criteria of 11-13, 87-91,
   132-3, 181-3, 227, *see* Desire
and mixed category 20, 181-5
a mixture of pleasure and intelligence 11-13, 181-5
Good man, and the gods' blessings
   36-7, 111-12
Gorgias 60-1, 129-30
Gosling, J. 213, 220, 229
Grammar *see* Letters
Gulley, N. 160, 229

Hackforth, R. 78, 98, 101, 104, 110,
   111, 116-17, 118-19, 121, 129,
   134, 143, 145-6, 160, 162, 186,
   187, 188, 191, 220, 229
Happiness *see Eudaemon*
Health 17, 43-4, 67, 204-5
Heavenly Tradition, the xiii-xv, 7-10,
   82-8, 153-81
Hekon 13, 89-90
Heracleitus 113
Hope 26, 31, 36-8, 107-8, 214-18
Hunger 25, 29, 56, 115-16, 126

Indeterminate *see Apeiron*
Infinite *see Apeiron*
Intelligence, Socrates' thesis ix-xiii,
   1, 10, 12-13, 62-3, 71-3, 103,
   132, 139-42, 181-4, 222-7
   see Cause, Divine, Good, *Peras*
Intermediate State *see* Neutral State
Irrationals 167-9, 199
Itching 45

Jowett, B. 156, 186, 229
Judgement, false 32-4
   and statement 35
Kalos (Kallos) see Fine

Katharos see Pure
Knowledge, blending with pleasures
    64-7, 133-4, 184, **222-3**
    forms of **4, 10-11, 57-62,** 126-132,
    222-3
    see Episteme, Intelligence

Letters 7-9, 162-4, 169, 171-2
Limit *see Peras*
Love 46-7, **50**

Malice **46-50,** 120
Mathematical objects 179-80
Mathematics, importance of **57,** 126,
    154, 166-81, 203-5, 222-3
    see Arithmetic, Geometry, Measure,
    Peras
Measure **16-18,** 68-9
    cause of mixture **68**
Measurement 58-9
    forms of 189
Meikton see Mixtures
Memory **27-31,** 103, 110-11
Method, philosophical, *see* Division
Microcosm/macrocosm **22-3,** 97-9,
    206-8
Mind, as a book **35,** 110-12
    as subject of desire 28-30, 104-6
    see Cause, Divine, Intelligence,
    Pleasure, *Psuche,* Soul,
    World Soul
Mixed category *see* Mixtures
Mixed life **11-14,**
    in the mixed category **20**
Mixtures **15, 17-20, 24, 68**
    as concepts 191-4
    as particular desirable states 192-4,
    200
    as spatial objects 186-8, 191
Monads *see* Units
Moore, G.E. 88
Music 8, **17, 57, 65,** 133-4, 162-4,
    169-71, 180, 197-201
    pure pleasures of **51-2,** 121-2

Nature, mistaken ways of studying **61**
    scientists on how to judge **43,**
    115-16
    and similarity 79-80

Necessary forms of knowledge **65**
    pleasures **66,** 133
Neutral state **26-7, 40-2, 56,** 102-3,
    210-11
Number *see Peras,* Arithmetic

Objects of pleasure and judgement
    108, 109, 215-17
On (ontōs) **26, 32-3, 51, 61-2,** 129,
    156-9, 213
    see Alethes, Truth
One and many **4-6, 8-9, 15, 16, 18,**
    78, **80-1,** 83, 86-7, 91, 143-53,
    202-3
Ontōs see on
Opposites **3-4, 17,** 76-7, 175
Owen, G.E. 95, 132, 229

Pain *see* Distress
Painter, simile of imagination **35-6,**
    111-12, 214-18
Painting **51-2,** 121-2
Pathos **29-31, 35,** 75, 110-11, 117
Penner, T. 215, 217, 229
Peras, x-xi, xiii-xix, 7-9, **14-15**
    expressions for 91-2
    and form xvi 156-9, 186-91
    and good mixtures 95, 135, 187-
    90, 200-1, 224-5
    and number 92-4, 164, 168-70,
    178-9, 197-205
    translation 84
    see Cause,
Perception **27-8,** 100-1, 103, 110-11
Phone 7-9, 85-7, 159, 162-5, 170-3
Phthonos see Malice
Philebus, his interjections **1, 2, 8-9,
    13, 20-1**
    the name ix, 73, 141, 226
    and sybaritism **2, 20, 42-6, 55-6,**
    102-3, 114-15, 136, 141-2,
    208-11, 220-1, 226-8
    his thesis ix-xiii, **1, 10, 12-13,
    62-3, 71-3,** 138-42, 181-4,
    222-7
Phusis see Nature
Physicists *see* Scientists
Pictures, true and false **36,** 108, 214-18
Plato, *Philebus*: structure viii, 96-7,

99, 207-12, 220-1, 226-8
references to dialogues
Apology 129
Cratylus 429-30, 108; 437b, 103;
439e, 103; 439-40, 113;
Definitiones 413c6-7, 134;
Epinomis 973c, 122; 977c-e, 126
Gorgias 462-5, 153; 491-4, 221;
496, 104; 495-7, 126; 503-4,
208; 508a, 178, 189; 508-10,
135; 526d, 135
Hippias Major 293d1-4, 127-8;
299d, 74
Laws 663c, 112; 668, 133; 715e,
83; 730c, 135; 732, 116, 124;
134, 223; 757, 178; 818, 154;
860, 91; 898, 207; 889-99, 97
Meno 71e, 121; 72-5, 74; 85d, 103;
86d-e, 109
Parmenides 129, 80, 143; 131,
143; 147c-e, 78, 80; 157b3-4,
110; 159a, 76;
Phaedo 65-7, 217; 70d-72d, 76;
73e, 217; 73-4, 103; 79-80,
100; 97-9, 95, 97, 208;
76-100, 131; 102, 81, 143;
104-6, 76
Phaedrus 245, 207; 246b, 207;
265, 82, 91; 270, 125
Politicus (*Statesman*) 262, 145;
284-5, 189; 293e, 145
Protagoras 331d-e, 78; 330-3, 76;
349, 132; 355, 116, 132; 356,
219
Republic 331c, 135; 332b-d, 121;
353, 125, 207; 413, 112;
431a-d, 130; 435a-b, 74;
436a-b, 104; 438c-d, 79;
436b-439d, 76, 80, 103;
441a-b, 122; 442-4, 130;
476, 130; 478b, 108; 479, 76;
485, 130; 493, 131; 505d-e,
90; 505, 139; 522c, 126, 154;
523-4, 76, 143; 525-6, 127;
534a, 94; 577e, 90; 579d-e, 90;
583, 103; 584c, 216; 585-6,
104, 122, 213, 221; 580-6, 75,
104, 130

Sophist 236a, 145; 237-40, 108,
114, 151; 243-5, 132; 248-9,
95, 110, 148, 151; 251-2, 80,
143; 253-4, 80; 250-5, 132;
255e, 79; 257c-d, 79; 257b-
259b, 76, 147; 261d, 148;
261-3, 204; 263-4, 88, 110
Symposium (*Banquet*) 204a, 213;
210-11, 146-7; 211-2, 130
Theaetetus 151c5-8, 120; 156-7,
103; 163d, 103; 167, 108;
172-7, 129; 181d, 103; 179-83,
113; 184-7, 88, 103; 188-9, 108;
189e-190, 110; 190, 88; 191-2,
103; 189-93, 114; 204b-c, 132
Timaeus 28-9, 94; 28-30, 125; 43,
100, 103; 48, 157; 64-5, 100,
104, 114
Pleasant, synonymous with 'good' x,
56, 126
Pleasure, anticipatory **26-7, 32-42,**
101-2, 106-8, 214-20
and *apeiron* **20, 24,** 96, 123,
193-4, 200, 228
blended with intelligence **62, 64-7,**
133, 183-4
bodily 115-16
and conceptual analysis 75-6,
213-14
degrees of **43-4, 53-4,** 124-5,
219-20
as effect xii, 3, 73-6
false **32-42,** 106-14, 214-20
as feeling 73-6, 113-14, 117-18
identified with activity 73-6,
113-14, 117-18
intensity **42-5, 67, 70,** 115-16,
136
issue *versus* intelligence 88, 139-42,
166-7, 181-5
kinds 210-12
knowing one's pleasure **12, 32, 63,**
88, 106-7, 216
mental *versus* bodily **26,** 100
mixed (mental) **46-51** (mental and
physical) **31,** 106 (physical)
42-5, 114-20
as motion 103

multiform 2-3, 73-6, 142, 143-53,
   176-7
nature of 43-4, 75-6, 104-6, 115-16,
   213-4
necessary 66, 133
perception of restoration 40-1,
   113-14
Philebus' thesis ix-xiii, 1, 10,
   12-13, 62-3, 71-3, 138, 139-42,
   181-4, 222-7
'pleased' 32-4, 107-8, 215-18
and reality 42-5, 114-15
as restoration 24-6, 100, 104,
   113-14, 122
and scientists 42-6, 114-15
sexual 115-16
a single thing, see multiform
translation 107-8
unmixed (mental) 52, 67, 70,
   122, 221 (physical) 51-2, 67,
   70, 121-2
Poson xvii
   see Peras, Quantity
Poste, E. 229
Precision 57-61, 128, 222-3
Prize-giving xi, 69-71, 135-8, 185,
   224-6
Proclus 94, 159
Prometheus 7
Psuche 1, 12, 18, 23, 25, 26-8, 30,
   35-8, 41, 44-8, 50-1, 56, 67-8,
   70, 207
translation 97-8, 116-7
Pure (purified) 53-4, 124-5, 184,
   212-13
   see Pleasure: unmixed
Pythagoras 83
Pythagoreanism 83, 99, 121, 165-81,
   196-205, 226-8

Quality, opposed to essence 109
   and quantity 86
Quantity 85, 91
   and quality 86
Quintilian 169

Rag-bag, theory viii, 226-8
Recollection 27-31, 103
Responsible see Cause
Rhetoric 60-1, 129-30
Robin, L. 160, 186, 191, 229
Robinson, R. 82, 229
Ross, Sir D. 160, 186, 187, 229
Runciman, W. 220, 229
Ryle, G. 110, 129, 223, 230

Schleiermacher, F. 127, 230
Schofield, M. 89, 115, 230
Scientists, Philebus' enemies 42-6,
   114-15
Scribe, similer of judgement 35-6,
   110-11, 214-18
Second prize 1-2, 13-14, 20, 64,
   69-71, 185, 224-6
Sick, and intense pleasures 43-5
Similarity xi-xiii, 2-4, 73-9, 142, 162,
   213-14, 226-7
Skill 6, 8-9, 153-4, 170-80, 196-205,
   227
Sorrow 46-7, 50
Socrates, his thesis ix-xiii, 1, 10,
   12-13, 62-3, 71-3, 103, 132,
   139-42, 181-4, 222-7
Soul, function of 207
   individuation of 207
   see Psuche, Mind, World soul
Sound, vocal 7-9
   see Phone
Species see Genus
Speusippus 89, 102
Spite see Malice
Stallbaum, G. 99, 127, 230
Stenzel, J. 191, 230
Striker, E. vi, 80, 83, 92, 98, 160,
   161, 163, 191-4, 230
Sybaritism ix-xiii, 2, 42-6, 54-6,
   69-70, 114-15, 136, 141-2,
   208-10, 220-1, 226-8

Taylor, A.E. 134, 160, 186, 187, 230
Techne, translation 153-4
   see Skill

Theuth 9, 171-2, 173
Thirst **25**, **29**, 100, 104, 126
Tragi-comedy **50**
Truth, degrees of 128-9, 222-3
    and pleasure **32-42**, **5 3-4**, **66-7**,
       106-14, 121
    unchanging **61**, **65**, 131-2, 222-3
    see Alethes, Aletheia, On

Units, and genus 84-5
    monads **4-5**, 82, 143-53
    see Arithmetic, One and Many,
       Peras
Universals 160-4

Unlike *see* Similarity
Unlimited *see Apeiron*

Wedberg, A. 160, 230
White **53**
Wicked, the, and false hopes **36-7**,
    111-12
Willing wrongdoing 89-91
Words, Primary and derivative uses 132
    synonymous 132
World soul **21-4**, 98-9, 227-8

Yearning **46-7**, **50**